Uprising

RHETORIC AND PUBLIC AFFAIRS SERIES

UPRISING

How Women Used the US West
to Win the Right to Vote

Tiffany Lewis

MICHIGAN STATE UNIVERSITY PRESS | *East Lansing*

Michigan State University Press
East Lansing, Michigan 48823-5245

LIBRARY OF CONGRESS CATALOGING-IN-PUBLICATION DATA
Names: Lewis, Tiffany, author.
Title: Uprising : how women used the us west to win the right to vote / Tiffany Lewis.
Description: First Edition. | East Lansing : Michigan State University Press, 2021.
| Series: Rhetoric and public affairs series | Includes bibliographical references and index.
Identifiers: LCCN 2020004641 | ISBN 978-1-61186-382-6 (paperback) | ISBN 978-1-60917-657-0 (pdf)
| ISBN 978-1-62895-417-3 (ePub)| ISBN 978-1-62896-418-9 (Kindle)
Subjects: LCSH: Women—West (U.S.)—History. | Sex role—West (U.S.)—History.
| Women—Suffrage—West (U.S.)—History.
Classification: LCC HQ1438.W45 L49 2021 | DDC 305.40978—dc23
LC record available at https://lccn.loc.gov/2020004641

Book design by Charlie Sharp, Sharp Designs, East Lansing, Michigan
Cover design by Erin Kirk
Cover photo: Suffrage states represented in tableau
near Central Park, New York City, 1915

Michigan State University Press is a member of the Green Press Initiative and is
committed to developing and encouraging ecologically responsible publishing
practices. For more information about the Green Press Initiative and the use
of recycled paper in book publishing, please visit *www.greenpressinitiative.org*.

Visit Michigan State University Press at *www.msupress.org*

For Gwen and Brooke

———◆·———

Contents

———•◆•———

Acknowledgments

———◆·———

When I enrolled in Sara Hayden's course on early feminist rhetoric as a graduate student, I would never have guessed I would be studying suffragists for so many years to come. I have been working on parts of this book for over a decade, so I have many people to thank. I am especially grateful for Kristy Maddux's insightful direction on early stages of this project. Her irreplaceable mentorship, feedback, and advice sharpened my work and transformed my career. More recently, the recommendations of the anonymous reviewers made this manuscript much better. Thank you for your time and thoughtfulness in improving this project. Marty Medhurst believed in my research since I was in graduate school, and his editorial support was instrumental to this book's publication. The team at Michigan State University Press, including Catherine Cocks and Anastasia Wraight, were helpful during the production process and made this manuscript much more polished.

This book became a possibility because of faculty mentors at multiple universities. As an undergraduate at the University of Washington, Valerie Manusov, Mike Peters, and Jody Koenig Kellas fostered my interest in research. The faculty at the University of Montana created a collegial and stimulating academic culture that makes many graduate students want to be academics: Steve Yoshimura, Alan Sillars, Sara Hayden, Steve Schwarze, Betsy Bach, Christina Yoshimura, and Jennifer Considine. After serving as my advisor, Steve Yoshimura remained a source of help and encouragement even as my research went in a different direction. Sara Hayden's rhetoric classes altered the course of my career, and I still benefit from her scholarship and support. At the University of Maryland, this project was encouraged from its inception. Kristy Maddux, James Klumpp, Shawn Parry-Giles, Trevor Parry-Giles, and Robert Gaines encouraged my interest in region and nudged me toward historical research, for which I am immensely thankful. Gay Gullickson's, Mari Boor Tonn's, and Elsa Barkley Brown's classes were especially valuable as I developed this project.

The leadership and faculty at the Marxe School of Public and International Affairs have created a department that promotes junior faculty members' success. I am thankful for the support of Dean David Birdsell and several supportive associate deans and chairs, including Jerry Mitchell, Dahlia Remler, Sanders Korenman, Jonathan Engel, and Patria de Lancer Julnes. David Hoffman and Don Waisanen have been wonderful communication colleagues who have looked out for me and made my job easier. Along with Diane Gibson and Tom Main, they recruited me to Baruch College and made me feel at home there, for which I am still appreciative. Hilary Botein, Cristina Balboa, and Susan Chambre were gracious enough to read multiple drafts of this manuscript and provided invaluable encouragement and accountability in the home stretch. I am incredibly grateful for their time, feedback, and thoughtfulness. Karl Kronebush, Jessica Greene, Ideen Riahi, Joselyn Muhlheisen, and Marco Desena have been fantastic colleagues. Anna D'Souza's friendship and reassurance as I put this manuscript together was irreplaceable.

Numerous grants, fellowships, and course releases made this project more feasible. Funding for this project was provided by PSC-CUNY Awards (jointly funded by the Professional Staff Congress and the City University of New York), the Eugene M. Lang Junior Faculty Research Fellowship, Marxe School Dean's Research Awards, and CUNY's Faculty Fellowship Publication Program. My colleagues in FFPP cheered this project along with their enthusiasm. My research assistants, Jessica Joffie and Aimee Roberge, were fabulous and a delight to work with.

I am immensely grateful for my peers from graduate school. My years in Missoula were that much more special because of Maria Blevins, Kira Jones, Jen Geist, Melissa Maier, Ryan Morton, Amy Pearson, Vailferree Brechtel, and Andrew Richards. My time at University of Maryland was made far better by Lindsey Fox, Robin Sholz, Terri D'Onofrio, Alyssa Samek, Elizabeth Gardner, Mara Hobler, Jim Gilmore, Steve Underhill, Tim Barney, Abbe Dupretis, Ben Krueger, Jade Olson, Sean Leuchtefeld, Katie Irwin, Stephanie Madden, Meridith Styer, and Yvonne Slosarski. Our numerous discussions, writing groups, shared experiences, and hours of debriefing were invaluable. More recently, this manuscript has been improved through the crucial comments, insights, and encouragement of Terri D'Onofrio, Alyssa Samek, Steve Underhill, Tim Barney, and Meridith Styer. Thank you for your generous readings and friendship.

This project was feasible in part because of archivists and librarians at the University of Oregon, Montana Historical Society, the Florence Bayard Hilles Feminist Library, the Library of Congress, the University of Maryland, New York Public Library, and Baruch College, City University of New York. Randall Lake's fabulous recovery and authentication work allowed me to make the chapter on Abigail Scott Duniway more thorough.

I have benefitted from the insights of many people in my field. The smart scholarship of Cindy Koenig Richards, Casey Ryan Kelly, and Sara Hayden first sparked my interest in this topic. Since then, my work has been improved and encouraged by numerous editors, reviewers, conference respondents, and helpful colleagues: Susan Shultz Huxman,

Martha Solomon Watson, Brian Ott, Greg Dickinson, Eric Aoki, Kristen Hoerl, Angela Ray, Belinda Stillion Southard, Leslie Harris, Karrin Anderson, Paul Stob, Bonnie Dow, and Danielle Endres. The chapter on antisuffragists was greatly improved by Joan Faber McCallister's response at a WSCA conference and the suggestions of Leslie Harris and other wonderful audience members.

The Western States Communication Association granted permission to reprint portions of chapter 1 that first appeared in "Winning Woman Suffrage in the Masculine West: Abigail Scott Duniway's Frontier Myth," *Western Journal of Communication* 75 (2011): 127–147. The Organization for Research on Women and Communication also granted permission to reprint portions of chapter 2 that first appeared in "Mapping Social Movements and Leveraging the U.S. West: The Rhetoric of the Woman Suffrage Map," *Women's Studies in Communication* 42 (2019): 490–510. Brian Ott and Kristen Hoerl's editorial guidance and their anonymous reviewers helped me sharpen both chapters.

During the years I worked on this project, I relied on dear friends. Like this book, my support system has been shaped by region. In the Pacific Northwest, my oldest friends have cheered this project on: Sarah, Susan, Kelli, Jenn, Jess, and Lily. In the Rocky Mountains, I was lucky to find Emma, Jenny, Maria, Kira, Jen, Steph, and Rachel. In Washington, DC, I relied tremendously on Lindsey, Robin, Emma, Tierney, Terri, Alyssa, Kelly Ann, and Mary Beth. And in New York City, I have been grateful for the friendship of Mary, Rachel, Alyssa, Emily, Mandy, Matt, Anja, Dana, and Matthew. Recently, I have especially appreciated the ongoing support and companionship of Maria, Terri, Alyssa, Lindsey, Emma, Anna, Shaun, and new friends from Archestratus and Greenpoint.

Across all of these different places, my family has remained a steady and constant support. My mom and dad, Robert, Walker, James, and Megan are my favorite Westerners. They have cheered, consoled, and celebrated at many steps along the way. My parents encouraged curiosity, perseverance, and an appreciation of region for many years before I began this project. I was lucky enough to meet Zach when I thought I was almost done with this manuscript, but still in fact had years more work to do. I'm thankful for the ways he believes in me and my work, loves archival texts as much as I do, and generally makes my life much nicer.

All of these people have made this project better. All the errors and omissions are my own.

Introduction

————•◆•————

On November 9, 1912, twenty-thousand demonstrators paraded down New York City's Fifth Avenue in the name of women's voting rights. More than four hundred thousand spectators filled the sidewalks from Fourteenth Street to Fifty-Ninth Street to witness the extravagant demonstration.[1] The parade was led by five large, horse-drawn golden chariots that represented the first five states where women won voting rights in the United States: Wyoming, Utah, Colorado, Idaho, and Washington.[2] Following the chariots, a parade float celebrated the newest states to enfranchise eligible women in 1911 and 1912: California, Oregon, Arizona, and Kansas. Next, a group of forty marching girls carried a giant yellow flag that featured a star for each state that had extended voting rights to some women, all of which were in the US West. Another float displayed a large US map that highlighted all the Western states that included women in their franchise. To make clear the message of the chariots, flag, and floats, marchers held signs that proclaimed, "Six hundred thousand women vote wisely and well in California. Why not in New York?" and "Women Vote for President in Wyoming, Colorado, Utah, and Idaho. Why Not in New York?"[3] As these protesters campaigned for woman suffrage in New York City, they celebrated white women's existing voting rights and the region where those voting rights were born: the US American West.[4]

Like the parade down Fifth Avenue, suffrage advocacy returned time and again to the US West. Suffrage activists verbally invoked the West in their speeches, pamphlets, and publications. Their imagery celebrated the region with flags, political maps, and cartoons. Their parades championed the Western states with floats and chariots, and their pageants and tableaus personified the Western states with women dressed in costume. Antisuffragists responded in kind by ridiculing the West and its enfranchisement of women. Both suffragists and their opponents leveraged the region as a persuasive resource in their national advocacy, but they did so in different ways. While suffragists imagined the West as exceptionally free, admirably modern, and crucially democratic, antisuffragists derided the West as unsophisticated and irrelevant.

I argue that the US West played a pivotal role in the campaign for women's enfranchisement in the United States. As suffragists deployed the region as a rhetorical resource, they contested and challenged the traditional meanings of the US West and East, which provided them with additional persuasive strategies.[5] Eventually, the West attracted such extensive national attention and scrutiny for women's voting rights that public discourse began identifying the region with women's freedom and using it as a symbol of their movement. The multiple ways suffragists used the West to advocate for the franchise illustrates the power of "region in protest"—the way social movements can tactically employ region to motivate social change. *Uprising* examines why and how the West influenced the national suffrage movement by tracing the ways Americans activated the region in their verbal, visual, and embodied arguments over women's voting rights, as well as the ways those rights shaped the meanings of the region. I focus on the campaign for women's enfranchisement in the United States, so I use the terms "the West," "Americans," and "the suffrage movement" to make claims almost exclusively about "the US West," "US Americans," and the "US woman suffrage movement." Overall, the West played a crucial role in the suffrage movement for at least three reasons: the West enfranchised women before the rest of the nation; Americans cared immensely about the region and its changing meaning at the turn of the century; and the West's regional rhetoric provided an invaluable persuasive resource for the suffrage movement.

Women's Voting Rights and Suffragists' Earliest Victories in the US West

The conventional narrative of the US woman suffrage movement begins in the Northeast.[6] In the 1830s and 1840s, women involved in reform efforts in the Northeast, who were typically white, educated, and middle or upper class, were condemned for going beyond their domestic sphere and excluded from groups that worked to abolish the institution of enslavement and oppose American Indian removal.[7] Abolitionists in Pennsylvania and Massachusetts, like Sarah and Angelina Grimke, found that to speak out against enslavement, they had to overcome objections to women participating in activism.[8] They had to justify their right to speak to effectively advocate for others. As Karlyn Kohrs Campbell explains, "In nineteenth century America, femininity and rhetorical action were seen as mutually exclusive. No 'true woman' could be a public persuader."[9] The nineteenth-century ideal of upper-class, white femininity did not include public advocacy. Women's activism challenged these ideals and made it radical and controversial for women to organize publicly. Through their protest of enslavement and Indian removal in the mid-nineteenth century, women learned to recognize their political agency, organize collectively, petition the government, and speak in public.[10]

Women involved in social reform in the Northeast began holding antislavery conventions for women, where they could also discuss women's rights, and they eventually organized conventions focused exclusively on women's rights.[11] In 1848, a women's rights convention was held in Seneca Falls, New York by Lucretia Coffin Mott of Philadelphia, and women from upstate New York, including Elizabeth Cady Stanton, Martha Coffin Wright, and Mary Ann McClintock. Three hundred men and women attended the Seneca Falls meeting, and signed a manifesto called the *Declaration of Sentiments*. Their declaration was modeled on the Declaration of Independence, but instead of decrying the British monarchy's tyranny over the thirteen colonies, they objected to men's tyranny over women, and declared that "all men *and women* were created equal." Their manifesto listed the rights they wanted, which included the right to vote. But the idea of women voting was so controversial that the resolution on woman suffrage was the only resolution that was not adopted unanimously, and it only narrowly passed the convention.[12] The ridicule and criticism that followed their convention was so intense that some of the one hundred men and women who signed the manifesto later asked to have their names removed.

After the Seneca Falls convention, more women's rights conventions were held in New York, Massachusetts, Pennsylvania, Indiana, and Ohio, only pausing during the Civil War.[13] These conventions gave them the opportunity to identify, explain, and debate their movement's goals, commitments, and ideology. As the movement grew, activists formed two organizations in 1869 that differed according to ideology and strategy, particularly in their stance on the Fifteenth Amendment, which enfranchised African American men. Stanton and Susan B. Anthony founded the National Woman Suffrage Association (NWSA) in New York City. Their organization opposed the Fifteenth Amendment because it did not include women, and focused on winning the franchise for women through a constitutional amendment. Lucy Stone and Henry Ward Beecher created the American Woman Suffrage Association (AWSA), headquartered in Boston. The AWSA supported the Fifteenth Amendment and focused their energies on winning suffrage for women at state and territorial levels because they thought it was more likely to succeed than a constitutional amendment.[14] These organizations eventually merged to become the National American Woman Suffrage Association (NAWSA) in 1890, headquartered in New York City.[15] After two more decades of activism, an additional suffrage organization split off from the NAWSA over another disagreement about advocacy tactics. In 1913, the National Woman's Party (NWP) separated from the NAWSA to focus on winning a federal amendment to the Constitution using militant tactics like White House protests and hunger strikes.[16] The NWP was based in Washington, DC, and led by Alice Paul and Lucy Burns. The NWP and the NAWSA together helped achieve the federal amendment to the Constitution in 1920. The Nineteenth Amendment technically enfranchised all women, but it functionally only enfranchised white women given the laws and practices that suppressed the votes of black, Asian, and American Indian men and women.

Because the traditional narrative of the US suffrage movement began in the Northeast, the national organizations were headquartered there, and the movement's most well-known leaders lived in the region, the majority of scholarship on the woman suffrage movement has focused on the movement's activism in the East.[17] This traditional narrative is disrupted when the West is centered in the story of women's voting rights.[18] While these movement leaders founded suffrage organizations in the East, Western territories began enfranchising women. In 1869—the same year that both the NWSA and the AWSA were founded in the Northeast—Wyoming Territory extended voting rights to women living thousands of miles to the west. Utah enfranchised eligible women in 1870, Washington followed in 1883 (although Washington's supreme court rescinded those voting rights in 1888), and Colorado and Idaho joined in the 1890s. Woman suffrage continued to spread regionally. By 1915, all twelve US states where women had equal voting rights to men were located west of the Mississippi River. Like states in the East and South, many Western states' electorates excluded American Indians and those who could not read and speak in English, which typically disenfranchised black and brown women and men. But these Western states included women and men who could meet their voting criteria, which differed strikingly from the East's exclusion of all women and the South's disfranchisement of women and African Americans.[19] Once the

West enfranchised women, they also began electing them to political office. While those in Eastern states were still campaigning for the right to vote, Utah, Colorado, and Arizona made women state senators, and Montana sent Jeannette Rankin to Congress.[20] When the Nineteenth Amendment to the US Constitution was adopted in 1920, fifteen states had granted women full voting rights, all of which were in the West except for New York, which adopted suffrage in 1917, and Michigan in 1919.

Thus, the West shaped the woman suffrage movement in part by enacting women's voting rights years before the rest of the nation. Why were the first suffrage victories in the West? The movement's success there was largely due to the region's fluid politics, women's innovative agitation tactics, and suffragists' coalitions with other reform movements.[21] The first territories to enact suffrage—Wyoming, Utah, and Washington—had small legislatures and were in the midst of attaining statehood. So they did not yet have state constitutions that required more complex procedures to redefine their electorate. Since these territories were still in the process of constructing their legal systems and did not have long-standing political traditions, woman suffrage was easier to pass.[22] In Utah, the Mormon Church influenced views on suffrage, and some non-Mormon citizens proposed enfranchising women to give them the political power necessary to end polygamy. In fact, Mormon elders approved woman suffrage to help protect polygamous practices, and for years, women voters helped keep polygamy legal in Utah.[23]

Suffrage activists' hard work and innovative agitation tactics were also essential to winning voting rights in the West. The earliest suffrage leaders in the West included Laura DeForce Gordon and Emily Pitts-Stevens in California, Abigail Scott Duniway in Oregon, Caroline Nichols Churchill in Colorado, Clarina Howard Nichols in Kansas, Emmeline B. Wells in Utah, and Clara Colby in Nebraska. Later in the nineteenth and early twentieth centuries, other regional leaders included Emma Smith DeVoe of Washington, May Arkwright Hutton of Idaho, Frances Munds in Arizona, Jeannette Rankin and Ella Knowles Haskell from Montana, Helen Reynolds of Colorado, Anne Martin in Nevada, and Ellen Sargent, Naomi Anderson, and Charlotte Perkins Gilman in

California. National suffrage leaders from the East also traveled to the West to give speeches, provide finances, and offer organizational and campaign insight, but they were not always appreciated by Western suffrage leaders, who sometimes viewed Eastern suffragists as interfering, controlling, or out of touch with Western culture. Activists toured the region to lecture on voting rights and organize suffrage associations. They also published women's rights journals, which were especially important for women in the Western states who were more separated in rural communities. Although each journal's content and style varied, they all helped build a sense of community among women and provided education, entertainment, and a trove of arguments and evidence for women's voting rights. Emily Pitts-Stevens began publishing the *Pioneer* out of San Francisco in 1869; Mary Livermore founded the *Agitator* in Chicago in 1869; Duniway founded the *New Northwest* in Portland, Oregon, in 1871; Caroline Nichols Churchill published the *Queen Bee* in Colorado; Emmeline B. Wells founded the *Woman's Exponent* in Utah; Clara Bewick Colby began the *Woman's Tribune* in Nebraska; and Emma and Ira Pack published the *Farmer's Wife* in Kansas.[24]

Suffragists were successful in part because of their strategic alliances with the populist and progressive movements. The Populist Party was a significant movement in the West that protested the region's economic subordination to the Northeast's organized capital. Populists called for the federal government to intervene and regulate the exploitation of the West by the Northeast's railroad companies, extractive corporations, and banks.[25] As women participated in the populist movement, they formed coalitions with populist organizations like the Grange and the Farmers' Alliance, and successfully gained populist men's support for woman suffrage.[26] The widespread appeal of populism in the West and populists' support of woman suffrage persuaded Colorado and Idaho citizens to adopt woman suffrage in 1893 and 1896 respectively.

Suffragists' coalition with the progressive movement helped win voting rights for women in Washington (1910); California (1911); Arizona, Alaska, and Oregon (1912); and Montana and Nevada (1914). Progressivism was a national movement that worked to address corruption in politics, regulate corporate interests, and support a host of issues including labor rights, prohibition, woman suffrage, and social welfare policies.[27] Progressives supported "direct democracy" reforms—policies like the referendum, the initiative, the recall, and woman suffrage—that empowered citizens to pass laws through their voting power and ideally limit corporate influence on the political process.[28] Many of these reforms were only adopted in the Western states. Woman suffrage was one of the few direct democracy reforms to eventually extend beyond the West. So, progressivism's direct democracy movement, and its success in the West, was a key agent in building Western support for woman suffrage.[29]

Finally, the regional development of woman suffrage in the West was not unique to the United States. Around the world, across continents and nations, women's voting rights first succeeded in places that were the most removed from centers of political, financial, and social power.[30] Although the instigating cause of women's enfranchisement varied, in each nation and region of the globe, women's rights first flourished far from the bases of imperial, financial, and political world powers. After women's voting rights were established somewhere within their nation or region, financial and political elites eventually followed the policies of those with lesser power. The initial experiments with woman suffrage eventually shaped national campaigns and spread women's voting rights to those centers of power.

The US West at the Turn of the Century

At the same time that Western states began enfranchising women, turn-of-the-century Americans cared tremendously about the West and its changing meaning because they were anxious about the perceived end of their frontier.[31] In 1890, the same year that Wyoming gained its statehood and became the first state to enfranchise women, Americans believed that the West had been settled. That year the US census revealed that every square mile of western land had a population of at least two inhabitants, excluding American Indians who were not taxed, and Americans interpreted this news to mean that the frontier was "closed."[32] Because there is little evidence that there was indeed a sharp break in Western American development in 1890, many contemporary scholars consider the supposed closing of the frontier irrelevant and critique the attention paid to the end of the frontier as a tendency to celebrate the tragic conquest of the region.[33] Yet, as David Wrobel argues, regardless of whether the frontier actually closed, Americans perceived that it had and acted on that perception.[34] Americans thought that by losing the frontier, they had also lost a source of exceptionalism, which they believed was detrimental to the future of the country. For generations, they had trusted that having a seemingly endless frontier was the basis of the United States' singularity, democracy, and individualism.[35] Benjamin Franklin, Thomas Jefferson, and Alexis de Tocqueville had depicted the unsettled land to the west as the key to American virtue and national health.[36] Americans feared that losing the frontier would destabilize the nation, increase poverty, decrease jobs and wages, and lead to overpopulation.[37] In 1893 history professor Frederick Jackson Turner famously expressed this concern at the World's Columbian Exposition in Chicago that the frontier had "explained America" and that having a frontier to conquer and land to settle was what had made the United States remarkable. But now that they believed it was gone, their unique source of excellence was gone too, and they thought the country would never be the same again.[38] Wrobel argues that the entire Progressive Era—which included the last thirty years of the suffrage movement—was marked by American anxiety over becoming a frontier-less nation.[39]

Americans began a critical effort to reimagine the new meaning of this western land, and that new meaning was contentious. Residents of the West and East had vested interests in contradictory visions of the region, and both attempted to shape it accordingly. Many Easterners wanted the West to remain a frontier, or at least their romanticized vision of the frontier they saw in Bill Cody's Wild West shows: a wide-open, "wild," and adventurous escape from the East.[40] For Easterners, the region's cultural appeal was its distinctness from the East. They wanted it to be a primitive place of freedom they could visit to be close to nature when they needed a break from social pressures and urban constraints.[41] So they held on to their image of the frontier past by revering the cowboy, hailing the heroic traits of pioneers, and celebrating the West as an undeveloped land of danger and adventure.[42] In contrast, the white people who actually lived in the West wanted to modernize and develop the region, draw more settlers, and make it more like the East. Many had migrated to farm land, build homes, and create communities, which required economic and civic structures, larger populations, and greater national representation. The more settled and populated the region was, the easier it was for white settlers to survive and prosper. In their language, their goal was to "civilize" the West.[43] Civilization was believed to be marked by whiteness, wealth, gender differentiation, and modern forms of technology.[44] To that end, they worked to make the West less rugged and more desirable to "civilized" settlers, featuring the region as a "white racial utopia," even though it was racially diverse.[45] They ran a decades-long booster campaign that depicted the region as a place of ease and modernity, which stood in stark contrast to the East's popular portrayals of the West as a wild frontier.[46]

As Americans reinvented the West, their conflicting visions were ubiquitous in popular discourse and made convenient rhetorical resources for suffragists. Americans used these contradictory meanings of the West to advocate and oppose women's voting rights. Suffragists like Abigail Scott Duniway (see chapter 1) capitalized on the nation's fascination with the West as a mythic frontier and the basis of American exceptionalism. Duniway associated Western women's voting rights with the freedom, exceptionalism, and heroism that Americans believed the region provided. In contrast, antisuffragists (see chapter 3) used the idea of the Wild West to portray the suffrage states as uncivilized and harmful to human development, rather than celebrating the frontier, and depicted women's voting rights as similarly unevolved and ignorant. In response, some Western suffragists went east to defend the West and promote woman suffrage as another aspect of the West's civilization, progress, and modernity. As Western suffragists defended women's voting rights (see chapter 4), they boosted the region's image in the East and depicted woman suffrage as another aspect of the West's ease, democracy, and technology—all aspects they believed to be part of civilization. Likewise, in the movement's imagery and performances (see chapter 2 and 5), suffragists used maps, parades, and pageants to depict the Western suffrage states as more civilized than the East. Eventually, suffragists used the West's civilized image and history of continental expansion to imply that women's voting rights were expanding across the continent. In their attempt to associate women's voting rights with civilization, suffragists' goal aligned with that of many Westerners: to construct the West as civilized in the national imagination.

In many ways, the meaning of the West and the woman suffrage movement grew up together. The nation was simultaneously debating the meanings of both the West and women's voting rights, and these debates inevitably influenced each other. While the nation was in the midst of remaking the meaning of this newly settled region, many Western states enfranchised women. And as Americans noticed the regional pattern in women's voting rights, public figures and the national press speculated on the reasons why the movement had succeeded in the West. So many people pointed to the Western suffrage states as support for their view of suffrage that a writer for *Woman's Protest* claimed in 1916, "I have heard the State of Colorado held up so persistently as an example on both sides of the fence that I think it must be showing signs of fatigue if not the actual wear."[47] Both suffragists and antisuffragists attempted to interpret the regional development of women's voting rights in ways that supported their viewpoint and their preferred meaning of the West.

As suffragists tactically deployed the West to motivate women's rights, they appropriated the racial and imperial rhetorics of civilization and continental expansion that shaped the region. Scholars have thoroughly demonstrated the ways white suffragists appealed to their audience's racist beliefs and imperial values in their efforts to persuade.[48] Many focused on gaining voting rights for themselves and others like them, and often embraced or ignored black and brown women's disfranchisement. In the end, white women succeeded in securing their voting rights in large part because they leveraged their racial and class privileges.[49] Suffragists' identification with the West made it even easier to appeal to the racist and imperial values of American voters since the region was often imagined as a white racial refuge from the East's growing immigrant population.[50]

Defining the US West as Regional Rhetoric

There are many definitions of the West in part because there is no consensus on the official boundaries of "the real American West," which is most obvious in attempts to identify where the Midwest ends and the West begins.[51] As scholars have argued over this point, they have proposed many potential eastern boundaries: the Mississippi River; the Missouri River; the Great Plains; the Rocky Mountains; a variety of state lines; and the 95th, 97th, 98th, and the 99th meridians.[52] Scholars also disagree on whether the Pacific Coast is part of the West, and if it is not, whether the West ends at the state lines of Washington, Oregon, and California, or at the point where the wetter land on the coast gives way to the arid land that marks much of the region.[53] Defining it according to its geographic location is also difficult because that location has shifted many times as a result of US colonial history. European settlers first referred to the Virginia's Piedmont region as the "far west." Then the "far west" shifted to the Kentucky-Tennessee region before the label was applied to land west of the Mississippi River or to the Rocky Mountains. For decades, the land that is now Minnesota and Wisconsin was considered the Northwest.[54]

Furthermore, the meaning of the West has been shaped by the colonization and conquest of North America. Indeed, the very term "West" presumes a European perspective of the North American continent, because for Europeans Americans coming from the Atlantic Coast, "the frontier *was* the West."[55] This name ignores the American Indians in the area, and erases the perspective of the Asian migrants who moved east to California, the Canadians who moved south to Montana and the

Dakotas, and the Latin American settlers who moved north.[56] The land that is now generally known as the West—the US territory west of the Mississippi—was legally created through the United States' purchase of Louisiana in 1803, the acquisition of the Texas and Oregon territories in 1845 and 1846, the Mexican cession of California and other territories in the 1840s, and the Gadsden Purchase of 1854.[57] Yet the language of "purchases" and "acquisitions" obscures the United States' accompanying racial violence, forced removals, seizure of land and resources, and attacks on culture and religion.[58] The West was created through conquest, continental expansion, and decades of racial violence and warfare. Patricia Limerick and Richard White—New Western Historians who led the scholarly effort to resist valorizing the United States' westward expansion—generally define the West as a place, product, and story of continual conquest.[59]

Given the numerous definitions of the West, it is helpful to understand the West as a kind of "regional rhetoric." Like many scholars, I approach regions as symbolic social inventions.[60] I agree with Douglas Reichert Powell that a region is not "a thing" with stable boundaries, official borders, or an "authentic" meaning, but instead, a region is a "cultural history, an ongoing rhetorical and poetic construction."[61] Instead of having official boundaries or borders, they are an "aggregation of places," or a network of sites that become bound to each other through the process of region-making: rhetorically connecting places to each other and assigning meaning to that network of places through observations, descriptions, analyses, and naming practices.[62] The very debate over the West's boundaries and meanings illustrates the contested nature of regions: each definition of the West attempts to link certain areas of land to each other, and to justify their relationship and definition. Since the meaning of a region is not grounded in physical territory, each attempt to define a region is "an attempt to persuade as much as to describe."[63]

So, when I talk about regional rhetoric, I am not talking about "local color" or "regionalized style."[64] Nor am I discussing solely speakers from the West, or arguments addressed to regional audiences. Instead, I define regional rhetoric as the symbols that connect local and material spaces—in this case towns, cities, and masses of land in the West—to each other, and to particular meanings, histories, and values. Regional rhetorics make at least two claims: these places are related to each other, and these places are related to particular meanings.[65] Inhabitants and outsiders cumulatively shape the dominant meaning of a region as they privilege certain definitions, histories, and values over others.[66] Whether it's the West, East, North, or South, or smaller regions like Silicon Valley, Appalachia, or the Bible Belt, those regional rhetorics are resisted, reimagined, and employed persuasively.[67]

By tracing the regional rhetoric that was prevalent in the controversy over women voting, I introduce the concept of "region in protest": the way social movements can strategically leverage and disrupt region to enact social change. Region—like other kinds of place—can function as a valuable persuasive resource for social movements, just as the West was rhetorically powerful for woman suffragists.[68] Since regional rhetoric creates relationships that connect places to each other and to ideas, it has the capacity to connect disparate sites, histories, values, and politics to create new or altered resources and strategies for activists. As rhetorics of relationships, rhetorical critic Jenny Rice explains, regions provide a means of reimagining places, political movements, and their relationship to each other and to other places, regions, politics, and powers.[69] Since regions are not stable entities, their locations and meanings can be unsettled for persuasive ends. Region in protest points to the way region can function as strategy—as a rhetorical resource that can be activated, disrupted, employed tactically, and leveraged for social change.[70]

Region in protest builds on Danielle Endres and Samantha Senda-Cook's conceptualization of "place in protest"—the way social movements strategically deploy the meaning of place as a persuasive strategy.[71] Endres and Senda-Cook have illuminated multiple ways that social movements employ place as a persuasive strategy: they craft "place-based arguments" that draw on the symbolic meaning of place verbally; they hold protests in places with symbolic power; and they reconstruct the meaning of a place by using it for persuasive purposes. Because regions are a kind of place, they can function similarly to place as a persuasive strategy for social movements.[72] Like with place, social movements can deploy region in protest through verbal arguments. But regions also fundamentally differ from place. Powell maintains that "region is in many ways categorically different from other conceptualizations of place" because "region must refer not to a specific site but to a larger network of sites." Powell clarifies that "regions are a particular sort of place, kind of a meta-place."[73] Rice agrees that regions are "not so much places but ways of strategically describing relationships among places."[74] So, as a unique kind of place, with its relational and networked nature, region must at times be deployed in different ways than place. For unlike place, social movement activists cannot employ or shape region by physically gathering together in a region, because it would likely invoke the meaning of the physical site in which they are gathered rather than the region. Rhetors seeking to invoke region, by contrast, must move beyond the materiality of the site to activate region visually or through other kinds of embodied performances, mediums, or strategies, as I will illustrate with the suffrage movement. Suffragists invoked and reimagined the West with their words, flags, maps, cartoons, pageants, tableaus, parades, and at least one cross-country road trip.[75]

In the end, suffragists employed and contested the West in a variety of ways as they protested women's unequal voting rights. As Thomas Farrell argues, "Rhetoric is the art, the fine and useful art, of making things matter," and advocates and opponents of woman suffrage made women's voting rights matter through their preferred visions of the West.[76] Both sides imagined and mobilized the West in disparate ways to convince others of the rightness or wrongness of woman suffrage. Through their words, visuals, and embodied performances, suffragists employed multiple regional rhetorics of the West—the mythic frontier, civilization, continental expansion, and Manifest Destiny—to appeal to Americans' fascination with the West after the US frontier seemingly closed.[77] Antisuffragists used an alternative regional rhetoric—a vision of the West as wild and woolly—to appeal to Easterners' romantic image of the West and depict women voting as uncivilized. Over time the suffrage movement challenged the traditional meanings of the West and East, which allowed them to compare the suffrage campaign's success with the process of the United States' westward expansion. Eventually, suffragists used their civilized image of the West to imply that the region's civilization and voting rights were spreading east, just as the United States expanded west from the Atlantic to the Pacific. By identifying the West with progress and civilization, and envisioning the East as an uncivilized and barbaric frontier, suffragists contradicted the image many Easterners imagined for themselves, the East, and the West. Advocates compelled Easterners to reexamine the meaning of women's voting rights and the West, and challenged longstanding visions of US regions and their relationships. These new visions of the West and its relationship to the East showcased suffrage advocates' new rhetorical tactic: the regional rhetoric of the US West.

CHAPTER 1

Mythologizing the West

ABIGAIL SCOTT DUNIWAY'S
MYTHIC FRONTIER, 1884–1905

———·◆·———

I n 1884, Western suffrage leader Abigail Scott Duniway (1834–1915) "created somewhat of a furor" when she spoke at the National Woman Suffrage Association (NWSA) convention in Washington, DC.[1] Visiting from the Pacific Northwest, she stood apart from the Eastern suffragists who lectured that week. The *Oregonian* reported that before she began, "there had immediately preceded her a Boston lady, a speaker whose words were carefully chosen, her modulation smoother, her *a*s and *ew*s given a scientifically correct sound, her gesticulations measured, her poise studied."[2] In contrast, Duniway:

> arose, stroked down the folds of her dress, walked to the middle of the platform as independently as a queen, and began her address in an off-hand manner that at once delighted her audience. Here was somebody novel to them. Force was substituted for excessive polish. As she proceeded, speaking in an unaffected, incisive, earnest, at times humorous

Figure 1. Abigail Scott Duniway.

manner, the audience cheered lustily. They were especially struck with her unique comparisons, the incidents of western life that she related. . . . Mrs. Duniway received more hearty and prolonged applause than any other speaker who addressed the body. . . . I [was] proud of Mrs. Duniway and Oregon.[3]

The reporter conveyed the distinctive nature of Duniway's regional themes and speaking style, and the appreciation of her audience for her uniqueness. Her singularity came in part from her vivid depictions of life in the West and what Randall Lake calls her western exceptionalism.[4] Given Americans' preoccupation with the changing meaning of the West at the end of the nineteenth century, Duniway's status as a Westerner captivated her audience's attention. She capitalized on their fascination by imagining the West as a mythic frontier to advocate women's voting rights.

Duniway—known as "the hardiest and tireless suffrage worker the Western states produced"—was a white lecturer, journalist, newspaper editor, and businesswoman who worked and lived in the Pacific Northwest (see figure 1).[5] She began her woman suffrage career by accompanying Susan B. Anthony on a lecture tour that covered two thousand rugged miles.[6] They took wagons, canoes, steamers, and stagecoaches through the Pacific Northwest's mud and rain to stay in primitive tents and rustic hotels. Even Anthony, who was accustomed to traveling by train and stagecoach on her lecture tours, described parts of the ten-week trip as "mortal agony."[7] When the trip concluded, she wrote home that she was "tired, tired" and returned east without raising the money she intended for the suffrage cause.[8] But Duniway was proud to have given Anthony "a taste of pioneering under difficulties that remained with her as a memory to her dying day."[9] More importantly, that lecture tour helped jumpstart Duniway's career as the most well-known suffragist of the West.

Duniway helped found Oregon's first suffrage organization in 1870, which became the Oregon Equal Suffrage Association in 1873, and started a human rights newspaper, the *New Northwest*.[10] From 1871 to 1887, her paper advocated woman suffrage and addressed economic injustices and discrimination toward women, American Indians, and Chinese immigrants.[11] She traveled, lectured, and published to such an extent that her contemporary biographers described her as "one of the most widely known women on the Pacific slope" in 1897.[12] After speaking at the conventions of the NWSA and the National American Woman Suffrage Association (NAWSA), Duniway earned a national reputation so great that Eastern suffragists sponsored an East Coast lecture tour for her and elected her to one of five NWSA vice presidents at large.[13] For many Eastern suffragists, she represented all Western women.[14] Lucy Stone, a leader of the American Woman Suffrage Association (AWSA), honored Duniway as "the pioneer Woman Suffragist of the great Northwest."[15] Her contemporaries described her speaking as "logical, sarcastic, witty, poetic and often eloquent" and her writing as "forceful and argumentative."[16] She was known for entertaining her audiences, making them laugh, and using her beloved West to persuade.

I argue that Duniway appealed to turn-of-the-century Americans' fascination with the West by leveraging the frontier myth as a regional rhetoric to champion women's voting rights. She invoked the dominant meaning of the West as a mythic frontier and reimagined it as a region of white women's liberty and equality. Duniway resisted the centrality of men in the traditional frontier myth and instead envisioned the West as a region created together by men and women, celebrating the sacrifices that women had also made. In her frontier myth, white women, like men, had survived their mythic trek west, proved their heroism, and earned their citizenship rights. She deployed the mythic frontier through three main strategies: she recognized Western women as frontier heroines who deserved the franchise; she excluded American Indians and Eastern women from the heroic status that merited suffrage; and she maintained the masculine ideals of the frontier myth and US politics as she celebrated white Western men and women in service of woman suffrage.

The West as a Mythic Frontier at the Turn of the Century

At the end of the nineteenth century, Americans were enthralled with the West as a mythic frontier. Myths are pedagogical narratives about exceptional people doing exceptional things.[17] Cultures repeat myths to account for their origins, teach their youth about their collective values, and celebrate models of exceptional action.[18] The traditional frontier myth is a narrative that elevated white frontiersmen as models to follow for future generations.[19] It chronicles the white men—hunters, trappers, traders, and explorers—who traveled west, fought and conquered American Indians, overcame many challenges, and transformed into American heroes in the process.[20] Facing epic struggles and violently killing American Indians was the transformative process of turning Europeans into true Americans and producing frontier heroes.[21] This myth imagined the West as a mysterious and endless testing ground to prove one's exceptionalism, and an opportunity for creating rugged, independent, and brave Americans.

The frontier myth is a persuasive and pedagogical narrative that has been used in many contexts and forms. John F. Kennedy invoked the frontier myth to advocate space exploration, George W. Bush used it to justify the War on Terror, and twenty-first century scientists continue to employ it to characterize scientific research.[22] Yet, the frontier myth also functioned as a form of regional rhetoric. In the nineteenth century, as it motivated Western expansion, it simultaneously shaped the meaning of the West. In 1893, historian Frederick Jackson Turner famously articulated the myth in his frontier thesis. He argued that the process of exploring, conquering, and settling the West had explained America as it taught Americans the pioneer virtues of independence and individualism.[23] Turner's thesis imagined the West as a frontier that could transform European men into true Americans who were good for democracy by challenging and testing them. Once they believed that the Western land had been settled, they feared that it no longer had the power of the mythic frontier to test and prove the mettle of European men. The narrative of exploration, conquest, and settlement had supplied white Americans with abundant evidence of US exceptionalism, so many of them mourned and feared this perceived change, and attempted to hold on to their preferred meaning of the West as a frontier. Americans' nostalgia and anxiety about the perceived "closing frontier" motivated them to recount the frontier myth in entertainment, art, and politics.

The frontier myth's prevalence in public discourse simultaneously functioned as a region-making rhetoric. Dime novels idealized the West as a frontier of outlaws, cowboys, American Indians, and saloonkeepers, and the legendary Buffalo Bill Cody's Wild West shows colorfully represented the West as a frontier from the 1880s to the 1910s.[24] Theodore Roosevelt celebrated it in his political speeches, performed the cowboy role through hunting and ranching in Dakota Territory, and formed the Boone and Crockett Club "to preserve a little of the old frontier spirit."[25] Owen Wister's best-selling cowboy novel, *The Virginian*, and Frederic Remington's murals depicted a West of heroic white cowboys and wild riders fighting American Indians.[26] The frontier myth's popularity and cultural power at the turn of the century influenced the ever-evolving meaning of the West as a region for years to come. Even after the land was claimed and settled by the United States, the frontier myth was used to envision the West as a frontier and valorize white Westerners as heroes. Given its prevalent and persuasive power, Duniway leveraged the myth's construction of the West as a frontier in her national advocacy for women's rights.

Yet, the traditional frontier myth was characteristically masculine.[27] The masculinity of the frontier myth has been discussed to such an extent by scholars that historian Susan Armitage calls the West Hisland.[28] Even as more women were populating the West, historian Susan Lee Johnson argues, turn-of-the-century Americans viewed the West as a refuge for white masculinity.[29] Literature often deployed feminine metaphors like virgin land to define the West as a frontier for men to forge, conquer, and own.[30] The traditional frontier myth celebrated white men as heroes, and told stories of Western travel and violence as romantic and heroic adventures from a white man's point of view.[31] Americans often understood westward expansion as an activity solely for white men, and many believed, as Roosevelt taught, that participating in western expansion and experiencing life in the rural West proved one's manhood and helped him cultivate manly virtues.[32] These masculine notions of the frontier myth would seemingly have been difficult for Duniway to deploy for women's rights. Yet, as she invoked the frontier myth for her persuasive purposes, she contested its traditional construction of the West and recast the region as a mythic frontier of freedom and heroism for women too.[33]

I illustrate this argument by examining twelve speeches in which Duniway employed and reimagined the West as a mythic frontier between 1884 and 1905.[34] She delivered six of the speeches in the East and the Midwest, when she addressed the US Senate Select Committee on Woman Suffrage in 1884;[35] the World's Columbian Exposition in Chicago in 1893;[36] the 1884 NWSA convention;[37] the 1889 NWSA convention;[38] the 1899 NAWSA convention;[39] and the 1900 NAWSA convention.[40] She delivered the other six speeches in the West, when she addressed the Idaho Constitutional Convention in 1889;[41] the Oregon State Equal Suffrage

Association's convention in 1897;[42] the fortieth anniversary celebration of Oregon's Admission to Statehood in 1899;[43] the Oregon Federation of Women's Club Convention in 1900;[44] the unveiling of the *Sacajawea* statue in 1905;[45] and the Lewis and Clark Exposition's celebration of Abigail Scott Duniway Day.[46]

Duniway's Reimagined West as a Region for White Women's Liberty

Duniway took advantage of the nation's nostalgia for the West as a frontier and deployed it strategically for women's voting rights. She invoked the meaning of the West as imagined by the frontier myth and challenged it by including white women as beneficiaries of the West's freedom and equality. She expanded the ideal of the frontier hero to include white Western women, and asserted that Western women had also been tested and transformed into frontier heroines who had earned their voting rights. But her celebration of white Western women excluded American Indian and Eastern women, and maintained the traditional ideal of white masculinity.

When speaking to the 1900 NAWSA convention in DC, Duniway claimed that "nowhere else, upon this planet, are the inalienable rights of women as much appreciated as on the newly settled borders of these United States."[47] At the 1899 NAWSA convention, she noted, "my state is the only one represented this year in this great convention in which an equal suffrage amendment is pending." She explained Oregon's pending suffrage amendment as evidence of the West's equality. In contrast to "the older states [in the East], crystalized with constitutions hoary with the incrustations of long vanished years," she celebrated the "liberties" white Western women had in "the free, young, elastic West."[48] She asserted that in the West, "our Constitutions are not ironclad but are sufficiently elastic to yield to the will of the majority of those who vote instead of those who refuse to vote, as in the older states, where it is almost impossible to amend a Constitution at all."[49] Duniway's West was politically malleable and easier to affect change than in the East.

Duniway's region-making suggested that white, Western women's liberty was derived in part from their location in the West. The frontier myth rests on the premise that freedom abides in the land, and Duniway likewise invoked these mythic conceptions about the region. She celebrated "the Pacific Northwest . . . as the original land of the Free and the Home of the Brave."[50] She maintained that in the West, "the spirit of liberty and patriotism . . . is in the air."[51] At times, Duniway's description implied that the motivation for equality of the sexes materially existed in the land of the West. She explained to Eastern suffragists, "There are lessons of liberty in the rock-ribbed mountains . . . There are lessons of freedom in our broad prairies . . . There are lessons of equality in the gigantic, evenly-crested forest trees . . . There are lessons of truth and justice in the very air we breathe, and lessons of irresistible progress in the mighty waters."[52] By depicting the West as a naturally equal and free space, Duniway suggested that women's presence there transformed them into women deserving of citizenship. Significantly, her depiction contrasted starkly with the traditional understanding of Western land as metaphorically feminine and as a place for men to conquer.[53]

Naturalizing white women's freedom in the Western land had the potential to undercut their agency, but it also deflected criticism for Western women's political involvement. Janice Hocker Rushing explains that the traditional frontier myth focused on the frontier to such an extent that it functioned as a main controlling factor to the hero's actions.[54] Furthermore, Dorsey observes that "when rhetors focused on the mythic frontier as a principle motivating force for human behavior, heroes were essentially absolved of any wrongdoing; their interaction with the frontier was being determined for them by the scene itself."[55] Likewise, in Duniway's myth, her focus on the freedom of the West may have helped exonerate Westerners from instigating gender equality and placed the responsibility for equality on the Western land. Furthermore, she reimagined the West as a region of women's freedom and equality in large part by re-envisioning the heroes of the mythic frontier and recognizing white Western women as exceptional.

INCLUDING WHITE WESTERN WOMEN
AS FRONTIER HEROINES

Typically stronger, smarter, and more spiritual than others, traditional frontier heroes left the civilization of the East to trap animals, battle American Indians, and create new communities in the Western wilderness.[56] They proved their exceptionalism through their ability to survive the uncharted wilderness alone and by passing successfully through a difficult rite of passage after great sacrifice.[57] The mythic narrative demonstrated how the frontier tested the hero who triumphed and offered lessons for future generations to follow by example.[58] Heroes earned the audience's awe and respect by acting exceptionally and giving their lives to something bigger than themselves.[59] In the traditional frontier myth, women were denied participatory, heroic roles and were instead positioned in opposition to the frontier values of freedom and adventure.[60] But Duniway's frontier included heroines who had also made their sacrificial pilgrimage and earned their voting rights for their struggle on the frontier.

Duniway praised the heroism of white Western women and positioned them as central protagonists of the mythic frontier. Her commemoration of frontier heroines was especially vivid in the speech she delivered at the celebration of Oregon's fortieth anniversary of statehood in 1899. At this ceremony, she addressed over one thousand Oregonians who were gathered in the statehouse in Salem. The state legislature hosted the event and planned the ceremony's program to include musical performances and speakers, including Duniway, Oregon's governor, and a former state governor. Duniway was the only woman to speak that day, and since the following year Oregonians would be voting on a suffrage amendment, she used this commemorative event as an opportunity to invoke the mythic frontier and recast it by celebrating white Western women as heroines who deserved their voting rights.[61]

While men and women had together made their pilgrimages west to Oregon, the famous frontier stories only featured men on the journey. Duniway attempted to rectify women's omission by "honor[ing] the valor of those intrepid mothers of the mighty men of today and yesterday, who

crossed the untracked continent in ox wagons or on horseback." Like
in the traditional frontier myth, Duniway praised "the valiant deeds of
Oregon's pioneer and public-spirited men" and recognized their "brave
hearts and firm footsteps" and "their deeds of daring, danger and endurance [that] have long been chronicled in song and story." Yet she
noted that "other speakers have extolled the . . . spirit which led men . . .
through a perilous, toilsome pilgrimage . . . But many were the *women*,
daily companions of these men of valor, with lives equal to theirs in rec-
titude and energy, whose names, as yet, have found no place in song and
story, who did their part as bravely as did any man; and their memory
remains today enshrined only in the hearts of rustic neighbors."[62] In her
frontier, both men and women faced struggles, endured sacrifices, and
risked danger, so both men and women deserved recognition and heroic
status.

Duniway celebrated white Western women as frontier heroines by
acknowledging the additional sacrifices of their westward pilgrimage.
She asked her Oregon audience to compare men and women's Western
experiences and agree that women's migrations included even more risks
than men's:

> The women of Oregon . . . have they not nobly and bravely borne their
> part as did the men? Were they not as faithful as [the men] in building
> up this vigorous young commonwealth of the Pacific Northwest? . . .
> It is now my grateful privilege to recognize woman's part, often more
> difficult and dangerous, because accompanied by the added terrors of
> maternity, and always as important as man's in building up a state from
> its crude beginnings into such fruition as we now behold.[63]

Every step of the way, women had also bravely left their homes and migrated somewhere new. But for women, migrating to a new home was
even more difficult under frontier conditions because of the terrors of
maternity they faced. As the mother of six children, five boys and one
girl, Duniway testified to the additional risks and dangers women faced
through childbearing on the frontier.

Duniway's heroines had also enacted the violence that Americans viewed as a distinctly American achievement. And like men, these women had contributed to American "progress" on the frontier and deserved a just reward. She recalled one such heroic woman: "We cannot forget the faithful bravery of the lone woman in her rough log cabin in the beautiful hills of Southern Oregon, who, when her husband lay dead at her feet, from the treacherous aim of a cruel savage, kept the howling despoilers of her home at bay with her trusty rifle until daylight came, and brought her succor from the neighboring hills."[64] Here Duniway presented a woman every bit as equipped as the traditional frontier hero. Gun in hand she defended herself and her home. Through her personal trial, she survived the violence of the frontier, triumphed over its testing, and proved her heroism. Richard Slotkin explains that the frontier myth hinges on violence and associates achievement and "progress" with violent action. According to Slotkin, the critical role of violence in the frontier myth is characterized as "distinctively 'American.'"[65] Likewise, Duniway highlighted the violence that proved the exceptionalism of white Western women as she declared, "We cannot forget the heroism of the women of the Whitman party, who were both victims and survivors of that horrible and historic massacre."[66] As she did in many of her speeches, she recognized women's contributions to war and violence by giving birth to soldiers. She quoted Oregon poet Joaquin Miller, "The bravest battle that was ever fought . . . Twas fought by the mothers of men," and she waved the bloody shirt as effectively as any politician of her day by remembering "the deeds of heroism that characterized the women who bore the soldiers who bore the arms."[67] Duniway's recollection of frontier battles showcased Western women's courage in the face of fear, loss, and violence.

Duniway featured frontier heroines whose place in the settling of the West was permanently inscribed on the Western consciousness. Women, like men, had earned their status as citizens through their triumph in the right of passage that brought them west to create a new life. To now turn their backs on their partners in the making of the West would deny the just completion of the women's frontier triumph. This not only deprived them of their rights guaranteed by the Declaration of Independence, but to refuse these women their citizenship violated the sacred promise of the frontier myth. Duniway reminded her Oregon audience of "Those mothers in Oregon, whose patient endurance of poverty, hardship and toil brought them naught of public and little of private recompense." She closed her speech at Oregon's anniversary ceremony by asking the men voters: "And shall Oregon . . . refuse, through her men voters, to ratify the [suffrage amendment] which has given them the glorious opportunity to . . . mak[e] it a year of jubilee for the wives and mothers of the pioneers, to whose influence the upbuilding of the state is, by their own confession, so largely due?"[68]

Although Duniway's commemoration of Western women was especially extensive at Oregon's fortieth anniversary ceremony, her other speeches often presented suffrage as a right that women had earned on the frontier. As she declared at the 1900 NAWSA convention, "These [Western] women . . . have royally earned their liberties."[69] Duniway's West had been secured by men and women together, she explained: "Men have had opportunities, in our remote countries, to see the worth of the civilized woman, *who came with them, or among them,* to new settlements . . . as their helpmates, companions, counselors and fellow-homemakers, rejoicing with them in the homes *they have earned together.*"[70] She posed the full quandary to men when she addressed the Idaho Constitutional Convention, seven years before the state enfranchised women: "Shall we, the women of this border land, who have shared alike your trials and your triumphs—shall we not be permitted to go up to the national capital bearing aloft the banner of our freedom?"[71] Duniway implied that Western men owed pioneer women suffrage for what they endured on the frontier. At an Oregon Pioneer Association meeting, Duniway introduced a resolution that the association adopted: "WHEREAS: The Oregon Pioneers of both sexes have equally shared the dangers and difficulties of subduing the Oregon wildernesses, therefore, be it Resolved, That we use all honorable means to secure to both sexes equality of rights before the law."[72] After surviving the trials and tests of the pilgrimage west and the violent defense of the land, white Western women had performed their true American identity, and frontier heroes owed it to them to recognize their sacrifice with the franchise.

Duniway also envisioned the West as a region of white women's freedom by personifying the ideal frontier heroine who had earned her citizenship through her mythic trek west, her extensive work on the frontier, and her return to the East. In her speeches and actions, Duniway drew on her ethos as a frontier heroine to legitimize her authority. In 1889, Duniway shared with her NWSA audience in Washington: "It is a matter of history that for fifteen years . . . your humble speaker had traveled alone, over Oregon, Washington and Idaho, enduring toil, hardship, privation, ridicule, sneers and vituperation, and steadily overcoming all sorts of obstacles."[73] To a convention accustomed to honoring those who fought for suffrage, she established her credentials by traveling alone like the frontier hero, enduring the trials as all those who made the West, and overcoming all the obstacles she faced as a suffragist.[74] All this worked to demonstrate the mettle that earns suffrage. Her confrontation with the earthly wilderness, as well as with the "ridicule, sneers and vituperation" she endured during her fight for suffrage, justified her assumption of the frontier hero persona. And to make certain her audience did not miss the point, she marked the states of the Northwest as her track, comparing her suffrage campaign trail to the Western trails traveled by pioneers.[75] By embodying the true rugged hero, she built her ethos on the model of frontier triumph, and demonstrated her mythic accomplishments.

Duniway also epitomized the ultimate frontier heroine through her life experience and western pilgrimage.[76] Like the traditional frontier hero, she had left the East and migrated west as one of the early Oregon settlers, and had faced the trials of frontier life.[77] At age eighteen, Duniway and her family left their farming village of Groveland, Illinois, and joined the Oregon Trail migration of 1852, one of the largest mass movements in US history.[78] Trying to escape the depression and widespread bankruptcies that followed the Panic of 1837, the Scott family traveled by covered wagon to join other relatives who had already moved to Oregon. During their five-and-a-half-month trip west, Duniway endured many sacrifices.

She lost her mother to cholera and survived the deaths of her brother, her cousin, and the man she had fallen in love with. Once she arrived in Oregon, she met and married Benjamin C. Duniway, established a home outside of Portland, and began having children. Duniway faced many more challenges of Western life. Her family lost their home due to her husband's poor financial decisions, and then her husband was injured so seriously by a runaway team of horses that he lost the ability to perform farm labor. Duniway enacted the independent and self-sufficient frontier heroine as she became the family breadwinner, and provided for her family through teaching, boarding, and opening her own millinery shop.[79] She had left her home and traveled west, survived her rite of passage in the Western wilderness, and endured physical and emotional sacrifices. By incarnating her argument, she attested to the veracity of her vision of the frontier.[80] Duniway's enactment of the frontier heroine functioned as proof that women could indeed attain elevated status.[81]

The years of work and sacrifice Duniway invested in the West and the woman suffrage movement enacted the mythic hero's superior strength and intelligence. Although she had no formal education other than some log-cabin schooling in Illinois, she demonstrated her exceptionalism by teaching herself enough to publish novels, poetry, and her own human rights newspaper. For sixteen years, she spent more than half of every year traveling around the Pacific Northwest giving speeches. She lectured three to five evenings a week and led women's clubs, all while publishing, editing, and writing articles for her newspaper, the *New Northwest*.[82] By 1897, Duniway had given 140 public lectures, traveled over twelve thousand miles, and distributed over half a million copies of the *New Northwest*.[83] Westerners recognized Duniway's exceptionalism. In 1905, Portland's Lewis and Clark Exposition celebrated Abigail Scott Duniway Day, making her the only woman to receive this honor for "embodying in high degree the qualities of the pioneer wives and mothers who had an equal share in the settlement of Old Oregon."[84] And the legislative record for the fortieth anniversary celebration of Oregon's statehood describes her as "known throughout the nation as perhaps the ablest champion now living of the claims of woman for equal political rights . . . Mrs. Duniway is a noble woman, of whom Oregon is justly proud."[85] Her sacrifices for the suffrage cause were also widely known. In 1897, her contemporary biographers maintained that she had "undoubtedly traveled more miles by stage, rail, river and wagon, made more public speeches, endured more hardships, persecution and ridicule, and scored more victories than any of her distinguished contemporaries of the East and middle West."[86]

Duniway also completed the mythic hero's cosmogonic cycle, which has endured as a central feature of the American frontier myth and consistently appears in many of the world's mythic traditions and sacred writings across continents and cultures.[87] The mythic formulation requires that after the protagonists experience their adventure in the new world, they return home and pass on their new knowledge to those they left behind. Duniway completed this cosmogonic cycle in several ways. During her own western migration on the Oregon Trail, she kept a daily journal of the trip to send back as a guide for future travelers.[88] She also returned to the East and shared with Eastern suffrage conventions the lessons she learned in the West. She reminded her 1900 NAWSA audience of "the Paradise of the Pacific Northwest, from whose summer lands and sun-down seas I have traveled four thousand miles to greet this brilliant gathering."[89] She noted that the NAWSA had asked her to speak to the audience about "the progress made during the century by the mothers of the race, in the far-off corner of our continent from which I come."[90] By personifying the frontier heroine, Duniway authenticated her experiences, elevated the credibility of her suffrage arguments, and served as evidence that women could undeniably fill the role of frontier heroine. She enacted her independence, her difference from Eastern women, and her exceptional nature. Performing her argument about white Western women's exceptionalism helped her employ and alter the mythic West as a persuasive resource in her activism.

Overall, Duniway's use of the frontier myth was a meritocratic argument for women's rights and was similar to arguments made about men's suffrage at other times in US history.[91] Reformers had argued that white men who served in the American Revolution or militia had earned the right to vote and that black men who served in the Civil War likewise earned the franchise.[92] Yet earned-rights arguments appear less often in the scholarship on woman suffrage arguments, which has focused largely on two types of arguments: natural rights arguments, which affirmed men and women's similarity and demanded women's rights according to their personhood and common humanity, and expediency arguments, which affirmed men and women's differences, emphasized their womanhood, and reasoned that woman suffrage would have a positive effect on political life.[93] Duniway's earned-rights arguments do not fit easily into either framework. She generally rejected the logic of expediency arguments, and although she shared the assumption of sameness basic to natural rights arguments by pointing out how men and women had endured the same trials and triumph, she also built her arguments on merit.

Duniway's arguments implied a test for citizenship: the rite of passage through the frontier. On one hand, as Lake argues, these earned rights can be read as further evidence that corroborates women's natural rights.[94] On the other hand, these earned rights can also be read as limiting. The suggestion that suffrage was something that one could or must earn undermined the concept of natural rights articulated in the Declaration of Independence and defined as self-evident and inalienable rights that existed in nature, independent of any government.[95] The logic of her frontier myth suggested that suffrage was owed to the exceptional who had proved themselves, rather than to all humans, based solely on their natural rights. Duniway still appealed to a sense of justice, but she depicted women's lack of rights in terms of the injustice of work unrewarded rather than universal rights denied. Thus, her frontier myth offered an altered natural rights argument. Furthermore, as the frontier myth only celebrated some people as exceptional, her regional rhetoric was also exclusive.

EXCLUDING AMERICAN INDIANS
AND EASTERN WOMEN

The traditional frontier myth defined the mythic hero according to two boundaries: conflict with American Indians and conflict with civilization. Duniway also used these boundaries to recognize white Western women as frontier heroines, characterizing them as distinct and superior to American Indian and Eastern women. This strengthened her ability to employ the myth for women's full citizenship rights, but it also perpetuated negative beliefs about American Indians and potentially amplified conflict with Eastern suffragists. Slotkin explains that Americans defined American Indians as one boundary of American identity by delineating that although they had learned to live in the wilderness and knew American Indians, they "were *not* savages." Heroes of mythical quests had to "know Indians, [but their] experiences, sympathies, and even allegiances fall on both sides of the frontier."[96] Heroes also had to feature their dissimilarity to their civilized counterparts. Originally, conflict with civilization existed between the American colonies and Britain. For the West, this conflict arose between the concerns of Westerners and those of the urban centers of power in the East. Therefore, in the frontier myth, the hero was distinct from the American Indians of the West and the "authoritarian politics and class privilege" of the civilization in the East.[97]

Duniway's frontier heroes and heroines were also distinct from American Indians. The violence through which her heroes and heroines had proved themselves was often with American Indians, like the "lone woman" she recognized who guarded her home with her "trusty rifle" after her husband was killed by a "cruel savage." In addition to valorizing the violence between her white heroines and American Indians, Duniway also at times specified her heroes' whiteness, such as when she praised them for having "the spirit of adventure characteristic of our Anglo-Saxon stock."[98] Other times she discussed the tensions of living with and among American Indians, while still being distinct from them. While boasting about Western women at a NAWSA convention, Duniway claimed: "The dusky wife of the aboriginal man [would not] be tempted to populate the new world with half-caste children, to become the Ish-maelites of new generations, like the son of one Argonaut I have in mind, who, when asked, after being convicted of murder, to state sentence of death should not be pronounced upon him, turned savagely upon his pious father and cursed him roundly for having married an Indian woman."[99] Here Duniway illustrated that white women in the West knew American Indians so well that they could live side by side with them. At the same time, she offered reassurance that her Western heroines would not consider American Indians as potential partners in Western life.

Yet after 1902 Duniway began, like other suffragists, to recognize Sacagawea as an American heroine. Sacagawea became widely known and valued for her role in Meriwether Lewis and William Clark's western journey in 1902, when Eva Emery Dye published her novel, *The Conquest: The True Story of Lewis and Clark*. Dye was a close friend of Duniway, and both of them participated in publicly commemorating Sacagawea. In 1905, Portland women commissioned a sculpture of Sacagawea, which was unveiled at the Lewis and Clark Centennial Exposition. Duniway spoke at the unveiling ceremony and honored Sacagawea alongside the white "pioneer mother who trudged across the almost untracked continent with her babe in arms and other little children clinging to her gown."[100] When Duniway spoke again later that summer, she included Sacagawea among a list of American heroes that included "Thomas Jefferson, Lewis, [and] Clark."[101] Her celebration of Sacagawea as "a new type of heroine" was notable for its inclusion and public praise of an American Indian woman. Yet she praised Sacagawea largely for "helping to upbuild a Pacific empire, upon whose borders the white man and the white woman would unite to perpetuate a nation." Duniway described Sacagawea "waving back the dark savagery to which she was born, [and] beckoning forward the advancing civilization to which she was wed."[102] So even as she recognized her as a heroine, Duniway celebrated Sacagawea's contribution to the conquest of the West and her role in creating a nation of white men and white women. As Cindy Richards argues, the commemoration of Sacagawea functioned to celebrate US expansion as "a story of progress rather than one of brutal conquest, suggesting that Anglo-Americans and American Indians worked together to 'civilize' the wilderness."[103] And although Duniway praised Sacagawea's endurance, courage, and "larger service to mankind," she did not include American Indian women as deserving of the franchise.

In addition to establishing a boundary between frontier heroines and American Indians, Duniway's mythic West also excluded Eastern women and traditional performances of femininity. Duniway's relationship with Eastern suffragists was often strained by disagreements over agitation tactics. The suffrage and temperance movements had worked in tandem for many years, and many Eastern suffrage leaders supported prohibition. But Duniway believed that connecting women's voting rights to temperance weakened the movement by arousing the opposition of liquor interests. She also believed that Eastern suffragists' public parades and events stirred up opposition and were less effective than her strategy of interpersonal maneuvering and one-on-one persuasion, which she called her still hunt method.[104]

Eastern suffragists often ignored Duniway's preferred agitation tactics when they went west to help with the Western suffrage campaigns. To defend her preferred advocacy strategies, Duniway used the frontier myth and its ideals of freedom to depict Eastern suffragists and their advocacy strategies as unfit for the West. She stated at a NAWSA convention that the people in Oregon "do not like professional agitators, but they love liberty."[105] To Duniway, professional agitators and well-funded suffragists from the East had no place in her mythic frontier, and she resented their interference in the West. In her 1889 NWSA address, she singled out and blamed the failure of a Washington Territory campaign on "the untimely invasion of Mrs. Clara B. Colby and other self-imported Eastern Suffragists."[106] When she spoke at the Idaho Constitutional Convention, she blamed Washington Territory's loss of woman suffrage on "a few peripatetic women, non-voters, from the East" who traveled to Washington and stirred up the liquor industry's opposition to woman suffrage when they privileged "coercion of men" over "liberty for [women]."[107] Duniway's mythic heroines earned their liberty through frontier trials, making Eastern suffragists' equality not only irrelevant to the freedom of Western women but also unearned.

Duniway delineated the differences between Western and Eastern women in her 1899 NAWSA address when she said:

> Women under normal conditions, are evolutionists, and not revolution-ists, as is shown by their conduct, as voters, in Wyoming, Colorado, Utah and Idaho. Your ideal, hysterical reformer, whose aim in life is to put men in leading strings, like little children, doesn't hail from any state where women vote.[108]

She described Western women who had suffrage as normal, while she drew on the gendered stereotype of women to portray Eastern women as emotional and irrational. Not only had Duniway's Eastern suffragists not yet earned their vote, they had also attempted to limit the freedom of men rather than expand liberty, contradicting the values of the frontier. Yet recognizing the bravery and endurance of Western women obscured the many Eastern women had also been intrepid when they left Europe for the colonies or the Eastern Seaboard for Tennessee, Kentucky, and Ohio. By employing the frontier myth in her suffrage arguments, Duni-way successfully portrayed Western white women as heroines deserving of suffrage, but in the process, she also depicted them as superior to American Indians and instigated conflict with Eastern suffragists.

CELEBRATING WHITE WESTERN MASCULINITY

Although Duniway's frontier included white Western women as hero-ines, she did not challenge the frontier myth's masculinity. Instead, she celebrated both white women and men's masculine performances in the service of women's voting rights. Like the traditional frontier myth, she championed white Western men as frontier heroes, but recast them as supporters of women's political equality. Duniway elevated "the men of our Pacific Northwest as a noble lot of freemen. The spirit of enterprise which led them across the untracked continent, to form a new empire

beside our sundown seas was a bold and free spirit."[109] Duniway connected Western men's heroism to their willingness to grant women suffrage. In 1884 she testified to her NWSA audience that "the hearts of the
men of the great Pacific Northwest were right toward women."[110] And
she stated in her Idaho address, "the freedom-loving spirit of our Western men is our proudest boast."[111] Western men were exceptional in part
because they valued the women who had tamed and transformed the
wilderness alongside them, and believed that they deserved citizenship
rights. She reported to her Eastern audience at the NAWSA convention,
"In our Pacific Northwest, the majority of the voters stand ready to grant
us the ballot whenever we demand it on the broad basis of individual
and collective liberty for ourselves."[112] Duniway depicted these heroic
and "never-fettered men of Oregon" as weary of gender inequality.[113]
Her frontier heroes acknowledged Western women's role in building the
Northwest and believed they should be rewarded with voting rights. Duniway claimed at the 1899 NAWSA convention that Western men appreciated Western women so much that they "wonder how they had endured
the old conditions, before the women joined them. Now, quite naturally,
they are learning to apply this rule to politics; and so our men of the
Pacific Coast are not alarmed [by women voting], as many men are in
other states."[114] Western men's heroism added legitimacy to Duniway's
argument and associated their exceptionalism with her cause.

Duniway's celebration of white Western men functioned differently for her various audiences. When she spoke to Western men, her
celebration of frontier heroes invited Western men to view their support for women's voting rights as heroic and admirable. In her speech
at the Lewis and Clark Exposition in Portland in 1905, she stated, "I
believe, as I address the honorable gentlemen . . . by whose courtesy
we are here assembled, that through your heroic, manly and chivalrous
action at the ballot-box next June, you will, in extending to Oregon's
pioneer women the right of suffrage, lay the foundation for an exposition on these grounds one hundred years from now in which your deeds
of moral chivalry and patriotic valor shall" be remembered.[115] Similarly,
when speaking to the state federation's biennial convention in Oregon,

she predicted that "When you, the chivalrous men of this mighty state, shall prove yourselves worthy of our great expectations by your votes for our amendment next Monday, you will rise higher than ever in the estimation of club women, who already like you and cannot help it."[116] She invited Western men to see themselves as heroes: men who deserved mythic status for their recognition of women as full citizens of the West that they created together through their shared struggle.

When she spoke to Western women, Duniway's praise of Western men as mythic heroes encouraged the suffragists in their activism. In 1897 Duniway addressed the Oregon State Equal Suffrage Association when they were meeting at her home in Portland for their twenty-sixth annual convention. After twenty-six years of advocacy, the Oregon suffragists needed assurance that their political goals were achievable and their efforts were not in vain. Duniway invoked the mythic frontier to reassure them that they could "expect to win our full, free and permanent enfranchisement through the vote of honorable men." Likewise, she reminded Oregon suffragists that all the progress that they had made in Oregon "concerning the rights and opportunities of women . . . [had] been made by men in whom the spirit of justice has proved stronger than prejudice or precedent." By depicting Western men as justice-minded, she motivated suffragists to "continue asking men to remove the same political disabilities from our shoulders . . . which we know they are destined to remove." Her portrayal of Western men as open to change and supportive of women's rights made Western activists' work seem more likely to succeed. She pointed to the men of Colorado and Idaho as evidence for her claim that "the spirit of liberty is strong in the men of our Western states and the enfranchisement of women when placed before them as an issue . . . always enlists their sympathy."[117] By casting Western men as heroic supporters of woman suffrage, she invited suffragists to recognize their capacity to enact political change and likelihood of achieving their goal.

When she spoke to Eastern men, Duniway positioned Western men as heroic exemplars to follow in their support of women's rights. In March 1884 she joined a delegation of at least ten women to address the US Senate Select Committee on Woman Suffrage and petition Congress for voting rights. Susan B. Anthony introduced Duniway to the committee as hailing "from the extreme Northwest," and added that Duniway was "the one canvasser in the great State of Oregon and Washington Territory, and that it is to Mrs. Duniway that the women of Washington Territory are more indebted than to all other influences for their enfranchisement," since Washington had enfranchised women the previous year.[118] As Duniway addressed the "Gentlemen of the committee," she invoked the freedom of the frontier myth with which they were already familiar: "My state is far away beyond the confines of the Rocky Mountains, away over beside the singing Pacific sea, but the spirit of liberty is among us there, and the public heart has been stirred." She encouraged the senators to view the nation's frontier heroes as suffrage supporters: "The hearts of our men have been moved to listen to our demands, and in Washington Territory, as one speaker has informed you, women today are endowed with full and free enfranchisement, and the rejoicing throughout that territory is universal. In Oregon, men have also listened to our demand, and the legislature has in two successive sessions agreed upon a proposition to amend our state constitution."[119] By expanding the vision of the West's mythic heroes to include a recognition of women's rights, Duniway associated the frontier that they longed for with women's political freedom and equality.

Duniway celebrated the frontier heroes, who the US senators already revered, "The men of the broad, free West are grand, and chivalrous, and free." Yet she accounted for these Western men's exceptional nature according to her altered vision of the frontier. These Western men were to be admired for their heroic experience on the frontier *and* their support of women: "They have gone across the mighty continent with free steps; they have raised the standard of a new Pacific empire; they have imbibed the spirit of liberty with their very breath, and they have listened to us far in advance of many men of the older States who have not had their opportunity among the grand free wilds of nature for expansion." In her frontier, the heroes proved their exceptionalism not only through their western pilgrimage and discovery of the West's freedom, but also for recognizing women's rights. Their support of suffrage was part of their heroic transformation. Once she had invoked and transformed the senators' image of the mythic West for her own purposes, she asked them to be like the frontier heroes that they already admired and "in the magnanimity of your own free wills and noble hearts, champion the woman's cause and make us before the law, as we of right ought now to be, free and independent?"[120] She called on Eastern men to follow the example of those who had gone west, proved their exceptionalism, and enfranchised women. Thus, she invoked the mythic frontier and its traditional masculine heroes to advocate women's voting rights.

Duniway also celebrated Western women as frontier heroines who deserved suffrage by describing them according to traditionally masculine characteristics related to physical strength, endurance, and violent frontier conquest. She recognized Western women for "proving themselves as strong in endurance and as intrepid in danger as their fathers, husbands and sons."[121] In some ways, celebrating women's performances of masculinity in the West expanded the possibilities of gender performances and challenged narrow gender ideals like the "cult of true womanhood." Duniway's positive depictions of Western women's masculinity on her mythic frontier demonstrated women's ability to participate in the rituals of manhood and made space for American women to live outside traditional gender restrictions. Yet, as she championed white men and women's performances of Western masculinity, she at times degraded traditionally feminine characteristics.

In contrast to her recognition of Western women, Duniway often depicted Eastern women who performed traditionally feminine roles in negative terms. In her 1900 NAWSA address, she asserted that Western men especially appreciated Western women compared to "the parasitic [Eastern] woman who inherits wealth, or the equally selfish woman who lies in idleness upon her husband's toil," who relied on the proceeds of their husbands' work, rather than earning their homes together with their husbands. She described these women as "hysterical reformers."[122] Her demeaning caricatures of Eastern femininity also disparaged "true women" as being unfit for political participation. Duniway regularly championed womanly women, but by celebrating the masculine performances of politically equal men and women and denouncing the femininity of women with fewer rights, she at times reinforced the culturally constructed relationship between politics and masculinity. As she implied that only the women who could prove their exceptionalism on the traditionally masculine, mythic frontier had the right to political equality, she encouraged women desiring suffrage to become more like men of the time and less like women, who were still seen as too weak to vote. Consequently, she did not work to destabilize the masculine assumptions of US citizenship; instead, she condemned traditional notions of true womanhood.

Conclusion

When they finally achieved suffrage in 1912, Oregonians honored Duniway by allowing her to be the first woman to register to vote in Oregon (see figure 2). She told the *Oregon Journal*, "I am so happy that now in the sunset of my life my fondest dream is beginning to be realized."[123] Within weeks of their success, hundreds of Oregonians gathered to celebrate Duniway's seventy-eighth birthday and recognize her for her decades of leadership and activism.[124] Despite enjoying such a place of honor and legacy in the West, she remained a controversial figure in the suffrage movement and experienced much conflict with national suffrage leaders (with the exception of Anthony). Duniway consistently viewed Eastern suffragists as invaders in the West. She wrote in her autobiography about being "side-tracked . . . by Eastern invaders [with] ways that are dark and tricks that are vain."[125] She believed that Western women may have won suffrage sooner "if left to themselves" rather than being "dominated" by the Eastern suffragists who took much of the money they raised.[126] She wrote to her son, Clyde, that she gave the Eastern organizers "a plain but courteous talk about combing the West of its cash in its hours of trial. I think they won't invade my bailiwick any more except by invitation."[127] She had faith that "the fatal mistake of the leaders in Oregon was that they imported the Eastern speakers, who took charge of the

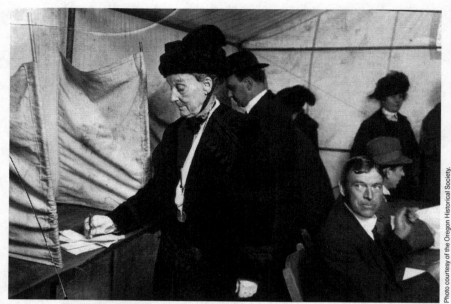

Figure 2. Abigail Scott Duniway voting in Portland, 1914.

campaign."[128] Eastern temperance women accused her of selling out to liquor, censured her for bringing "disgrace on the woman suffrage cause," and undermined her still hunt method by hiring prohibitionists to campaign for suffrage in the Northwest without her knowledge.[129]

After Duniway's protest of prohibition in her 1889 NWSA convention speech, there was an "intrigue" of women against her at subsequent conventions and the national leaders treated her as though she was unwanted and unnecessary. Suffrage leader Clara Colby sought to remove Duniway from her leadership position by organizing a "secret conclave," and Duniway exchanged negative words with multiple Eastern suffrage leaders.[130] In a letter to the NAWSA president Anna Howard Shaw, Duniway called Colby a "fool" and an "old tramp," and accused Shaw of having misplaced priorities: "You and your ex-officers and agents are evidently working for organization, glory and salary. I am working for success."[131] Duniway went so far as to threaten that if Shaw "again set foot in Oregon," she would make her "face the legal consequences" for her lies and her confiscation of suffrage campaign funds.[132] Thus, some histories of the suffrage movement cast Duniway in a negative light and blame her for the numerous suffrage defeats in the Pacific Northwest.[133] In an editorial, Duniway wrote that she had no use for the sentimentality of "eastern poetesses" who knew nothing about of the "Women of the Border," but she hoped that someday history would appreciate the "unknown heroines" of the West.[134]

Although much of Duniway's conflict with Eastern suffragists revolved around clashing methods of agitation, her regional rhetoric may also have contributed to that tension. Her depiction of liberty residing in the West was likely more empowering for Western women than for Eastern suffragists, who could not claim that they had earned their voting rights on the frontier. The logic of her earned rights argument and her negative attitudes toward Eastern suffragists may have impacted the movement years later. In 1914, the Congressional Union for Woman Suffrage (cuws) sent organizers to the nine woman suffrage states in the West to campaign against the Democratic presidential candidates as punishment for not enfranchising women. Like Duniway, many Western voters protested "outside interference" from Easterners.[135] Ultimately, the re-election of President Woodrow Wilson (1856–1932), a Democrat and the only candidate who did not publicly endorse woman suffrage, symbolized a large failure for the cuws's strategy in the West.[136] The Easterners' inability to marshal Western women's support for this campaign may have had roots in Duniway's region-based suffrage arguments.

Duniway may have employed the mythic frontier to protest women's disfranchisement more extensively and specifically than others, but she was not the only suffragist to deploy the West as a mythic frontier in their advocacy. Her region-making of the West seemed to resonate with activists nationwide because elements of her mythic frontier appeared in arguments for women's rights around the country. In 1910, as Washington and Oregon prepared to vote on suffrage amendments, *Votes for Women*, a woman suffrage newspaper published in Washington, proclaimed the freedom of the West in an article titled, "The Spirit of the West": "Freedom has always come out of the West—the West which has always been peopled by those free souls who gladly gave up the luxuries of the East in order to escape its slavery."[137] *Votes for Women* invoked the West and imagined it as a region of freedom to encourage suffragists in the Northwest that their activism and advocacy would be rewarded with the franchise. Similarly, in 1911, Chicago suffragist Bell Squire explained in the *Chicago Tribune* California's decision to enfranchise women:

> Out in the far west, where there is space to breathe and move about freely, out in the open as it were, men welcome new ideas and new ideals. They are open to new thoughts. The same spirit of adventure that drove them to penetrate the western plains and deserts, to climb the western mountains and find an outlet to the western sea, makes them desire to change their ways, if a change of ways seems desirable. The spirit of fair play is there, for fair play is the essence of adventure, the spirit that moves the real adventurers of the earth.[138]

Squire imagined Western women's voting rights as an extension of the freedom, openness, and adventure of the Western spirit.

Suffragists around the country also elevated the heroism of Western men. In Chicago, Squire praised Western men who "welcomed new ideas and new ideals" and were "open to new thoughts." Likewise, *Votes for Women* valorized Western men as heroes partly because of the way they appreciated Western women: "The women of Washington want political equality with their brothers, not because they have been badly treated, but because they have been well treated. It is only those classes of people who have enjoyed rights and privileges who know how to appreciate them, and work for more."[139] Similar to Duniway, *Votes for Women* celebrated Western men's appreciation of Western women as evidence of their frontier heroism. In 1905, Ida Husted Harper of Indiana appealed to the exceptionalism of Western men at the NAWSA Convention held in Portland, Oregon. Amidst Oregon's campaign for a state suffrage amendment, Harper proclaimed, "It is to the strong, courageous and progressive men of the western States that the women of this whole country are looking for deliverance from the bondage of disfranchisement. It is these men who must start this movement and give it such momentum that it will roll irresistibly on to the very shores of the Atlantic Ocean. Today the eyes of the whole country are on this beautiful and progressive State."[140] She made the Western men the heroes of the suffrage story who could deliver women from their bondage: "Would it not add the crowning glory to this greatest period in your history if the free men of Oregon should decree that this shall be, henceforth and forever, the land also of free women?"[141] Harper appealed to Westerners' pride in their exceptional West and urged them to secure Western men and women's freedom forever with their votes.

Discussions of Western women's voting rights often celebrated them as frontier heroines. Squire argued that Western women deserved the most recognition for their sacrifice and fearlessness: "Nor is it strange that California should give its women the freedom that they craved. Motherhood should not be counted as a crime, but as a great, transcendent service to the commonwealth, equal, if not greater in dignity, than that which any soldier can ever give. To give life and to risk life in giving it, is surely as brave and honorable as to take life, and risk life in taking it."[142] Like Duniway, Squire recognized Western women's childbearing as brave, and compared it to the valor and honor of military service.

Even Roosevelt's masculine frontier myth celebrated Western women's frontier heroism at times. For despite his celebration of manhood and masculinity, he also figured frontier women as strong and virtuous, as long as they served the nation by bearing children. Leroy Dorsey argues that when Roosevelt discussed women's voting rights in the early twentieth century, he invoked elements of the frontier narratives that he had popularized at the end of the nineteenth century. Dorsey explains that Roosevelt "still tapped into his decades-old myth although he was not always as specific with his frontier references when discussing modern women."[143]

Perhaps the frontier myth was prevalent enough in suffrage advocacy that it strengthened suffragists' perceived differences between Eastern

and Western women. For in 1911, when the *San Francisco Call* published
the "Ballad of a Suffragette," it not only celebrated the freedom of the
West and its exceptional Western women, it elevated Western suffragists
above the aristocratic women of New England:

> There's a grander type of women than New England ever nurtured.
> Though lofty types your early years could boast;
> There's a sweeter task for ladies than to be aristocratic,
> And there's something on the free Pacific Coast
> That shall make the whole world better when the fair shall call it hither,
> And the eastern states shall travel home again.
> With the lesson of our progress, the example of our women,
> And the state that called them equal with its men.[144]

It is doubtful that all these visions of the mythic West in national suffrage discourse were based solely on Duniway's frontier myth. Yet they
illustrate the way the meaning of the West as a frontier circulated and
influenced the national woman suffrage movement. The mythic frontier
in suffrage discourse interpreted and promoted Western women's voting
rights as a sign of the heroism, exceptionalism, and freedom of woman
suffrage and the West.

As suffragists imagined the West as a frontier of freedom for white
Western women, they characterized them as heroines who had earned
their right to vote through their western pilgrimage. They challenged
the centrality of men in the frontier by recasting the traditional hero to
include heroines and Western men who supported women's rights, while
maintaining the masculinity of the mythic frontier. By imagining the
West as a region of white women's political equality, they elevated white
Western women, while often excluding American Indian and Eastern
women from that same heroic status, which set Western and Eastern suffragists in opposition. Overall, invoking and reimagining the West as a
frontier was just one of multiple ways that suffragists deployed region in
protest of women's disfranchisement.

CHAPTER 2

Visualizing the West

SUFFRAGE MAPS' IMAGERY OF LEGITIMACY, CIVILIZATION, AND CONTINENTAL EXPANSION, 1907–1917

———————•◆•———————

I n the early twentieth century, US woman suffragists began using a new advocacy strategy: the suffrage map.[1] These maps used black and white shading, and sometimes colors, to mark the places where eligible women could legally vote.[2] In 1907, Chicago suffragist Bertha Damaris Knobe published one of the earliest suffrage maps that designated all five kinds of voting rights that existed for eligible women at the state level: equal suffrage, municipal suffrage, school suffrage, tax-paying suffrage, and school and tax-paying suffrage (see figure 3).[3] Supporters found Knobe's map such an "effective way to advertise the cause" that they called it the "suffrage success map" and began making their own maps to post at their headquarters, outdoor celebrations, and public protests (see figure 4).[4] Eventually, the maps became ubiquitous, as suffragists displayed them in city streets and open-air meetings, made them into parade floats and billboards, and wore them in public demonstrations (see figures 5 and 6).[5] They distributed the maps in numerous

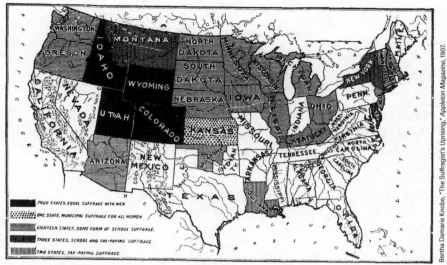

Bertha Damaris Knobe, "The Suffragist's Uprising," *Appleton Magazine*, 1907.

Figure 3. Map of the United States showing the status of woman's suffrage legislation. Black indicates the four states where women had equal suffrage with men. Gray indicates the twenty-two states where women only had municipal, school, or tax-paying suffrage. White indicates the states where women could not vote in any elections.

Photo courtesy of the University of Missouri, Western Historical Manuscripts Collection, Columbia Research Center.

Figure 4. Volunteers working near map hung in the Missouri state suffrage headquarters.

Figure 5. Suffrage map hung over a street in Nevada, 1914.

Figure 6. Suffrage map painted on the brick wall of a building opposite the Republican Convention, held in the Chicago Coliseum, 1916. Mrs. James W. Morrison, recording secretary of the NAWSA, and Mrs. Harrison Monro Brown, president of the Illinois Equal Suffrage Association, are shown putting the finishing touches on the map.

forms—as calendars, in the baseball programs at New York Giants games, and on fans, flyers, and leaflets.[6] Geographer Christine Dando argues that the suffragists' use of maps between 1907 and 1920 "represents the most extensive use of a single iconic map image for persuasive purposes in the United States, save perhaps the outline of the United States itself."[7]

Like suffrage cartoons, performances, and image events, maps were compelling visual arguments for women's voting rights in the early twentieth century.[8] Suffragists frequently claimed that of all their arguments and advocacy strategies, the maps made their "strongest argument," and suffragists insisted that they proved their movement was a success.[9] For Henrietta Livermore, the maps convinced her that "Woman Suffrage is Inevitable . . . It is not a question of *whether* but a question of *when* equal suffrage will come."[10] And after comparing and contrasting suffrage maps from 1869 and 1917, the *Woman's Journal* concluded, "we hazard the prediction that by 1920" woman suffrage will be achieved across the country.[11] Suffragists also attested to the map's affective power. In 1912, a writer for the *Woman's Journal* asked the reader, "Can you look upon the map unmoved?" The author professed, "You cannot be a suffragist without feeling your heart swell with pride as you look at this map!"[12] That these maps had the power to make suffragists feel proud of their achievements, and convince them that their success around the country was inevitable, points to the maps' ability to persuade suffragists of their agency to enact large-scale social change.

I contend that by visualizing white women's voting rights in the West, the US suffrage maps depicted the movement as unstoppable and constituted suffragists as powerful political activists who had the agency to secure the franchise nationwide. Scholars have established maps' persuasive ability to shape readers' perceptions, and thereby motivate or deter actions and choices.[13] Maps function constitutively, as well as instrumentally, to shape users' identity.[14] As cartographers select what information to include and exclude on a map, their choices influence readers' perceptions of the world they live in, the possibilities and options they perceive as available to them, and, in the process, the map user's agency.[15] Timothy Barney argues that a map's particular framing of the world gives map makers and users "a position of power."[16] Likewise, as suffragists used maps to imagine their movement and the possibilities available to them, the maps helped them recognize their capacity to effect change nationally.[17] This chapter examines how the maps convinced suffragists of their political agency, in part by functioning as regional rhetoric that activated, challenged, and persuasively deployed the meaning of the West to protest women's lack of voting rights.

I argue that the maps asserted suffragists' agency and constituted the activists as powerful political actors through maps' ability to provide legitimacy, exaggerate importance and influence, and activate region as a rhetorical resource. Amidst the Progressive Era's infatuation with modernity and scientific evidence, the increasingly common medium of the map provided suffragists' claims an image of scientific objectivity and credibly legitimized the existence of women's voting rights as a reality, rather than a wishful fantasy. Furthermore, the thematic map's ability to flatten data exaggerated the suffrage movement's significance and power in national politics. Finally, the suffrage maps invoked, disrupted, and leveraged the West to advocate suffrage in the East and depict their success nationwide as inevitable. The maps presented the growth of women's voting rights as continental expansion, suggesting that they were destined to reach the Atlantic.

This case study extends the existing scholarship on suffrage maps begun by geographer Dando, who recovered many of these maps and documented their production, circulation, and racial implications. In addition to establishing the suffrage maps' prevalence and importance to the movement, Dando recognizes the maps as a groundbreaking example of critical cartography that used a traditionally masculine form to claim public space for women. Here, I build on this work by analyzing the suffrage maps according to theories of maps' rhetoricity and region to illustrate the way these maps legitimized the woman suffrage movement, exaggerated the movement's power, and activated the meaning of the West. The suffrage maps reimagined the meanings of the West and East, and suffragists employed these refashioned images of both regions to advocate suffrage nationwide. The maps, however, were not the first or last medium that suffragists used to visualize women's voting rights. Seventeen years before the suffrage map's creation, advocates began visualizing Western woman suffrage with flags.

Flags and Stars as Predecessors to the Suffrage Maps

As soon as Wyoming Territory was granted statehood in 1890 and retained woman suffrage in its state constitution, suffragists around the country began celebrating their first suffrage state with flags, badges, and pins that symbolized the state with a star. Some flags, like "the beautiful new flag" created to fly over the Iowa State Fairgrounds, had "one grand star in the centre of the blue space, with the name of the 'First Free State'—Wyoming—in large white letters."[18] But many of the flags, like the one adopted by suffragists in Los Angeles, looked like the red, white, and blue US flag, except for having "only one star in the blue field—indicative of the fact that only one State out of the forty-four now in the Union, had secured 'Liberty and Equality' to all its citizens."[19]

The practice of updating and altering the US flag with new stars for new states was still fairly common in the nineteenth century. The United States used at least twenty-one different designs for their flag as the number of stars in the blue field grew from thirteen stars in 1777 to forty-four in 1891. Americans regularly used the flag to visually recognize the legitimacy of a new state. Just as suffragists had altered the American Declaration of Independence to present their manifesto as the Declaration of Sentiments, they adapted the US flag to celebrate women's voting rights. On both the suffrage and US flag, the white stars represented states. Thus, Los Angeles suffragist M. V. Longley argued that the inclusion of only one star on the suffrage flag indicated "there is only one State true to the principles on which the government was founded, we have that one only represented on our flag and badge—glorious and faithful Wyoming!"[20] Likewise, Emma Smith DeVoe wrote in 1891 that Illinois suffragists were "determined to procure a beautiful silk flag, bearing one

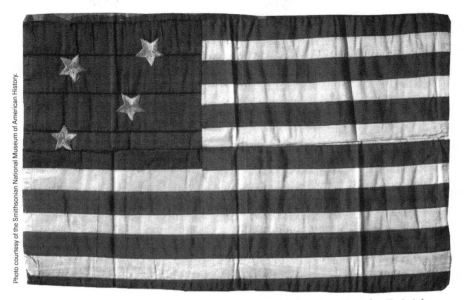

Photo courtesy of the Smithsonian National Museum of American History.

Figure 7. Handmade silk woman suffrage flag made by Mrs. Douglas Reinicker, 1900.

star—typical of the first true republic, and at the World's Fair to unfurl it to the breeze, and thus tell the whole world that there is one State in this Union, namely, Wyoming, that is indeed a true republic."[21] Because the flag appealed to the patriotic ideals and principles of the nation's founding, suffragists used it to argue that those ideals and principles were only truly practiced in the equal suffrage state of Wyoming.

The flag declared that within the United States, a true republic that valued men and women's votes equally already existed within the nation's borders, and provided suffragists cause for rejoicing. They called the one-starred flag their Star of Hope because it served as a source of encouragement, and the *Woman's Journal* claimed that the flag symbolized a hopeful vision of women's voting rights in the future when the flag's "field of blue shall be dotted with every star that represents a State of this Union."[22] By 1896, they had added stars for Colorado, Utah, and Idaho, and supporters put the stars of the four "free states" on flags, postage stamps, pins, buttons, pillows, leaflets, handouts, and posters (see figure

7). As a California suffragist explained, until all the states were represented on the suffrage flag, these stars were "encouraging and cheering
us in our battles, and leading us on to victory" in their campaign for
suffrage nationwide.[23]

Although the starred suffrage flag lifted the morale of supporters,
who understood its meaning, its ambiguity made it less understandable
to the public. In 1909, when Alice Stone Blackwell advised suffragists in
the Midwest on how to decorate their state fair exhibits, she suggested
twenty potential items to display. She specified that the "big 'Votes for
Women' flag—yellow, with the words in white or black letters [was] pref-
erable to the four-starred flag, because everybody knows at first sight
what it means."[24] But her top recommendation for display was the suffrage map. Suffragists continued to display the flag and added a star for
every additional state's adoption of suffrage, and eventually for every
state's ratification of the Nineteenth Amendment. However, they found
that the maps were more readily understood by all viewers than the flag.
Furthermore, the maps' ability to legitimize, provide credibility, and
employ the meaning of the West made the them especially useful.

Suffrage Maps Provided Legitimacy

The suffrage maps asserted activists' collective agency through the ability to provide legitimacy and scientific authority. Their persuasive power
comes in part from their capacity to legitimize and assert ontological
claims. Attempting to explain and demystify the rhetorical power of
maps, Denis Wood and John Fels maintain that every map makes "a
powerful existence claim—*this is.*"[25] Not only do maps claim that *this exists*,
they also say that it exists *there*. In doing so, those claims "reinforce each
other" and imply "a reality test, that you can go there and look." As
Wood and Fels put it, maps ask the reader, "Why would we put it there
if it weren't so? Check it out if you want!" Maps' existence claims are so
persuasive because of the "indexicality vouchsafed" by the map. They
assert their own credibility by implying that users can test maps' claims

and verify for themselves whether maps are true. So by asserting that something *is* there, maps are also "a uniquely powerful way of insisting that something *is*."[26]

Maps also persuade because they are perceived as objective, neutral, and credible.[27] As Mark Monmonier explains, "People trust maps."[28] Even though maps make persuasive arguments, they often appear to be value-free, impartial representations of reality, partly because they always assert their own truth and objectivity.[29] They insist on their own authority with everything on and around them, including the titles, captions, and accompanying texts and images.[30] Jeremy Black argues that even blatantly political or propaganda maps can have an appearance of objectivity "thanks to the resonance of cartography as an objective medium."[31] Barney emphasizes that they are both science and art. Although maps present themselves as objective representations of the world, mapmaking is also an "art and artifice" that can emphasize some truths, perspectives, and ideologies over others.[32] But maps' appearance of objectivity hides the role of mapmakers and can present maps as objective truth.

Maps' seemingly objective form was especially appealing to Progressive-Era reformers. At the turn of the century, objectivity and systematic observation gained increasing authority, and social science informed government, industry, education, and social reform.[33] Progressives were, Ellen Fitzpatrick argues, "enamored with scientific fact," and worked to inform and justify their activism and reform with social scientific research.[34] Progressives frequently appealed to social science in their public argument, and maps' appearance of scientific objectivity made them ideal justifications for social reform efforts.[35] Because of their appearance of objectivity and new technologies that made them easier to reproduce and distribute, maps became a popular way for Progressive-Era reformers to visualize rates of social problems like illiteracy, crime, disease, and disenfranchisement.[36]

The suffrage maps provided authority and legitimized the existence of women's voting rights at a time when woman suffrage was often viewed as a failing movement. When Knobe published her 1907 map in *Appleton's Magazine*, suffragists were in the midst of what historians call the movement's doldrums, a period of fourteen years when no state suffrage campaign succeeded. Yet Knobe used the map to support her essay, "The Suffragists' Uprising," which countered the prevailing perception that the movement had stalled. Given that equal suffrage had "been granted by no state since Idaho gained it in 1896," she acknowledged that suffragists were "disheartened . . . over [the] stagnant condition" of the movement. However, she used her suffrage map to challenge the perception of the movement's failure and presented evidence that "on the contrary, [suffragists had] every cause for congratulation." She argued that although the movement appeared to be thwarted, in fact, it was in the midst of an "uprising." Knobe's map and essay asserted that despite the long gap in women's legal gains, "the suffragists' world do move" by pointing to women's existing voting rights. The map was proof that their movement was succeeding, lawmakers' attitudes were changing, and "indeed, everything seems to be coming the suffragists' way" as support was "growing amazingly."[37] The maps' ability to assert the ontology of suffrage legitimized the presence of women's voting rights in the United States and framed the movement as succeeding.

Maps' powerful ontological claims illuminate why the suffrage maps may have been so persuasive. The suffrage maps argued that *this*—women's voting rights—*is*. Woman suffrage existed, and it did not just exist *somewhere*, it existed in the West. The suffrage maps validated the existence of women's voting abilities and shifted the debate from a hypothetical to a real possibility. They challenged the perception of woman suffrage as a wish or fantasy, and instead legitimized it as a reality already practiced in the United States. White women's voting rights had been implemented and tested, and they worked. Just look at the maps and see for yourself.

The suffrage maps helped normalize the existence and practice of women's voting rights, which made them less likely to be questioned or resisted. Like the map, the suffrage flag had also proclaimed the existence of women's voting rights, but the meaning of the stars was not clear without explanation. The power of the flag was only apparent to those who already knew what it meant. Furthermore, maps made a second reinforcing claim that *it exists there*. The maps' indexicality implied a reality test that the flag did not. The suffrage maps had the legitimizing power to say, "Women's voting rights exist in the West. Go and check it out if you don't believe me!"

Given the importance of objectivity in the Progressive Era, maps also made convincing instruments for suffragists' ontological claims because of their scientific authority, giving women's claims credibility.[38] Although most Americans already knew women voted in the West, seeing it visually represented "in the guise of scientific disinterestedness" made the existence of women's voting rights seem that much more valid.[39] Suffragists exploited maps' appearance of objectivity for authority and legitimacy, and borrowed from the form's perceived credibility to present their arguments in a seemingly objective light, assert their legitimacy, and project their power.

The maps provided suffragists with so much credibility and legitimacy that they circulated them widely. One month after Knobe's "Uprising" article was published, the *Woman's Journal* reproduced the map on their front page.[40] Her map generated so much interest that within months, *Harper's Weekly* published another suffrage map by her, and the National American Woman Suffrage Association (NAWSA) began selling the maps printed on tracts for 2 cents per copy.[41] After reading about her mapmaking process in the *Woman's Journal*, suffragists began making their own maps, posting them in public, and trading mapmaking strategies for use in schools, at state fairs, and as wearable sandwich boards.[42] Alice Park insisted that "the use of the map is obvious, both on the wall at Suffrage Headquarters, and as a portable object-lesson to display at meetings."[43] In Oregon, suffragists trusted that the map's argument was so self-evident that they tacked a large suffrage map to the wall of a barbershop, where men were "lathered and helpless before one, unable to answer back."[44] Suffragists believed that the maps persuaded men to support their cause. Lavinia Dock reported that when she displayed the map, "Men are much impressed by the ocular proof of our advance, and after little talks in groups of three to ten, many sign slips" that stated they believed women should be granted the vote. Dock believed the maps were so persuasive because "many people receive impressions

Figure 8. Woman showing suffrage map to a crowd during the Liberty Bell Tour, 1915.

Figure 9. Suffragists use map at a backyard meeting in Marthasville, Missouri, 1914.

more strongly through the eye than the ear."[45] Suffragists found the maps so legitimizing that they instructed with them at schools, displayed them when they spoke before crowds, hung them at the steps of their city hall and state legislatures, and used them in congressional testimony (see figures 8 and 9).[46]

Furthermore, the authority of maps obscured the role of suffragists as mapmakers, and appeared to let the impartial facts speak for themselves. Perhaps because the maps provided complex information in a seemingly objective light, newspapers frequently published updated suffrage maps when they reported on successful state campaigns to visualize which states had enacted women's voting rights. These maps appeared in publications across the country, including the *New York Times, Lexington Herald, San Jose Mercury, Trenton Evening Times, Salt Lake Evening Telegram, Kalamazoo Gazette, Duluth News Tribune, Idaho Daily Statesman, Times-Picayune, Miami Herald,* and *Wilkes-Barre Times Leader.*[47] When the maps were published in black and white without obvious suffrage endorsement, they appeared more like census maps and unbiased evidence than political arguments and propositional claims.[48] The suffrage maps' argument functioned similarly to the naturalistic enthymeme that Cara Finnegan identifies in photographs—viewers assume their truth unless given reason to do otherwise.[49] The legitimizing power of maps reflected on the collective identity of suffragists, as they recognized themselves as part of a credible movement.

Suffrage Maps Projected the Movement's Political Power

The suffrage maps also asserted suffragists' agency by projecting their movement's political power through thematic and dynamic maps. Thematic maps are designed to provide information for analysis, so they visualize the distribution and spatial pattern of a specific phenomenon or theme—like women's voting rights—by assigning a value, color, or characteristic to each individual territory. Because they generalize data by category and across spaces, they must "abstract, exaggerate, simplify, and classify data," which unavoidably obscures the complexity of the spaces represented by ignoring factors like population size, and density. Obscuring this data shapes the perception of political significance.[50] As Jeremy Black illustrates, thematic maps can overstate the role of sparsely populated areas and downplay the importance of areas with heavy populations or political power.[51]

Dynamic maps can suggest that the world represented is changing and transitioning. Barney argues that when maps are regularly redrawn, updated, and altered, dynamic maps can "connote a sense of constant movement," and encourage readers to consider not only what is, but also "what could be."[52] A sense of movement can persuade readers that social change is underway, and enable them to imagine an alternative world. Rhetoricians have demonstrated how movement can function rhetorically in a variety of contexts—through the rhetoricity of embodied performances, mobility discourses, and mobility ideologies.[53] Visualizing the mobility of women's rights on suffrage maps represented the movement's power as growing and expanding, enabled map readers to imagine how the world *could be*, and convinced activists of their capacity to enact social change.

The thematic map's ability to flatten data visually overstated the suffragists' political power. At the turn of the century, only four states had enacted equal suffrage: Wyoming, Utah, Colorado, and Idaho. But all four states were large in terms of area size and land mass. Since they expanded over 3.1 million square miles of US territory, they covered a significant portion of the US map—about 12 percent of the square mileage of the contiguous United States. Suffragists interpreted and emphasized the large size of the suffrage states as an indication of national support for their movement. When the map was published for the first time in the *Woman's Journal*, the only accompanying commentary was, "It is instructive to see how *large* a part of our country women now have some share of suffrage."[54] And in 1913, the *Woman's Leader* posited that the maps gave "food for reflection to the sceptical mind when it realises the *tremendous hold* the question of Women's Suffrage is obtaining on popular opinion."[55] Their comments indicate that the size of the areas representing woman suffrage on the maps countered most Americans' beliefs about the stalled and failing status of the movement by suggesting that it had significant support and endorsement.

But the large size of the Western suffrage states on the maps exaggerated their significance. Although the four states were spatially large and extended over a sizable portion of the continent, they all had extremely small populations and little political influence. In 1900, only 1.4 percent of the US population lived in one of these four states.[56] So the suffrage maps represented the movement as more significant than other representational strategies would have—such as the percentage of the US population or states with equal suffrage. The overstatement of the movement's significance was mostly due to the nature of the thematic map. The mapping suppressed the small population size and influence of the Western states, which visually amplified their apparent significance and helped project the import of woman suffrage to the nation.

The suffrage maps magnified the movement's influence to such an extent that they provoked numerous responses from antisuffragists trying to refute them. The *Observer* asserted that "it is not territory that counts on election day, but voters. The suffrage map is a fraud."[57] Antisuffragists tried to highlight the maps' exaggeration of the suffrage states' significance by calling attention to their small population sizes, and even created their own images to counter them, including pie graphs that emphasized the small percentage of the population with equal suffrage, rather than territory. Antisuffragists repeatedly published tables that compared the population sizes of the Western suffrage states to Eastern towns and cities to underscore the West's insignificance and assert that they, like a 1915 writer to the *New York Times*, were more "interested in people than inanimate clod."[58]

Antisuffragists' tables and pie graphs were likely compelling to their audiences, as they also appealed to progressives' desire for scientific evidence and objectivity, and would have supported most Eastern residents' perceptions of the West as sparsely populated. Yet as Susan Schulten has noted, data presented in tables "required the viewer to calculate and convert in order to make sense of the information," in contrast

to maps that presented data "in a way that was immediately recogniz-
able and meaningful."[59] In addition to being easily understood, maps
also provided more complex information than pie graphs by showing
precisely *where* women now voted. The map's complexity and indexicality
concretized the abstract idea of woman suffrage in a form that was more
readily accessible than tables and more meaningful and complex than
pie graphs. As Walter Clark, chief justice of the North Carolina Supreme
Court, wrote in a letter to suffragist Maud Younger: "I thank you very
much for the hundred copies of your splendid map. They are very effective, and are a condensed argument which anyone can understand."[60]

In addition to the size of the suffrage states, suffragists also used
the changing maps to feature the power of woman suffrage as mobile
and growing. As more state campaigns succeeded, suffrage newspapers
emphasized the dynamic nature of maps by heralding the growth of
their movement as they claimed more territory. In 1912, the front page
of the *Woman's Journal* announced, "Nation Hails Change of Map," and
in 1914, the *Suffragist* ran "The New Suffrage Map" on their front cover.[61]
The NAWSA had to print new maps so often to keep them accurate that the
costs of publication grew increasingly expensive. Eventually, the state
"suffrage victories, the thing the company was working for, meant its
financial loss." By 1917, the National Woman Suffrage Publishing Company "was 'bankrupted' trying to supply 'suffrage maps' up to date."[62]
"The newest" label on updated maps suggested that suffrage was moving
and would continue to spread in the future.

Suffragists emphasized the mobility of women's voting rights by
displaying sequences of time-elapsed maps to illustrate expansion of
voting rights over time.[63] When iterations of the maps were placed side-
by-side, they functioned like a moving picture book that showed the
changes happening before the readers' eyes (see figure 10). Women's
voting rights appeared fluid on the map, spilling over the state borders
to their neighboring states and inevitably washing across the nation. As
Leslie Harris argues, "mobility connotes possibility, freedom, flow, and
advancement," and suffragists promoted that possibility and advancement visually and verbally.[64] One NAWSA map poster announced: "Votes

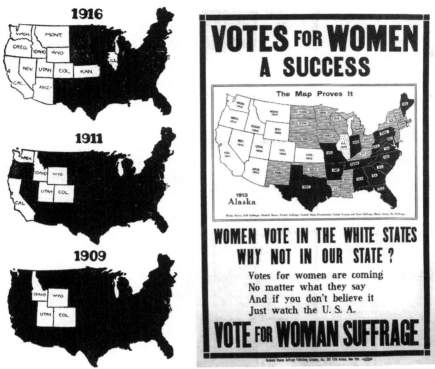

New York: National Woman Suffrage Publishing Company, 1914.

Figure 10 (*left*). Time-elapsed suffrage maps printed on the front page of the *Woman's Journal*, March 10, 1917. Figure 11 (*right*). "Votes for Women: A Success," map.

for women are coming, No matter what they say, And if you don't believe it, Just watch the U.S.A." (see figure 11).[65] The changing map image on the poster helped them depict woman suffrage as coming rather than going, and growing rather than stagnating. Discussing suffrage as coming reflected the connotation of arrival, approach, and future success. Suffragists underscored the speed that suffrage was moving with their frequent rallying cry to "hurry and get on the suffrage map."[66] As Alyssa Samek explains, "Velocity can be rhetorically, ideologically, and politically charged."[67] She asserts that sometimes faster movement indicates strength and power, and suffragists celebrated the moving maps as a sign of growing power, success, and freedom.

With thematic maps' ability to exaggerate the influence of the suffrage movement, and mobile maps' implication that their power was advancing, the maps gave suffragists a means to promote the legitimacy and influence of their movement, which constituted suffragists as powerful political agents. By visualizing women's voting rights' ontology (this is) and inevitable success nationally (this will be), they encouraged suffragists in their activism, assured them that their triumph was near, and convinced them of their collective agency to attain their goal. Although activists had been working for their cause for half a century, suffragists no longer identified as members of a "disheartened [or] stagnant" social movement, as Knobe had described them prior to the first suffrage map.[68] Instead, the maps positioned them as powerful and successful political activists with the agency to achieve equal voting rights nationwide, regardless of the population size that endorsed them. The victorious image of the suffrage map was amplified by the regional development of suffrage policies.

Suffrage Maps Activated and Reimagined the West

Suffrage maps simultaneously invoked and deployed the meaning of the West. By visualizing the suffrage movement spatially, the maps vividly displayed the regional pattern of women's voting rights. In 1915, all the equal suffrage states were west of the Mississippi River and bordered each other, so the suffrage maps produced an image of a coherent and united Western region of Washington, Oregon, California, Idaho, Nevada, Utah, Montana, Colorado, Arizona, and Kansas. The line running north and south down the maps separating the Western suffrage states from the rest of the country visibly resembled the frontier line on the nineteenth-century US Census maps.[69] As Belinda Stillion Southard notes, the 1913 suffrage map provided an image of the nation that was "divided and fractured" over woman suffrage, and the division was between the West and the East.[70] The apparent frontier line on the suffrage maps visually invoked the meaning and history of the West as a

Francis Amasa Walker, Statistical Atlas of the United States Based on the Results of the Ninth Census 1870. J. Bien, lith., 1874. Photo courtesy of the Library of Congress, Geography and Map Division.

Figure 12. Map showing the distribution of the US Constitutional population in 1870 (excluding American Indians not taxed). This black-and-white version of Walker's map obscures the yellow used on the original map to highlight American Indian reservations, which are not visible here.

frontier, activating the traditional rhetoric of the West as a frontier (see figure 12).

In the nineteenth century, European Americans' practices and rhetorics of conquest and continental expansion defined the West as a region in need of a violent civilizing process. As white Americans killed and displaced American Indians, they justified continental expansion with the discourse of Manifest Destiny. Manifest Destiny asserted that Anglo-Saxons were the superior race and destined by God to spread Christianity and "civilization" around the world, particularly across the North American continent from the Atlantic to the Pacific Ocean.[71] John Gast's *American Progress* painting visualized the dominant image of the West as an unsettled frontier to be civilized (see figure 13). Gast represented the violent civilizing project of continental expansion as an allegorical white woman who wore the "Star of Empire" on her forehead and held a school

Figure 13. John Gast, *American Progress*, 1872. Printed by George A. Crofutt as a chromolithograph in 1873.

book in one hand and the nation's telegraph lines in the other.[72] From the East to the West, the goddess-like woman led the light of civilization, white settlers, Christianity, and the social order of education and technology. He featured the West as a darkened wilderness where American Indians, bison, and other wild animals fled the approach of civilization. The painting was reproduced widely as colored prints and published in popular guidebooks.

Yet, the suffrage maps challenged the traditional image of the West as a frontier and reimagined the region as more civilized than the East through the imagery of light, whiteness, and social order.[73] The maps visualized this partly through their coloring. Although some maps were published in color, most were in black, white, and gray. The earliest suffrage maps, like Knobe's, shaded the four equal suffrage states in black, the non-suffrage states in white, and the partial-suffrage states in gray. But

Figure 14. At a parade in Omaha, Nebraska, horses draw a float decorated with a suffrage map proclaiming "9 States of Light Among 39 of Darkness." "Celebrating the 'Ratification,' by the Ninth State."

as more states enacted equal suffrage, the colors were reversed so that the maps identified the non-suffrage states in black, and the equal suffrage states in white, yellow, or gold. The light and dark shading of the maps featured the equal suffrage states more favorably than the non-suffrage states with the archetypal metaphors of lightness and darkness, which evoke strong positive and negative associations. As Michael Osborn explains, for centuries, light has been associated with vision, safety, and warmth, and darkness with night and limited sight, which can increase vulnerability and danger. Osborn argues that when lightness and darkness are used in persuasion, the metaphors often "express intense value judgments."[74] On both the suffrage maps and nineteenth-century images of continental expansion, civilization was represented as light shone into darkened, "uncivilized" places. In 1912, Omaha suffragists decorated a parade float that declared, "9 States of Light Among 39 of Darkness."

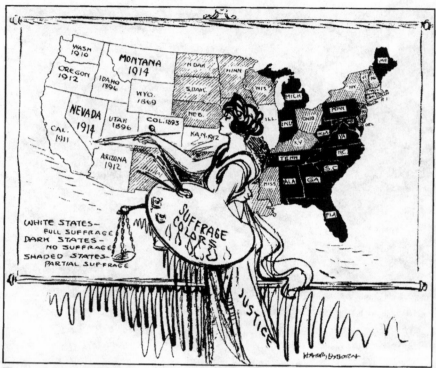

Figure 15. Harry Osborn, "Two More Bright Spots on the Map," *Maryland Suffrage News*, November 14, 1914.

The large lettering accompanied a map of the nine white suffrage states gleaming their light next to the darkly shaded Eastern and Southern non-suffrage states (see figure 14). Similarly, when Maryland suffragists appealed to their voters, they included a white woman painting a map with the "suffrage color" of white to celebrate "two more bright spots" (see figure 15).[75] Like the imagery of Manifest Destiny that visualized the light of civilization, the suffrage map's light-dark metaphor featured the suffrage states as civilized, in contrast to the Eastern non-suffrage states marked by primitive darkness.

The suffrage maps were a kind of moral map, which was a well-known visual medium at the time. Nineteenth-century and Progressive-Era reformers used lightness and darkness on maps to mark the counties or states where social problems were most prevalent. These maps were called moral maps because they reflected the moral judgments of the mapmakers. Darker shades were usually used to identify whatever the mapmaker viewed as immoral—high rates of disease, poverty, prostitution, enslavement, or crime, or low rates of education, literacy, or charity.[76] So the coloring of the suffrage map encouraged readers to associate suffrage with morality, another component believed to be a marker of civilization, and view the lack of suffrage as a social problem. In the United States, the most famous moral maps visualized enslavement of African Americans in the nineteenth century and women's voting rights and prohibition in the early twentieth century. Abolitionists' maps used black to shade places where African Americans were enslaved.[77] The similarity in coloring between the prevalent enslavement maps and suffrage maps may have further affiliated women's disfranchisement with the lack of civilization since abolitionists frequently described enslavement as a "relic of barbarism."[78] The maps' coloring also associated the suffrage states with the criteria considered most essential for civilization: whiteness. Based on a social Darwinian model of human progress, the Progressive-Era discourse of civilization was racialized. European Americans believed that white people were the ideal of humanity and the highest level of evolution a human could reach. The presence of white residents was often perceived as an indicator that a place was civilized, and North America was believed to be civilized as white settlers expanded west.[79] White was also used to describe suffrage states because once the maps became prevalent, states' voting policies were discussed in terms of their color on the map. Although some maps used yellow or other colors to represent suffrage states, white was used most often, so suffrage states were often called white states. The maps were also commonly accompanied by the appeal, "Women vote in all the white states. Why not in this state?"[80] When more states adopted woman suffrage and were added to the map, the *Lexington Herald* announced, "The World Grows Whiter" and the *Miami Herald* reported on "the rapidly whitening suffrage map of the United States."[81] Some suffragists used the white and black colors of the maps to suggest that their cause would ensure white supremacy.[82] For

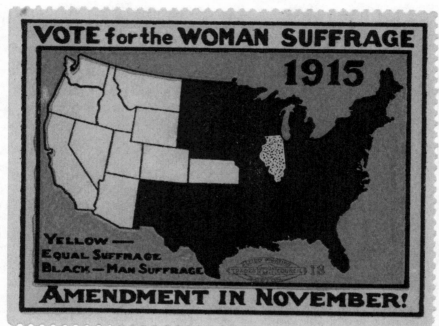

Photo courtesy of Cornell University Library, PJ Mode Collection of Persuasive Cartography.

Figure 16. "Vote for the Woman Suffrage Amendment" poster stamp, 1915. This black-and-white version of the poster stamp depicts the suffrage states in gray rather than yellow.

example, Texas suffragists published the map with large lettering that asked voters, "Won't you help us make Texas white?"[83] And suffragists of Richmond, Virginia, paired a map with their adopted slogan, "Help Us to Whiten Virginia."[84] These color euphemisms would have been easily understood by white Southern voters, since many believed that woman suffrage would increase or restore the white majority in the electorate of the Southern states and protect Jim Crow laws.[85]

Frequently, suffrage maps only marked and named the states in which women could vote. So the Western suffrage states were often delineated with borders and names, looking like developed, "civilized" places. In contrast, the non-suffrage states in the East and South were sometimes represented as a dark and formless mass, lacking borders, names, identifying features, or any sign of settlement or social order (see figure 16). Thus, the suffrage maps transposed the image of early US maps, which represented the Eastern states as settled and the Western land as undeveloped. By reversing the imagery of early US maps, the suffrage maps depicted the Eastern non-suffrage states as a primitive and undeveloped frontier that still needed to be civilized by women's voting rights, equating suffrage with progress and order.

By activating the meaning of the West and East, the maps forced Americans to consider the incongruity presented therein: the suffrage maps visually identified the West with progress, whiteness, social order, and civilization, and identified the East with barbarism, people of color, and the unsettled wilderness. The suffrage maps' image contradicted how many Easterners viewed themselves, the East, and the West. By reversing the imagined relationships with which Americans were familiar, the maps encouraged Easterners to reexamine the meaning of women's voting rights, and challenged longstanding meanings of both regions.

The suffrage maps' activation and recasting of the West also featured the growth of women's voting rights as continental expansion, which suggested that suffragists' national success was as inevitable as Manifest Destiny. As Samek argues, the rhetoricity of place and mobility interact and transform each other.[86] The maps featured the movement's growth as continental expansion in part with the maps' mobility and light-dark metaphor. At a NAWSA fundraiser held at Carnegie Hall in 1913, Anna Howard Shaw planned to promote the movement of women's voting rights with a "moving picture show"—a performance with a series of moving images and dynamic maps.[87] The *Woman's Journal* explained her plan for the show:

> The first map will be as black as Egypt. Then two little gray specks will show the beginning of school suffrage. The first glow of dawn will come in the West—first in Wyoming. The whole western part of the United States and the Pacific Coast will gradually be illuminated with the golden light of victory. Succeeding maps will show the gold extending in great floods of color after the elections of 1913, 1914,

and 1915, until, at the beginning of 1920, only one black spot is left—
namely, Vermont.[88]

Shaw planned to use the maps' movement to depict with certainty that
"The United States at the end of 1920 will have a cloudless map, all gold
and no black." The picture show may not have turned out as active as she
hoped. The *New York Tribune* coverage of the event did not mention the
movement of the maps, but described her "cloudless map of 1920 [as] a
huge slide, with the map of the United States as it 'MAY' be then—every
state full suffrage."[89] Yet her plan indicates that suffragists were aware of
the moving map's rhetoricity and attempted to emphasize that movement to depict suffrage as inevitably spreading across the continent.

Furthermore, Shaw's moving picture show was designed to commu-
nicate the inevitability of their success using the light-dark metaphor to
naturalize the transition to suffrage states. As Osborn argues, the light-
dark metaphor can also imply inevitability, as well as "confidence and
optimism," because the light and dark qualities in nature evolve chrono-
logically from night into day and winter into spring. Shaw's language
reveals an additional layer of meaning. She described the spread of suffrage as gradually illuminating the non-suffrage states that were "as black
as Egypt" with the "golden light" of suffrage rights. "As black as Egypt"
was a nineteenth-century expression and biblical allusion to Exodus
10:21, when Moses imposed darkness on the Egyptian pharaoh.[90] Yet the
phrase simultaneously invoked other common phrases at the turn of the
century, including "the dark continent" and "darkest Africa," which were
used to describe Africa and anywhere that was considered uncivilized.

Both suffragists and antisuffragists appealed to the same racial
ideology that constructed whiteness as the preferred race in the United
States to make different arguments about woman suffrage moving east.
As Samek notes, faster movement has the capacity to "signal invasion,
threat, or danger."[91] Antisuffragists viewed the suffrage maps' movement as a dangerous threat, and sometimes described its contagion
as "yellow peril."[92] The "yellow peril" description evoked the symbolic
color of the suffrage movement, Chinese and Japanese exclusion, and

American xenophobia. Antisuffragists used the term to associate the eastward movement of woman suffrage with the eastward migration of East Asian immigrants, and defined the presence of both as dangerous and unwanted.

Suffragists imagined their maps' mobility as conquest, which also evoked the rhetoric of continental expansion. When the *Woman's Journal* discussed "The Changing Map" in 1916, they argued, "The suffrage map must now be changed again—for the fourth time this year. It changes almost as fast as the map of Europe. But the suffrage victories are bloodless, and represent only slain prejudices."[93] Likewise, Crystal Eastman Benedict described the white states on the maps as a "triumphant, threatening army."[94] Describing the maps' mobility in terms of war and violence depicted women's voting rights as an empire claiming territory. Some antisuffragists also seemed to read the suffrage maps in terms of war and imperial power. Antisuffragist Mrs. William Forse Scott acknowledged in the *New York Times* that after looking at the 1915 suffrage map, she could see that "feminism is rampant now, and suffragists are boasting of alleged successes all along the line." In the *Reply*, Forse admitted, "It is time to face the *danger*. The solid block of suffrage states . . . stares at us from the suffrage map."[95] The imperial implications of the maps gestured to opponents that their defeat was near, and opposition was futile.

Suffragists used the maps' movement and colors to invoke imagery of continental expansion by emphasizing the eastward direction women's voting rights were moving. As the *Woman's Journal* headline promoted in 1915, "Suffrage Moving Steadily East."[96] Blackwell asserted that on the suffrage maps, "the movement is ALL ONE WAY . . . There can be no doubt as to which way the procession is moving."[97] When Crystal Eastman Benedict spoke before the House Judiciary Committee in 1914, she shared suffrage maps with the committee and told them, "Our plea is simply that you look at the little map again. That triumphant, threatening army of white States crowding *rapidly eastward* toward the center of population is the sum and substance of our argument to you."[98] The perception that suffrage was moving east was so common that the *Boston*

Transcript asked, "Is woman suffrage a thing that always moves from the west eastward, occupying the ground as it goes, like a storm centre, and 'area of depression'?" The *Woman's Journal* answered the *Transcript*'s question in the affirmative, arguing that across the United States, even at the county level, suffrage was moving from west to east.[99] Samek maintains that "the directionality of movement matters," and the eastward mobility of the white states implied that suffrage was expanding across the continent.[100] But instead of bringing the light of "civilization" to the West, the maps asserted that the light and civilization of woman suffrage was inevitably expanding to the East. The rhetoricity of the West transformed the meaning of the maps' mobility to suggest that women's voting rights were not just growing—they were expanding across the continent, bringing the civilization of woman suffrage to the new Eastern frontier.

Some of the suffrage maps and their accompanying discourse explicitly compared the movement's growth to Manifest Destiny. In 1917, the *General Federation Bulletin* published the newest suffrage map and explained: "This is the latest suffrage map. All the white States are suffrage States. The *Star of Empire that looks its way Westward* till every Territory had become a State is making its return trip East to encourage the States to enfranchise all citizens . . . We have added seven States to our suffrage list since January. Soon our whole map will be white."[101] Not only were the white suffrage states expanding inevitably across the continent, but the *Bulletin* argued that the force bringing suffrage to the East was the same "Star of Empire that looks its way Westward till every Territory had become a state." The "Star of Empire" was a nineteenth-century euphemism for Manifest Destiny. Adapted from George Berkeley's poem, "Westward the Course of Empire Takes Its Way," the phrases "Star of Empire" and "course of empire" were often used interchangeably.[102] Berkeley's verse was used to encapsulate the ideals of Manifest Destiny and inspired many murals of continental expansion, including Gast's *American Progress* and Emanuel Gottlieb Leutze's *Westward the Course of Empire Takes Its Way*.[103] Gast's allegorical feminine figure wore the "Star of Empire" on her forehead as she brought civilization eastward.[104] The phrase also had multiple meanings for suffragists, since they used stars to symbolize the equal suffrage states on their flags, badges, and pins.[105]

The association between woman suffrage and continental expansion became so strong that it appeared in suffrage discourse even when the maps were not present. In 1915, *Current Opinion* played on Berkeley's verse with their headline, "Eastward the Tide of Woman Suffrage Takes its Way."[106] Likewise, during the Ohio campaign for a state suffrage amendment, suffragists "explained that Ohio will be the next State to adopt woman suffrage. Eastward the star of civilization takes its way!"[107] This declaration predicted that suffrage was successfully moving east, and imagined the spread of women's rights as the "star of civilization"—the symbol of continental expansion and Manifest Destiny. The belief that the "civilization" of woman suffrage was moving east featured the Eastern states as the new "frontier." In 1914, when the *Woman's Journal* covered the campaign for suffrage in Ohio, their front page announced, "Ohio Eastern Frontier of Suffrage Movement—Success Means Landslide in 1915."[108] As the *Journal* predicted that "Ohio Will Unlock the East," they imagined the East as the "new frontier" they were destined to soon claim. As Americans mourned the closed frontier and longed for the old West that gave them their perceived exceptionalism, suffragist's rhetoric of continental expansion gave Americans a new frontier to conquer, and asserted that women's voting rights were destined to succeed in the East.

The suffrage maps' regional rhetoric of the West and continental expansion were salient and prevalent enough to circulate in political cartoons. In 1913, when Illinois's house of representatives passed a bill that enabled women to vote in presidential and local (but not state) elections, John T. McCutcheon, a cartoonist for the *Chicago Tribune*, drew a map of Illinois with suffragists walking across the state with suffrage flags held high, claiming it imperially for their cause, like John Freemont did when he planted the US flag on the Rocky Mountains and claimed them as territory of the United States (see figure 17).[109] And in February 1915, Henry "Hy" Mayer published "The Awakening" in the two-paged centerfold of *Puck Magazine* (see figure 18).[110] The cartoon parodied the suffrage maps by adding the symbolic figure of a white woman striding

Figure 17. John T. McCutcheon, "The First One East of 'The Mother of Waters.'"

Figure 18. Henry "Hy" Mayer, "The Awakening," *Puck*, February 20, 1915.

confidently across the Western states in an eastward direction. The woman's sash was labeled "Votes for Women," and she held a lit torch that brought the light of women's political progress into the darkened East. The cartoon invoked the image of Gast's *American Progress* painting as both images depicted cross-continental movement of large, allegorical feminine figures bringing light to darkness. But rather than leading the light of America's "progress and civilization" to the darkened West, "The Awakening's" feminine figure led the light of woman suffrage to the dark and formless East, which was filled with a sea of women reaching longingly toward the West for voting rights. "The Awakening's" inversion of *American Progress* asserted that woman suffrage was moving progressively to the East, just like the suffrage maps suggested. Suffragists seemed to view "The Awakening" image as empowering, since the National Woman's Party published the image on the cover of the *Suffragist* the following year, albeit in altered form—they removed the sea of Eastern women reaching desperately toward the West.[111] The circulation and parody of the suffrage maps in political cartoons suggest that the public was familiar with the maps and recognized the rhetorics of continental expansion they communicated.

Conclusion

In 1913, following a suffrage pageant in New York City, Theodore Roosevelt spoke before a crowd and "asserted that the fact that it was possible to hold such a gathering here in New York was the best proof that 'civilization was slowly creeping from the West.'" According to the *New York Times*, he predicted, "I don't think the East is going to always lag behind the West in darkness . . . I think civilization is coming East gradually . . . There is no surer sign of advancing civilization than the advanced respect paid to woman."[112] Roosevelt, who was by then a proponent of woman suffrage, verbalized the argument that suffragists made with their maps: that woman suffrage was "civilized," the West was civilized because it had enacted women's voting rights, and the West's civilization was surely expanding east across the continent just as the United States had expanded west.

By visualizing women's voting rights geographically, the maps constituted suffragists as powerful political agents and asserted their capacity to achieve the franchise nationwide. The rhetoricity of thematic and dynamic maps legitimized the existence of women's voting rights as a reality, exaggerated the suffrage movement's national influence, and activated and reimagined the meaning of the West. Reimagining the non-suffrage states as the new frontier suggested that suffragists would inevitably succeed in the East and expand women's voting rights across the continent. The maps also illustrate that the West had persuasive power nationwide, and could be employed by suffragists around the country, not just advocates who lived and worked in the West, like Duniway. Since regional appeals can be used for nationalist claims, the maps could advocate women's citizenship rights nationwide in part through their regional rhetoric.[113]

The maps' characterizations of the West and the East varied distinctly from Duniway's depiction of those regions, in some ways reversing her vision. Rather than imagining the West as a frontier as she had, the maps depicted the East as the new frontier, set apart from the civilized West. Both Duniway and the makers of the suffrage maps featured the West and East as distinct from each other, and the West as better than the East, though in different ways. Duniway's West was exceptional for its mythic heroes, frontier heroines, and inherent freedom. The maps' vision of the West was superior to the East for its woman suffrage policies and civilization. She looked down on Eastern women as interfering, weak, and dependent on men. The maps envisioned the East as barbaric and uncivilized—the nation's new frontier. Mayer's "Awakening" cartoon did both, by depicting the East as a primitive and undeveloped wilderness, filled with desperate and dependent women waiting for help from the West.

The suffrage maps provided advocates the opportunity to appropriate and exploit the history of continental expansion in the West as a tool of persuasion. The implication that woman suffrage was inevitably and certainly expanding east across the continent underscored the map's claims of the movement's success and power. Just as Duniway leveraged the meanings of the mythic frontier to suggest that Western women had earned the right to vote, suffragists exploited the meanings of continental expansion and Manifest Destiny to assert the woman suffrage movement's power and inevitable victory nationwide. Other suffragists also promoted a vision of the West in line with the map, as a region that was civilized, progressive, and superior to the East, in part because of its politically active women. Eventually, suffragists took the map's rhetoric of continental expansion and performed it through a months-long transcontinental car trip that embodied the promise that Western women were bringing suffrage to the East, just as they depicted it on their maps. Yet those who opposed women's voting rights did not accept these visions of the West as inherently free or as civilized. Antisuffragists also invoked regional rhetoric in their opposition to woman suffrage. Through a variety of arguments, antisuffragists tried to refute the significance, power, and civilization of the Western suffrage states, instead envisioning it as unimportant and uncivilized with the regional rhetoric of the wild and woolly West.

CHAPTER 3

Dismissing the West

ANTISUFFRAGISTS' WILD AND WOOLLY WEST, 1903–1919

———•◆•———

In the spring of 1913, the *New York Times* published a letter to the editor responding to the newest suffrage map and the enfranchisement of women in the West. In his letter titled "No Eastern Suffrage States," Walter C. Taylor, a man from Brookline, Massachusetts, explained his opposition to women's voting rights: "Not a single State east of the Mississippi River ha[s] adopted woman suffrage: every 'white' State on the suffrage map is in the weird and woolly West . . . Woman suffrage has been adopted only by the crude, raw, half-formed Commonwealths of the sagebrush and the windy plains, whence have come in endless procession foolish and fanatical politics and policies for a generation or two."[1] To oppose the growing success of the woman suffrage movement, and respond to the powerful image of the suffrage map, he took aim at the West and exploited another regional rhetoric. Instead of imagining the West as mythically free, the crucible of American exceptionalism, or a place of progress and civilization, as had Duniway and the suffrage mapmakers, Taylor envisioned the West as "weird and woolly."

Like this Massachusetts man, many Eastern antisuffragists denied the significance of women's voting rights in the West and dismissed the suffrage states as unimportant and uncivilized. Antisuffragists—who called themselves "antis"—attempted to refute the suffrage maps' projections of power by region-making the West as "wild and woolly" and emphasizing the West's small population size. This chapter focuses on how antisuffragists imagined the West in the periodicals they published between 1903 and 1919.[2] I argue that, by presenting an alternative image of the West, Eastern antis discounted Western women's voting rights as unimportant, and rejected the idea of following the West's precedent as "ludicrous."[3] They imagined the region as uncultivated and unevolved with the racialized, gendered, classed, and mobility-based discourse of civilization and the woolly West.

Historian Billie Barnes Jensen argues that studying antisuffrage texts gives us a window into how Easterners viewed the West in the early twentieth century.[4] I build on her argument and add that these texts also show how antisuffragists shaped and constructed Easterners' views of the West for their persuasive goals. As rhetorical critic Thomas Rosteck explains, historical texts are not only windows for viewing ideas of a certain time period, they were also vehicles for shaping ideas of the time.[5] The antisuffrage texts encouraged Easterners to view the West and women's participation in politics in specific ways.

The New York Times *on Suffrage in the East and West*

In October 1915, Eastern voters were preparing to decide whether to enfranchise women at their upcoming state elections in Massachusetts, New Jersey, New York, and Pennsylvania. The *New York Times* weighed in on the issue in an editorial titled "Suffrage, East and West."[6] Although the editorial never used the phrase "woolly West," the *New York Times* opposed enfranchising Eastern women by imagining the Western suffrage states as less advanced than the East. The *New York Times*'s use of regional rhetoric to oppose woman suffrage is representative of many anti arguments, so I examine it here more closely.

The article opened by documenting the Western suffrage states' rurality with figures and tables: "Outside of California . . . and Illinois . . . the equal suffrage states are mostly sparsely settled." For evidence, the reader was directed to "Look at this list" of suffrage states' populations in 1910. The list included ten of the twelve suffrage states at the time, excluding California and Illinois, the two most populous suffrage states.

STATE	POPULATION, 1910
Arizona	204,354
Colorado	799,024
Idaho	325,594
Kansas	1,696,949
Montana	376,053
Nevada	81,875
Oregon	672,765
Utah	373,351
Washington	1,141,990
Wyoming	145,963
Total	*5,817,918*

The author compared the list to the populations of four Eastern states that were preparing to vote on suffrage amendments that fall.

STATE	POPULATION, 1910
Massachusetts	3,366,416
New Jersey	2,537,167
New York	9,113,279
Pennsylvania	7,665,111
Total	*22,681,973*

The editorial summarized the point of the lists: "Ten states, whose combined population was nearly two million less than that of Pennsylvania . . . Is it from this handful of people that these four great States are to learn the art of 'ideal democracy' and improved government?"

The author provided a separate list for the population sizes of the two most populous suffrage states, California and Illinois, which were similar to states in the East.

STATE	POPULATION, 1910
California	2,377,549
Illinois	5,638,591
Total	*8,016,140*

The editorial disregarded the two states because "California adopted woman suffrage in 1911 against the wishes of a majority of the women of the State," an argument often used by antis, and Illinois only let women "vote for all offices not created by the State Constitution." In 1915, women in Illinois could vote in federal elections but not in state elections, so the author suggested that Illinois did not really trust women voters.[7]

Then the article went through all the suffrage states one-by-one to provide reasons why each state's suffrage policy should be disregarded by Eastern voters. Some of the states were again dismissed for their population sizes: "Arizona wouldn't make two New York Assembly districts." But the other states were imagined as less cultivated for their unsophisticated politics: "Kansas, with all its virtues, has had from the first an emotional temperament, a disposition to shudder at imaginary 'calamity,' to get wild over crank political specifics, to worship and then break grotesque political idols. For many admirable things can the Sunflower State be praised, but not for sound judgement." The author pointed to the widespread support of populism in Kansas and characterized the state as radical, lower-class, and as emotionally unpredictable as a toddler. Similarly, Oregon was described as a politically immature teenager: "Oregon is the experiment station of all sorts of bewildering and bedeviling whimsies." The state had implemented many direct democracy policies, and the editorial used them as evidence of the state's inexperience and rudimentary politics. California was also stalled in its advancement, deemed politically unevolved, and easy prey for uncivilized influences, the editorial argued: "From California . . . the East has nothing to learn except avoidance of radical and *half-baked* 'reforms.'" Colorado and Idaho were dismissed as models for action because of their struggles with "peace and orderliness," apparent in the labor strikes and resulting violence, like the Ludlow Massacre that had taken place the previous year. And Utah was dismissed as unevolved according to polygamy: "Utah's long devotion to plural feminism is not forgotten."

After dismissing each of the Western suffrage states, "Illinois remain[ed] the only 'equal suffrage' State where anything like a parallel environment and conditions to those of New York, New Jersey, Pennsylvania, and Massachusetts exist," but these women had only been voting for two years, since 1913. The editorial summarized that "If the woman suffrage coterie in the East were as rich in judgment as it is in enthusiasm, . . . it would have waited until time has ripened and careful observation examined the good, the evil, or the indifferent effects of the Illinois experiment."[8] The suffrage policies in Illinois were still maturing and evolving, lagging behind the East, and were not yet "ripe" enough to follow as examples.

As the author featured the West's lack of cultivation, the editorial listed the many ways woman suffrage had harmed the West and its advancement toward civilization. Since California had enfranchised women, "The legal status of women has actually been made worse. The so much hymned moral benefit has not occurred." Countering the prevalent expediency arguments of the time, the author argued that woman suffrage was not making politics better. Instead, "San Francisco women [had used their new direct democracy rights to recall] a Judge and got in his place 'a Magistrate with very scant knowledge of the law and of such a weak character that he would never appeal to any but women voters.'" Furthermore, "It should be added that an extraordinary increase of State and county taxation has occurred under, if not because of, woman suffrage." The Western voters were not yet as mature and experienced as the East, so they were making politically ignorant errors like raising taxes and electing inexperienced judges, which the editorial depicted as stalling the West's progress and advancement, and causing the region to devolve toward barbarism. The editorial proclaimed that "*The Times* . . . oppose[s] the initiative and referendum and the recall of judicial decisions so beloved in some of the suffrage States."[9] The author derided the direct democracy policies popular in the West to feature the region as uninformed, ignorant, and primitive.

Finally, the editorial closed by maintaining that even though "the public mind is occupied with problems much more vital and engrossing [than women's voting rights], the suffragists seek to drive their obsessing idea through in four great, populous, complex Eastern States." In addition to characterizing women's voting rights as trivial and suffragists as obsessive, the editorial featured the "four great, populous, complex Eastern States" as much more advanced, populated, and important than the West. Eastern voters were encouraged to "Wait and weigh" before enfranchising women. "Don't thrust upon the East a still doubtful speculation in government."[10] By invoking the East and the West, and envisioning the regions as distinct from each other in population size as well as political advancement, the *New York Times* urged Easterners to avoid following the West's unevolved and experimental practice of enfranchising women. The editorial resembled a common rationale of antisuffragists.

US Antisuffrage Organizations and Rationales

Like the woman suffrage movement, the antisuffrage movement was founded and headquartered in the Northeast. In the late nineteenth century, women and men in New York and Massachusetts began organizing associations to collectively oppose the movement for women's voting rights. Over the years, state associations grew in size and influence, and antisuffrage associations formed on the West Coast and in the Midwest.[11] In 1911, various state associations joined forces to form the National Association Opposed to Woman Suffrage (NAOWS) and based their headquarters in New York. By 1916, the NAOWS had grown into an organization of 350,000 members across twenty five states.[12] The members were typically white, and although some men were involved, women were more active. They led the antisuffrage organizations and wrote most antisuffrage books, articles, essays, pamphlets, and periodicals, including the *Remonstrance*, the *Anti-Suffragist*, and the NAOWS's official organ, the *Woman's Protest* (renamed the *Woman Patriot* in 1917).[13] Antis also distributed postcards that visualized many of their arguments against suffrage through cartoons that reached a broad population.[14]

Antisuffrage scholars agree that there was a significant change in the antisuffrage movement in 1917. That year, the NAOWS moved its headquarters from New York City to Washington, DC, and replaced their president, most of their national officers, and most members of their executive committee.[15] Beginning in 1917, the discourse of the NAOWS also broadened from a focus on women's voting rights to oppose all forms of radicalism, including feminism, socialism, and bolshevism.[16] Antis' discourse from 1917 to 1920 became much more paranoid and aggressive, which Kristy Maddux explains is common for groups that perceive that they have lost power or become oppressed. Maddux and Thomas J. Jablonsky reason that antis most likely perceived they had lost power because the suffrage movement was getting so much national attention due to the Congressional Union's White House pickets, demonstrations, and arrests, and Carrie Chapman Catt's "Winning Plan" to focus the NAWSA on winning a federal amendment for women's voting rights. Furthermore, in the fall of 1917, New York became the first Eastern state to enact equal voting rights for men and women. New York's new suffrage policy made it much more difficult to dismiss women's voting rights as solely a phenomenon of the West. Prior to 1917, however, Eastern antis commonly disparaged the Western suffrage states as uncivilized and insignificant in comparison to the East.

Antisuffragist discourse often focused on the ways the vote would harm women and their families, create barriers to enacting reform, and endanger society and civilization.[17] Antis used a range of pragmatic arguments to assert that suffrage was not practical or useful because women did not want to vote, they did not need the vote because their husbands' votes represented them, and they were too busy caring for their homes and families to go to the polls. These arguments suggested that voting would add another burden to their busy lives and would threaten their position in society as it would allow "bad" women (usually meaning women of color, women who immigrated to the United States, and women engaged in sex work) to vote.[18] The threat of enfranchisement as a danger to enacting reform was effective because many antis were committed to social progress, women's advancement, philanthropy, and public activism, but did not think the vote was necessary to enact such reform. They believed that women were better reformers and had more public power because they were not enfranchised and functioned in a separate sphere that was untainted by politics and men.[19] These antis reasoned women would be more effective at influencing public policy through strategies other than the vote.

The most common rationale against woman suffrage was the separate spheres ideology. Historian Aileen Kraditor argues that antisuffragists primarily opposed women's right to vote based on beliefs that men and women had different roles in society and were meant to function in different spheres. Because women were supposed to function in the home, woman suffrage would disturb their societal role and therefore hurt women, their families, and society.[20] Many Americans believed that advanced civilizations depended on these separate and distinct spheres, which would be disrupted if women left the private sphere to vote and participate in politics.[21]

Industrialization contributed to the reality of separate spheres for many middle- and upper-class people. The separate-spheres model became an ideal amidst industrialization in Europe and the urban areas in the US East, where it became more common for men to leave their homes to labor for wages while women performed unpaid labor at home. Yet this was less common in unindustrialized places, like the rural West, where many men and women worked alongside or near each other and their families. Even though some Westerners subscribed to the separate-spheres model and families often divided their labor along gender lines, most Westerners' lives did not appear like the industrial ideal of separate spheres, a fact that antis used to depict the West as uncivilized and harmful to women and their communities.[22]

The separate spheres ideology was based on theological and biological arguments about men's and women's distinct roles in society, citing Genesis and Paul's letters in the New Testament. Proponents argued that God created men and women to fulfill different roles in society. God designed women's bodies for reproduction and dominance in the private sphere, and men, whose bodies were not designed for reproduction, were meant to function in the public sphere.[23] Likewise, women's primary role in life was caring for children. Antis claimed that because women were physically weaker, they could not undertake the physical demands required for political participation. According to Catherine Palczewski, Americans believed that "physical power was needed in order for a vote to carry any force," so women were unsuitable because they "lacked the physical power necessary to enforce the vote."[24] Yet these biological arguments did not hold up as well in the West, where many women supported themselves and their families through hard, physical labor.[25]

Like suffragists, antis blatantly appealed to racist, xenophobic, and anti-Catholic sentiments.[26] Scholars have identified numerous ways that antis charged that woman suffrage could threaten white supremacy or the Protestant American way of life, both of which they reasoned would hurt white Americans.[27] Yet examining the antis' visions of the West illustrates that antis also appealed to anti-Mormon sentiment, since the suffrage states of Utah and Idaho had large Mormon populations.[28] Although many Mormon women supported women's right to vote, national suffrage discourse generally avoided associating woman suffrage with Mormonism because they were commonly discriminated against in the United States. Many Northeastern Americans were concerned that Mormon theology did not support a separation of church and state, and viewed it as a threat to American democracy, values, and institutions in the West.[29] Furthermore, the Mormon Church was also associated with polygamy because the church practiced and endorsed it during much of the nineteenth century. Despite major federal legislation to restrict polygamy, it was still practiced until 1890, when the church's president Wilford Woodruff promised that the church would stop so that Utah could be granted statehood.[30]

Interestingly, polygamy and woman suffrage were intertwined in several ways in Utah. Antipolygamy advocates endorsed woman suffrage because they assumed that women would vote to eliminate polygamy. Yet once Utah women were able to vote, many of them supported polygamy. In the nineteenth century, the practice in the Western territories provoked as much, and potentially more, national indignation and disapproval as the institution of enslavement. The Republican Party called polygamy and enslavement the "twin relics of barbarism."[31] Americans believed that slavery's "Twin Sister" endangered the United States' "free institutions" and many believed it needed to "be wiped out in blood."[32] As Americans opposed these practices, their antipolygamy rhetoric unrelentingly depicted polygamy as morally debased, barbarous, and a threat to civilization.[33] As I will illustrate, antis linked women's voting rights with the practice of polygamy by featuring both polygamy and woman suffrage as practices of an unevolved West.

The Regional Rhetoric of the Woolly West

Antis often described the Western suffrage states with the rhetoric of the "wild and woolly" West, an image that was prevalent in the American public's imagination and discourse. At the turn of the century, "wild and woolly" was used to describe things that were barbaric, rude, lawless, uncultured, or uncivilized.[34] If civilization was the "highest form of humanity" on the evolutionary scale, then "wild and woolly" was the lowest form, used to describe the "primitive humans" who had only slightly evolved beyond animals.[35] In contrast to civilization, which was marked by whiteness, gender differentiation, and sophistication, wooliness was believed to have several markers: people of color, the blurring of gender differences, lower socioeconomic class, and associations with violence or lawlessness. Wooliness implied a lack of elements associated with progress, reform, or modern advancement.

In the nineteenth century, "woolly" was often used to describe animals. Shepherds might call their sheep "woolly backs," or families may refer to their pets as the "woolly dog."[36] But it was also a racial descriptor. In the 1850s, the phrase "wild and woolly" often described both animals and people from Africa, Australia, Polynesia, or New Guinea.[37] White Americans often called African Americans' hair "wool," which associated African Americans with animals. US enslavers described people they enslaved according to the style or length of their "wool."[38] "Woolly-heads" became such a commonly used synonym for blackness, that African Americans and their supporters appropriated the term.[39] When Phineas T. Barnum advocated "Negro Suffrage" in 1865, he described African Americans according to "their woolly heads," and at an American Equal Rights Association event in 1869, Frederick Douglass referred to himself when he said, "this woolly head of mine."[40] Even into the mid-twentieth century, "wool" continued to be used to describe African American hair.[41]

In the nineteenth-century context of social Darwinism, describing African Americans as woolly or having woolly hair differentiated blacks from whites as a different species and as less civilized and evolved than whites. The animalistic term "woolly" positioned African Americans as somewhere in the evolutionary development between animal and civilized human. Scientists often classified "woolly"-haired people with dark skin as the bottom rung of the human evolutionary ladder.[42] Woolly hair and dark skin became associated with lower levels of intelligence, civilization, and humanity.[43] These and other physical traits of African Americans were used as scientific evidence for racial difference and hierarchies that justified enslaving people and treating them differently.[44]

In the West, wooliness described black and white men differently. As a discourse of civilization, woolly rhetoric could be used to legitimize and challenge a variety of kinds of power, people, and causes. For black men, wooliness was evidence of their barbarism, primitiveness, and animalism. But for white men in the West, wooliness signified masculinity and served as evidence of their manhood. For example, the four African American units of the US Army that were stationed in the West were called Buffalo Soldiers on account of "their woolly heads" that appeared "so much like the matted cushion that is between the horns of the buffalo."[45] William Cody, the white American scout and eventual performer, was also given the name "Buffalo." But Buffalo Bill Cody secured his nickname by supplying buffalo meat to the Kansas Pacific Railroad workers and by winning a buffalo-shooting match with William Comstock, killing sixty-eight buffalo to Comstock's forty-eight. The white Cody won the "buffalo" title for killing buffalo, while the black "Buffalo Soldiers" received their name for looking like the buffalo.[46] The buffalo moniker illustrates the way being "wild and woolly" was believed to make white men more manly, but displays of wooliness by non-white men were used as proof of their barbarism or animalism.[47]

Americans also began to use woolly to describe white cowboys, desperados, and Westerners who appeared unkempt, partly because many Western pioneers had wool that showed on the outside of their sheepskin coats.[48] By the end of the nineteenth century, white cowboys were described as "wild and woolly" in books like Adair Welcker's *Tales of the "Wild & Woolly West"* (1891), and the woolly West was often visualized by a white mustached cowboy with a pistol, large hat, and cigar.[49] White men in the West began to be considered woolly according to their lack of refinement, resistance to the law, and associations with violence.

Many Easterners enjoyed depictions of the West as wild and undeveloped. By 1917, the woolly West was the subject of several films, including *The Wild and Woolly West*, *Fearless Freddie in the Woolly West*, and a silent comedy titled *Wild and Woolly*.[50] Easterners also liked pretending they were in the uncivilized West at parties and in clubs. In 1909, a benefit held at the Waldorf-Astoria hotel in Midtown Manhattan was Western-themed, complete with a shooting gallery, bows and arrows, a violent wild west show, waitresses dressed as cowboys, and decorations of the Rocky Mountains and grizzly bears. The *New York Times* commented that "the idea of the wild and woolly West at the Waldorf-Astoria is funny in itself."[51] In 1915, young professionals of New York City created an outdoors organization called the Inkowa Club, and at their first "great council fire" in the Bronx's Van Cortlandt Park, the *New York Times* reported, "The effete East and the woolly West came together" as the club members dressed up as "young squaws" and "indian chiefs . . . and sang somber Indian songs to the notes of the tom-tom."[52] The *New York Times* accounts illustrate the ways Easterners were at once fascinated by the idea of the uncivilized West and viewed it as drastically different than the East. Similar to Theodore Roosevelt, Owen Wister, and Frederic Remington, many Easterners liked envisioning the West as distinct from the East and less civilized.[53]

Region-making the West as woolly imagined a distinct spatiotemporal construction, understood to be a temporary phase in the ongoing evolutionary process of civilizing the United States and the rest of the world. In descriptions of white cowboys and the Far West, Americans used "wild and woolly" to describe a region that was not yet civilized, but would inevitably be transformed and lost due to evolutionary progress. In 1902, when Cody recalled Roosevelt's 1883 trip to "the then 'wild and woolly' town of Little Missouri . . . in the heart of the 'bad lands,'" Cody said the Dakota Territory town "contained at that time some of the worst 'bad men' and outlaws to be found outside the borders of civilization."[54] Cody's recollection placed the wild and woolly town outside of civilization and the law, and illustrates the perception that the West was changing as it became more civilized and less woolly. When the *Woman's Protest* praised the newly "clean, well-ordered city" that Chicago had become by 1915, they recalled its "'wild and woolly' condition" ten years earlier, before it was civilized.[55] Recollections of the woolly West often included references to violence, outlaws, and sparse populations. In 1917, when *The Boy Scouts' Year Book* recalled "the days when the west was wild and woolly," they described the sheriffs as violent "man-killers."[56] All of these descriptions of the woolly West featured it as passing or having passed, a period of history that could not endure. In 1908, *Outlook* magazine predicted, "Within a few years it will be seen of all men that 'the West is no longer a wild and woolly sort of No-Man's Land, where spurred and pistoled bravos do nothing all day long but fling defiance in the face of Heaven and its laws."[57]

As a discourse of civilization, I argue that the regional rhetoric of the woolly West was a mobility-based rhetoric. The region-making of the West was done partly by constructing the movement toward civilization as distinct from other parts of the country. At the turn of the century, civilization was considered a process—"a *movement* from barbarism to refinement."[58] Americans believed that the United States was evolving from primitivism to sophistication, but the image of the woolly West asserted that the region was at a different point in the evolutionary process than the rest of the country. Rhetorical critic Leslie Harris argues that rhetorical mobility in a space shapes the meaning of that space. Since both time and space are rhetorically constructed, spaces gain their meaning in part through discursive constructions of the movement and time within a space. The region-making of the West as woolly was done partly by constructing the West's movement from barbarism toward civilization as stuck, behind, or moving more slowly than the East or South. Harris argues that rhetoric can construct spaces as moving differently, or at different rates, sometimes so much so that communities in certain places "can be perceived as dislocated either spatially or temporally."[59] The rhetoric of the woolly West constructed the West partly through a unique rhetorical mobility that featured the region as temporally dislocated from the rest of the nation.

The wild West referred to a certain region at a certain moment in time that was changing and would not last forever. Change can evoke nostalgia, which Harris defines as "a spatio-temporal longing"—the way many Easterners felt about the West. As Americans believed that the West was changing, they found themselves nostalgic for the way it was while it was still distinct from the East, prior to cultivation. In the Eastern imaginary, the ideal West was frozen in time at a moment in the ongoing development of the United States. As Liza Nicholas argues, this Eastern ideal of the West was "Turnerianism interrupted"—"a West in which Frederick Jackson Turner's famous, and inevitable, march of civilization, settlement, and progress [had] proceeded only so far." While Easterners valued white civilization and believed it to be the ideal of humanity, their preferred concept of the West "conveniently paused right after the Indians had been subdued and before the settlers and their civilizing agenda invaded their pure and sanctified space."[60] In 1903, a writer for the *Chicago Tribune* bemoaned, "What has become of the Wild and Woolly West" since it was "reformed." As he lamented the passing of the "rough and tumble pioneer life," he "confided [his] grief at finding effete civilization invading the West."[61] Yet while Easterners romanticized their vision of the wild West and viewed the woolly West with nostalgia, they did not view it as a model for the future of the East. They wanted the West to remain distinct from the East; they did not want the East to become more like the West.

Antisuffragists' Woolly West

The "wild and woolly West" functioned as a convenient rhetorical resource for Eastern antis. Antis could easily persuade Easterners that the suffrage states were uncivilized, because it was an image of the West that many Easterners wanted to believe. Antis positioned women's voting rights as another characteristic of an unevolved region. Rather than nostalgically yearning for the time when the West was an unsettled frontier, antis instead envisioned the West as temporally dislocated from the rest of the nation and therefore still primitive and not-yet developed. Sometimes they fashioned the West's primitivism as causing woman suffrage, suggesting that it was a practice of a barbaric and not-yet civilized region. Other times, antis featured Western women's voting rights as causing the West's barbarism, which required rhetorically constructing the West as temporally moving backward in the evolutionary process. Either way, these visions of the primitive West featured women's voting rights as a component of the entire nation's primitive past, and irrelevant to the nation's progressive future.

THE WESTERN SUFFRAGE STATES' RURALITY

Eastern antis constructed the Western suffrage states as unimportant because of their small population sizes, which they used to prove the West's insignificance to the nation at large in order to refute the suffrage maps' visual projections of the suffragists' growing power. In 1915, an antisuffragist wrote in the *Utica Observer*, "Here are some things to remember when they show you the 'suffrage map' and talk about the 'march' of the 'votes for women' movement. The 'march' of suffrage has been over the prairies and through the mountainous regions of the West, where there are few men and fewer women." The author listed the populations and densities of the suffrage states to show that even when all the suffrage states were combined, they still had fewer residents than the state of Massachusetts. The author concluded, "It is one thing for territory to adopt woman suffrage. It is quite another thing for people to adopt it. New York has people. The West has territory, with a man here and there and little more than half a woman to every man."[62] These arguments attempted to discredit the suffrage maps' exaggerated claims and feature the West as unimportant and irrelevant to the East.

Antis often published tables that compared the population sizes of Western suffrage states to Eastern towns and cities to depict the West as insignificant. In 1911, the *Anti-Suffragist* published an article titled "Facts That Speak for Themselves" that listed the populations and electorate size of the first four suffrage states and compared them to New York state. The *Anti-Suffragist* summarized the statistics to show that New York's population was "seven times as large as all the woman suffrage states combined."[63] In 1909, the *Anti-Suffragist* emphasized the disparity in population by comparing the Western states' populations to Eastern cities': "Buffalo, with a population as large as that of Idaho and Utah combined! Rochester, with a population larger than that of Wyoming or Idaho! Syracuse and Albany, each with a population larger than that of the State of Wyoming!"[64] Antis also created their own visual representations of Western women's voting rights, like the "Population Diagram" pie graph (see figure 19).[65] These graphs clarified that the proportion of

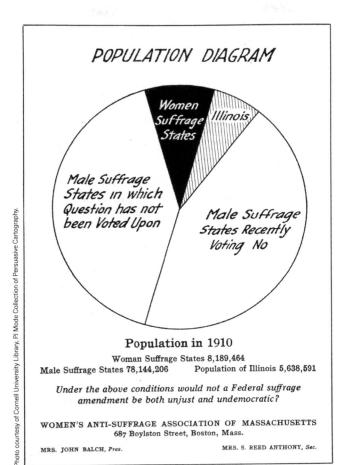

POPULATION DIAGRAM

Women Suffrage States

Illinois

Male Suffrage States in which Question has not been Voted Upon

Male Suffrage States Recently Voting No

Population in 1910
Woman Suffrage States 8,189,464
Male Suffrage States 78,144,206   Population of Illinois 5,638,591

Under the above conditions would not a Federal suffrage amendment be both unjust and undemocratic?

WOMEN'S ANTI-SUFFRAGE ASSOCIATION OF MASSACHUSETTS
687 Boylston Street, Boston, Mass.

MRS. JOHN BALCH, *Pres.*   MRS. S. REED ANTHONY, *Sec.*

Figure 19. "Population Diagram," Women's Anti-Suffrage Association of Massachusetts, 1916.

the US population with equal suffrage was much smaller than the proportion of territory with equal suffrage.

To underscore the West's unimportant and small population, antis emphasized the rural nature of Western life. The *Anti-Suffragist* argued, "Wyoming adopted woman suffrage in 1869, but as it was and is an immense grazing region with sparse population, only one person to the square mile, it received little consideration from the country." This discussion included densities of New York and the first four suffrage states:

- New York, 1 square mile to 150 persons
- Colorado, 1 square mile to 5 persons
- Wyoming, 1½ square miles to 2 persons
- Idaho, 1 square mile to 2 persons
- Utah, 1 square mile to 3 persons

Emphasizing the West's rurality in comparison to New York was meant to undermine suffragists' claims to power, triumph, and success. Yet Americans largely valued rurality and country life at the time. Disparaging rural areas countered popular ideals articulated by Roosevelt's Country Life commission (1908) and the millions of American farmers and upper-class urban residents who sought out country life as an escape from cities.[66] Americans often idealized country life and viewed farmers and those in rural areas as more moral, natural, and in touch with the land than city residents. Likewise, many Americans viewed dense and urban areas as corrupt, immoral, and artificial. Many cities had reputations as places of vice, danger, and moral depravity.[67] Thus, dismissing woman suffrage according to the West's rurality only got antis so far.

Beyond disputing the suffrage maps' claims to power and influence, antis also positioned the West's rurality as uncivilized, less cultivated and advanced than the older, urban societies in the East. In 1915, Mrs. Simon Baruch noted in the *General Federation Bulletin*, "Suffrage . . . spr[a]ng up in the virgin soil of the wild and woolly west, [but] was defeated in eight of the more cultivated States."[68] Rather than depicting the West's space and country life as idyllic, wholesome, or mythically American, antis imagined the West's rurality as unsophisticated and separate from the East. The *Atlantic Monthly* argued that "the experiment of the four crude and sparsely settled states in which there is full suffrage affords no adequate tests for full suffrage in the great centers of civilization, and in vast and crowded communities, with immense and diversified interests."[69] The *Atlantic* specified that the first suffrage state of "Wyoming is a state of cowboys and cattle-ranges," and therefore inconsequential to the urban and industrialized states in the East.

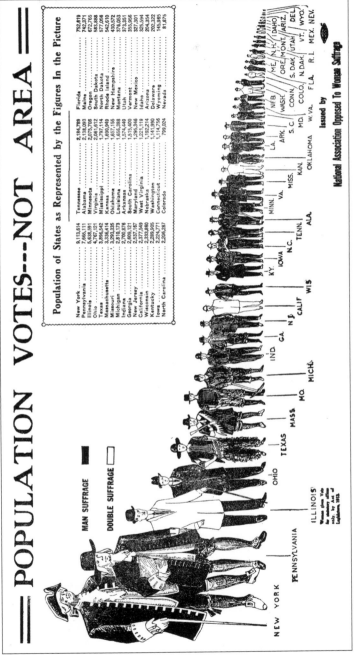

Figure 20. "Population Votes—Not Area," National Association Opposed to Woman Suffrage, 1915.

Antis imagined the Western suffrage states' rurality as an element of the West's primitivism. Out of the four states that had adopted woman suffrage, some Easterners considered Colorado the only "fair test" of woman suffrage, because it was the most populated and therefore most "nearly resembl[ed] the order of civilizations," according to the *Atlantic Monthly*.[70] But the *Anti-Suffragist* even disregarded the "most important State of the four, Colorado," for its rurality because it has "an average of about five persons to the square mile!"[71] When Nevada and Montana adopted woman suffrage in 1915, antisuffragist Mrs. Baruch assessed the new policies in the *General Federation Bulletin* as insignificant because the two states' "population equals that of two of our mediocre cities."[72] For Mrs. Baruch, a state needed urban life to demonstrate social progress and advancement. Antis also dismissed Idaho's two "cities" Boise and Pocatello, as not large enough to be considered cultivated or metropolitan, refusing to accept that Idaho was civilized. In the antis' imagination, the West had not yet developed enough to have large cities and populations.

In 1915, antis visualized their assertion that dense and populated states were more mature than rural states with an image that proclaimed, "Population Votes—Not Area. Area Does Not Vote" (see figure 20).[73] The image featured drawings of men to represent each state, scaled to reflect the population size of the state. New York and Pennsylvania were the largest men, representing states where only men could vote. On the other end of the line, the men representing suffrage states were so tiny they were barely visible. By visualizing and comparing state populations in this manner, the antis depicted the suffrage states as insignificant, as well as immature and childlike, while depicting the non-suffrage Eastern states as the adults with authority and importance.

THE WESTERN SUFFRAGE STATES
AS TEMPORALLY BEHIND THE EAST

Although Americans viewed the United States as civilized and continuing to progress forward in the evolutionary process, the antis' vision of the West positioned the region as temporally stuck, slow, or behind the

East by comparing the regions in terms of age, wealth, and politics.[74] The *Anti-Suffragist* compared the four suffrage states admitted into the Union between 1876 and 1898 with "the State of New York. . . . A portion of the country that may soon celebrate its three hundredth anniversary!"[75] Their 1911 article asserted that "the Old State of New York" had been evolving longer than the "new" suffrage states, and was therefore ahead of the Western states in the process of enlightenment and cultivation.[76] The antis contrasted the wealth of the East's economies as clear evidence of their cultivation compared to the Western suffrage states. In 1909, the *Anti-Suffragist* listed the debt of each suffrage state, all of which were well below seven million, and then compared them to New York, "a state so wealthy that it can afford to have an indebtedness of over $430,000,000." Antis suggested that refined and enlightened places like the East had larger debts and budgets. To further illustrate the West's undeveloped economies, the *Anti-Suffragist* listed states' interest rates, showing that New York's "legal rate of interest—so important to the poor man—of 6 per cent," was superior to interest rates in the West. They even took a swipe at the salary of the West's government officials when they ridiculed Utah's governor for "receiv[ing] a salary of $2000." According to the *Anti-Suffragist*, the Western states' youth and still-budding economies were signs that the West had not yet advanced into a civilization worth considering or following.

The antis also described Westerners as politically inexperienced and ignorant. The *Woman's Protest* characterized Westerners as an "uninformed electorate" that did not know any better than to enact equal suffrage. It claimed, "The new [Western] voters were all wholly inexperienced and, in a very great measure, unqualified in political activity." According to the antis, Westerners did not yet have the political experience or expertise to enact smart public policy. They were such political neophytes that "even the mechanical process of casting a ballot is still an unsolved mystery to most of them." Only the older states, with their "wise and enlightened statecraft" who were farther advanced on the evolutionary spectrum understood "the underlying principles of government" necessary to make decisions about the electorate.[77] In contrast to Duniway's vision of a democratic West, antis envisioned the West as not evolved enough for democracy, the region's primitivism preventing advanced political processes.

Some antis cast the adoption of woman suffrage as a result of the West's susceptibility to political chicanery and trickery. The *Woman's Protest* reasoned that the West's citizens were so uninformed that they were fooled and manipulated by the politicians and propagandists that hailed their states.[78] The *National League for the Civic Education of Women* insisted that "Woman Suffrage was secured in Wyoming . . . through the political trickery of an illiterate and discredited man, who was in the chair."[79] The *Woman Patriot* agreed that the only reason Wyoming enacted woman suffrage was because "one woman . . . was able to influence a weak kneed governor into passing a woman suffrage bill."[80] The *Woman Patriot* claimed that "suffragists won the state of Washington, by using a proposed amendment which did not refer in words to woman suffrage at all," which caused "yet some doubt expressed by lawyers as to whether the adoption of the amendment was legal."[81] By calling into doubt the legality and transparency of the political processes that enacted suffrage in the West, they constructed these Western states as politically inept and easily misled. Since the West was temporally stalled behind the East along the evolutionary trajectory, antis implied that Westerners were so primitive they could be duped into enfranchising women.

With the imagined lack of political maturity and advancement in the West, antis argued that Westerners were predisposed to the influence of other uncivilized movements, like populism and Mormonism. Many Easterners viewed populism as a radical movement of the rural working class even though populism shared some of the same reform goals as progressives organizing in industrialized parts of the East.[82] Populism, however, focused on affronts to farmers, whereas progressives tended to prioritize urban problems.[83] So progressivism was, as Kansas editor William White claimed, "populism with the whiskers shaved off," which was another way of saying that progressivism was viewed as an upper-class cause and populism as working class.[84] Although some progressives were also populists, Eastern progressives and Western populists had reason to be skeptical of each other because many Eastern corporations made money by exploiting Western labor and resources, which Western populists had resisted. Antis drew on Eastern skepticism and perceptions of populism as a rural, lower-class, unsophisticated cause in order to construct Western woman suffrage states as radical, easily influenced, and uncultivated. Mrs. Guide's column of the *Anti-Suffragist* reported, "Colorado adopted [woman suffrage] in 1893 at a time of intense depression, when the Populist Party was in full control of the state."[85] A statement in the same publication, written by Miss Phoebe W. Couzins, held Colorado's "Populist legislature" responsible for Colorado's 1893 enfranchisement of women.[86] Similarly, the *National League* attributed Idaho's adoption of woman suffrage to the 1894 decision of "the Populist party of Idaho [to] put a plank in its platform, favoring the submission of a Woman-Suffrage amendment to the people." Then, when the "Free Silver Populist Movement swept the state" in 1896, Idaho also enfranchised women.[87] Antis discredited Western woman suffrage as a phenomenon of the West that they had imagined—young, inexperienced, and undeveloped enough that they were easily swayed by the radical and primitive populists.

Similarly, antis envisioned the Western suffrage states' immaturity allowing them to become controlled by the Mormon Church. The *National League* argued in 1910 that "The Mormon church is the greatest political power in any of the four Suffrage states."[88] Likewise, the *Reply* claimed that "all the Western States that have Woman Suffrage are . . . entirely or partially under the political control of the Mormons."[89] The *Anti-Suffragist* characterized the Mormon Church as Utah's supreme power that "no political organization has been able to make any headway against."[90] Antis were able to use the prevalent anti-Mormon sentiment to discredit woman suffrage as yet another institution unique to the West. The *Woman's Protest* called woman suffrage a "Mormon institution," and the *Anti-Suffragist* charged, "In Utah the granting of the ballot to women was brought about in 1896, chiefly by the Mormon Church, which thereby greatly strengthened its power. In Idaho it was granted the same year through the same influence."[91] Antis represented the Mormon Church's influence as radical, un-American, and threatening to "a Constitutional or Republican form of government."[92] Because of Mormonism's influence in Utah, "the introduction of Woman Suffrage within its borders was not only undemocratic, it was anti-democratic."[93] The antis' vision of the West as a theocracy depicted woman suffrage as an outcome of undemocratic life.

In another attempt to persuade America of the West's barbarism, antis envisioned it as a polygamous region. As the *National League* argued, "The only form of the Turkish harem found in this country is in this Suffrage state" of Utah.[94] An anti living in Idaho testified in the *Woman's Protest*, "Our becoming pro-suffrage was not so accidental as it seemed. There were plenty of plural wives in South Idaho at that time."[95] Antis highlighted the ways that woman suffrage "was a great advantage to the Mormon who had several wives while the gentile neighbor had one" and therefore linked the practice of polygamy with the passing of woman suffrage.[96] The antis' associations of Western woman suffrage with polygamy largely portrayed both as results of the West's barbarism and lack of social evolution. Yet other times, they also suggested that woman suffrage perpetuated the practice of polygamy. The *Atlantic Monthly* reminded its readers that "in Utah, the women-voters, under the lead of Mormonism, have voted steadily in favor of polygamists and law-breakers, who have been sent to Congress, in defiance of the law, by the votes of women."[97] They argued that woman suffrage promoted and protected polygamy, implying that polygamy could only be eradicated by ending women's voting rights in the West. Therefore, antis constructed the West's temporality and movement toward civilization in multiple ways. Sometimes they depicted the West as progressing behind the East in their social advancement, and at other times, the antis featured the West as moving backward because of women's voting rights.

THE UNGENDERED WESTERN SUFFRAGE STATES
MOVING TEMPORALLY BACKWARD

When antis featured the West's primitivism as the result of Western women's voting rights, they suggested that woman suffrage had caused the stages of social evolution to move in reverse. Instead of evolving toward the human ideal like the rest of the United States, the antis' West was spatiotemporally dislocated, moving backward in time and in an entirely different direction. As evidence of the West's devolvement toward wooliness, antis envisioned the West as distinct from the East according to Western women's masculinity. In the *Woman's Protest*, Verna Witherall wrote, "'Votes for women' in Colorado has . . . brought into the foreground numbers of masculine women, in whom all gentleness and womanliness is dead or submerged."[98] In *Outlook*, Elizabeth Mc-Cracken was convinced that the voting women in Denver had become "less womanly" since their enfranchisement.[99] Americans in the early twentieth century believed that societies with blurred gender roles were uncivilized and therefore less advanced than societies with feminine women and masculine men.[100] Antis reported on the West's crude, and therefore ungendered, women by emphasizing their differences from Eastern women. McCracken explained that although Eastern women may not have had as much political power as women in Colorado, Eastern women were "perhaps also a little less crude, and more than a little less rasping" than Western women.[101] Antis fashioned an image of rough and uncivilized Western women. In the 1909 suffrage hearing before the Joint Judiciary Committee, an anti testified, "I've been [to the West] and seen the women drinking in the saloons with the men."[102] By emphasizing Western women's crudeness and lack of morality, here demonstrated by their alcohol consumption, antis imagined the West as distinctly less civilized than the East. Women's voting rights had so severely harmed the West's progress that it was now backsliding toward barbarism, marked by a gendered and racialized vision of the West.

The antis' mobility rhetoric described the Western suffrage states as moving down the evolutionary scale toward primitivism, as demonstrated by the un-gendering of enfranchised women.[103] Anna Richardson described in the *New York Times* the West's "unsexing of woman through the coarsening of the voting booth."[104] The *Anti-Suffragist* published commentary that Western woman suffrage had instigated "men and women becoming more alike," which they saw as "*sink*[*ing* the population] to a lower common level" rather "than *ris*[*ing*] to a higher" level.[105] Antis charged that over time, Western women were changed by the franchise into worse mothers and poorer housekeepers. McCracken argued that Colorado women "have become less fitted to guide the children growing to manhood and womanhood in their State," too "marked by self-interest," and "her ideals have been lowered; the delicacy of her perception of right and wrong has been dulled."[106] Some antis, like Mrs. Anna Kelley in the *Reply*, were concerned about "whether a woman can repeatedly soil her skirts figuratively speaking at the polls and remain as delightfully feminine as before." Kelley testified, "I have seen timid women shrinking at the first visit to the polls grow as brazen as the very young women of the street after a few years of voting." Antis envisioned the West as a place where women's femininity had been diminished by the vote, leaving only envious, brazen, and masculine Western women. Kelley claimed that since woman suffrage was adopted in Colorado, "the sweet faced old lady is gone. I have seen the good housekeeper and contented wife neglect her home and grow envious of her husband's political job."[107] Rather than nostalgically longing for the passing woolly West, these antis were mourning the loss of feminine and civilized women, because women's voting rights had brought about the deterioration of civilization in the West.

Although the rhetoric of the woolly West was common, the antis' use differed from most as it did not associate women's crudeness with the temporary phase of Western life that most Americans assumed would be inevitably civilized. Rather, in the antis' primitive West, masculine women were being coarsened by voting and were reversing the West's civilizing progress, causing its civilization to devolve rather than evolve. Imagining the Western suffrage states as "woolly" invoked racialized meanings of the West, which would have threatened the femininity and civilization of the white women who lived there. Historically, white women's femininity and markers of civilization were jeopardized by associations with African Americans. For example, in 1850, when white abolitionist Ernestine L. Rose attempted to speak at an American Anti-Slavery Society meeting, hecklers booed her off the stage for cohabiting with African Americans. One man shouted, "I have always respected the presence of ladies, but I doubt very much whether white women who cohabit and mix with the woolly-headed Negro are entitled to any respect from a white man."[108] As Palczewski has argued, white members of the National Woman's Party who were imprisoned for their suffrage advocacy were read as defeminized merely through their proximity to black women's bodies.[109] If being in the vicinity of non-white bodies detracted from white women's femininity, then the antis' racialized vision of the West as woolly would have further contested the femininity and sophistication of the white women who lived in these states and delegitimized the political goals they supported.

Antis also viewed equal suffrage as harming the West in gendered terms—making it a feminized West that had been weakened by women's voting rights. The *Anti-Suffragist* offered their condolences to the men of Western suffrage states: "Our sympathy goes out to those women, and men too, of the state of Washington, who for lack of active and organized resistance allowed their state to become 'feminized.'"[110] The *Anti-Suffragist* pointed to "the bad effects of overfeminization on the schools of Colorado" as evidence that woman suffrage was feminizing the West's public services.[111] As Palczewski has illuminated, antis in the East commonly depicted women's voting rights as the "emasculation of manhood" that would feminize men and require them to care for their home and children while their wives left the home to vote.[112] But antis went further to apply the emasculation argument to the region, depicting it as dependent on the federal government. Antis recalled the times that labor strikes in the West became so disruptive that Western state governments called in federal troops for support. When Western mine worker strikes became violent, federal troops got involved in Idaho in 1907, and they supported Colorado in 1904 and 1914. In 1914, the *Reply* asked, "might it be just possible that in a state not weakened by woman suffrage, a mass meeting of men would not have cried for outside help? Men would have fought for their state, and men would have upheld 'states' rights' and 'Colorado's dignity' in the eyes of the nation."[113] This charge challenged the masculinity and physical strength of Western men, suggesting that the reliance on federal troops indicated the Western states' fragility, which the antis blamed on the West's suffrage policies. The National Anti-Suffrage Association blamed the disorder and unrest in Colorado on "the impotency and indifference of a feminized electorate."[114] The antis' gendered language depicted the West's government as feminized by women's voting rights and appealed to the fear that the United States as a whole would be endangered and unable to protect itself if women's voting rights were to expand beyond the West.

Conclusion

The antis' woolly West arguments may have shaped some Easterners' impressions of the West. When the Biennial of the General Federation of Women's Clubs held their 1898 meeting in Denver, "Some of the delegates who had never been here [to Denver] before cherished a lingering impression that the West was 'wild and woolly,' and were surprised to find a city so full of all the modern improvements." The *Woman's Journal* reported that delegates "had an idea that they might do missionary work" in Colorado. But in contrast to their expectations, the women found that in many ways:

> Denver was ahead of the East. Above all, they found an intelligent, orderly, cheerful community, none the less civilized for being wide-awake and progressive. They saw happy homes, healthy children, well-fed and contented-looking husbands, and women who showed no signs of being unsexed; they found the wheels of the social order revolving as smoothly as elsewhere; above all, they found the courtesy of men towards women in no wise diminished. Many of the delegates had honestly believed that equal suffrage would bring about a sort of inferno. It can never again be to them that vague and unknown horror.[115]

Eastern women visiting the West had expected to find that woman suffrage had made Colorado less civilized, ungendered, and lacking social order to the point of becoming an inferno. Similarly, when Harriot Stanton Blatch arrived in Chicago in 1916, she said, "You women of Illinois do not look one bit more masculine than you did before you got the vote. How dare you upset that old argument of the anti-suffragist so brazenly?"[116] In 1916, Carrie Chapman Catt recalled that "when California obtained woman suffrage, in 1911, . . . people began to sit up and take note. . . . Before that, they regarded the suffrage States as only the wild and woolly West."[117] These accounts are not evidence that the antis' arguments caused these Eastern women to expect the West to be "wild and woolly," but they demonstrate that these depictions were circulating in public discourse. Some Western suffragists found the woolly depictions of the West so upsetting that they traveled East to refute them.

To dismiss Western women's voting rights as insignificant and uncivilized, antis leveraged the regional rhetoric of the woolly West and positioned the West as distinct from the rest of the nation in their spatiotemporal progress toward civilization. They featured woman suffrage as another characteristic of a barbarous region—like populism, Mormonism, and polygamy—that flourished in undeveloped societies. They emphasized the West's rurality as evidence of the West's lack of advancement. And at times, antis also portrayed the West as moving backward in their social progress, being dragged toward barbarism by the existence of woman suffrage. In the end, they imagined a racialized, gendered, and classed image of the West.

The antis' marshalling of the regional rhetoric of the woolly West drew on Easterners' idealized image of a wild West and their desire for a frontier to exist distinct from Eastern civilization. But different imaginations and constructions of the West served some groups better than others. Imagining the West as woolly and uncivilized served the interests of Easterners from an economic and cultural viewpoint, and also served antis' claims about the effect of woman suffrage on civilization. Not only did the woolly image of the West counter suffragists claims, it also maintained differences between the regions that positioned them hierarchically—with the East depicted as more culturally, politically, and economically advanced and powerful than the West.

Amidst the national scrutiny of the Western suffrage states, both suffragists and antis marshalled their preferred meanings of the West for
their own purposes. But in addition to disagreeing about women's voting rights, Western suffragists and Eastern antis also disagreed about the
meanings of the West, and the antis' imagination of the region differed
markedly from those of Duniway and the suffrage maps. Both Duniway
and the antis featured the West as unsettled and uncivilized, an image
of the West that many Americans romanticized and wanted to maintain.
Yet Duniway's unsettled West was the United States' mythic frontier, the
creator of American exceptionalism, the proving ground for exceptionally heroic men and women, and a land of equality and freedom. The
antis' uncivilized West was barbaric, primitive, and socially unevolved.
Instead of growing increasingly more civilized, the anti's West was de-
layed, behind, and backsliding through the stages of social evolution.
Both portrayals likely appealed to Easterners' preferred vision of the
West as unsettled and uncivilized, but the antis included no ideals of
exceptionalism, heroism, or freedom in their images of the West.

The antis' woolly rhetoric especially countered the suffrage maps'
vision of the West as more moral and civilized than the East. In many
ways, the woolly West rhetoric responded to the suffrage maps by employing the rurality and unimportance of the Western suffrage states.
Yet beyond refuting the suffrage map's assertions of the suffrage states'
importance, power, and influence, the antis also attempted to refute the
map's portrayals of the West as more civilized than the East. As the maps
offered a vision of the East as the new frontier, the antis provided piles of
evidence that the West had not yet been settled and was still in need of
civilization. Still, suffragists did not let these woolly charges stick. The
accusations antis made about the West eventually motivated Western
women to go east to disprove the antis' charges about woman suffrage
and the West. To prove that the suffrage maps were true and the antis
were wrong, Western women went east to defend and boost the West's
civilization and progress.

CHAPTER 4

Defending the West

HELEN RING ROBINSON'S AND JEANNETTE RANKIN'S
WESTERN DOMESTICATION AND BOOSTERISM, 1913–1918

———— · ◆ · ————

On January 19, 1914, 1100 members of New York City's Economic Club gathered in the grand ballroom of Manhattan's Hotel Astor to see Colorado state senator Helen Ring Robinson (1860–1923) debate equal suffrage. Robinson was introduced as the "first woman state senator in the United States," hailing from one of the eleven suffrage states at the time. Attendees of the debate included cheering suffrage leaders, "a sprinkling of women who were positive antisuffragists," and many men who loudly supported her opponent, Mrs. A. J. George, field secretary of the Massachusetts Association Opposed to Woman Suffrage. As Robinson "ridiculed some of the anti-suffrage arguments," she "frequently had to ask for silence when the points she scored on the anti-suffragists were applauded."[1] Four years later, further uptown, US Representative Jeannette Rankin (1880–1973) of Montana "stepped out before the applauding crowds at Carnegie Hall" and spoke about woman suffrage. More than three thousand New York City

95

residents attended her address to see "the first woman ever elected to the legislative halls of the United States" and hear her sing her "Praises for 'Her West.'"[2] Both Robinson and Rankin held positions of political leadership in Western suffrage states, championed progressive causes, and delivered remarkably similar messages to their New York audiences. As they championed women's participation in politics, they surprised their audiences with their femininity, boasted of the exceptionalism of their home states, and depicted the West as a model for the rest of the nation to follow.

Robinson and Rankin were just two of the women elected to political office in the Western suffrage states during the last decades of the US suffrage movement. While women in Eastern states were still campaigning for the right to vote in general elections, Utah chose Martha Maria Hughes Cannon as their state senator in 1896, Colorado elected three women to their House of Representatives in 1894, and Arizona voted Frances Willard Munds into their state senate in 1914.[3] Because women in positions of political power were such a novelty at the time, many of these politicians were scrutinized and featured in the national press. But state Senator Robinson and US Representative Rankin received an exceptional amount of national and international attention. Both of these political leaders of Rocky Mountain states were eloquent and popular orators who accepted invitations to speak on women in politics around the country and made many public appearances in the East.

Robinson was frequently celebrated on the East Coast as the first woman to become a state senator, even though she was second to hold the position, following Cannon of Utah.[4] She grew up in Providence, Rhode Island, before living and working in Colorado for more than thirty years before she was elected to one of Denver's three at-large seats for state senate in 1912.[5] National newspapers heralded her election as a sign of US women's political progress and reported on her performance to their Eastern audiences. On Robinson's first day in the Colorado Senate, the *Washington Post* reported that she "caused excitement and curiosity, even among the senators themselves . . . When the body assembled the solons turned toward the desk where sat Mrs. Helen Ring

Robinson, making her debut as a lawmaker" and "bowed profoundly."[6] When she visited New York that spring, the *Daily News* announced her presence and noted that senators were not "rare birds in New York. But Senator Robinson is different. She has the distinction of being the only woman state senator in the United States or that ever has been."[7] Given her unique status, she was "wined and dined and lionized as the first woman senator in the land by suffrage leaders and followers in the East."[8] Suffrage organizations invited her to the East to speak about her experiences in political office.[9] In the summer of 1913, Eastern suffragists organized a "strenuous two months 'on the stump' tour" for Robinson through Maryland, Pennsylvania, New York, New Jersey, and Rhode Island. She "made upwards of sixty suffrage speeches" on this tour and spoke "before audiences of men and women once and sometimes twice a day."[10] She returned to the East for additional lecture tours later in 1913, 1914, 1915, and 1916, and spoke before large audiences in Baltimore's Lyris Theater, Philadelphia's Lyceum Theatre, Boston's Symphony Hall, and New York City's Hotel Astor.[11]

Just a few years later in 1916, when Montana elected Rankin to the office of US Representative, her status as the first woman in Congress won even more media attention than Robinson. Rankin got her start in politics in the suffrage movement and led Montana's successful 1914 suffrage campaign. Born and raised in Montana but educated in the East, she came from a wealthy family and had a politically powerful brother, Wellington Rankin. She won her unlikely campaign for one of Montana's two at-large congressional seats through her talented and relentless campaigning, the support of women voters and prohibitionists, and her brother's money, power, and political maneuvering.[12] Following her historic election, she was featured in national newspapers and sought after for interviews, photographs, advertising endorsements, lecture tours, and movie deals.[13] Rankin's attention was so extraordinary that she went into hiding for several months following her election to avoid reporters and photographers.[14] Eventually Lee Keedick, a tour manager from New York, negotiated a speaking contract for her to perform in twenty cities in the Northeast prior to the beginning of her term in Washington.

Keedick explained that Rankin had "received so many requests from women in the eastern states asking that he use his good offices to iduce [*sic*] Miss Rankin to lecture in Carnegie hall that he made a special trip to Montana to deliver in person the invitation."[15]

National suffrage leaders championed Robinson's and Rankin's political achievements as proof of women's political capabilities and recruited them for national suffrage advocacy in the East. In addition to her Eastern lecture tours, Robinson played a prominent role at the 1913 annual convention of the National American Woman Suffrage Association in Washington, DC. She gave the principal address of the day on "Women as Legislators" and introduced the resolutions that called upon President Woodrow Wilson to adopt the woman suffrage amendment to the Constitution.[16] Likewise, suffragists claimed that Rankin's election to US Congress was a significant "victory for the women of the country" and looked to her to advance their cause and represent them well during a critical point in the campaign for the federal amendment.[17] Anna Howard Shaw and Carrie Chapman Catt "saw her as the savior of suffrage" and depicted Rankin's election as a sign of the suffrage movement's nearing success.[18] Soon after her election, Rankin announced, "I am deeply conscious of my responsibility as the first woman to sit in Congress. I will represent not only the women of Montana but also the women of the country."[19] Keedick told the press, "The women of America consider Miss Rankin as their national representative in congress . . . They are anxious to see and hear this woman who has reflected so much honor on their sex and whose opportunities for the promotion of the cause of woman's suffrage and the advancement of legislation relating to the problems that vitally concern women are unsurpassed."[20] As Eleanor Flexner and Ellen Fitzpatrick argue, Rankin was "a visible embodiment on the House floor of the growing pressure on that body for political legitimacy for her sex."[21] Both Rankin's and Robinson's performances in political office and on their Eastern lecture tours would positively and negatively shape the nation's perception of women's political capabilities and affect the likelihood of the suffrage movement's success nationally.

Robinson's and Rankin's unique statuses and national notoriety gave them a platform to champion woman suffrage. However, once they were on stage, they used the opportunity to shape the reputations and meanings of their home states of Colorado and Montana. They countered Eastern antis' imaginings of the West as unevolved with their own visions of it as a model of progress, democracy, and civilization for the rest of the nation to follow. Their audiences expected them to account for their historic elections and explain the regional pattern of Western woman suffrage. In contrast to the antis' woolly West rhetoric, Robinson and Rankin used woman suffrage to connect the West to ideologies of progressivism, modernity, and civilization. Both politicians used their elections and voting rights as vehicles for redefining the West, domesticating its image, and presenting the region as temporally ahead of the East in its advancement toward civilization, and thus, a model for the nation to follow. Robinson defended the region against the slurs from Eastern antis by depicting her home state as "civilized," free from corruption, and marked by progressive legislation and traditional gender roles. Rankin used a rhetoric of Western boosterism to imagine Montana as a promised land for future settlers, complete with the most modern technologies, plentiful natural resources, and progressive politics. Both women domesticated the West by performing traditional white femininity and constructing women's political participation as a fulfillment of their uniquely feminine roles.

Domesticating and Boosting the West

Countering the Eastern antis who depicted the West as wild and woolly, Robinson and Rankin domesticated the meaning of the West and redefined it as settled, civilized, and modern. Domesticating is "a rhetoric of control that tames and softens," or conquers and disciplines what is seen as unfamiliar, unknown, natural, or wild.[22] In the nineteenth century, domesticating discourse was prevalent among white settlers because they viewed the West as "an untamed space that threatened civilization and needed to be domesticated."[23] Domesticating rhetoric assisted them in taking and inhabiting land that was not theirs, as it helped them make it more homelike and familiar. Amy Kaplan calls the domesticating discourse of the nineteenth century "manifest domesticity," because it helped white settlers in the project of Manifest Destiny. The rhetoric of manifest domesticity motivated and justified their presence in the West by "rendering prior inhabitants alien and undomesticated and by implicitly nativizing newcomers."[24] White women writers in the nineteenth century often used domestic terms to imagine the Western land as a setting for a glorified domesticity in their public fiction and nonfiction writing as well as their private letters, diaries, and travel accounts.[25] Therefore, domestic discourse of settlers in the nineteenth century was at the heart of the imperial project of civilizing the West as it positioned American Indian residents as subjects to be dominated.[26]

In the early twentieth century, many US settlers sought to domesticate the image of the West further to encourage more people to move there and to prove its significance to the nation.[27] Most Western states struggled with their disadvantaged economic, social, and political status relative to the East. The East's powerful corporations, railroads, and banks had dominated the West's economy and left these states with little economic or political leverage.[28] To grow their economic and civic structures, Western states needed a larger population and greater national representation. Greater populations guaranteed an expansion of trade, industry, transportation, and culture, which would raise the values of the property and maintain the growth of their communities, businesses, and governments.[29] So, they worked to depict the West positively to other potential settlers in the East. To ensure that farming communities would continue to grow, Westerners like George H. Beasley worked to discard the "mistaken image of the West . . . of brigandage, horse thievery, wild and wooly west rot" and create a new meaning of the West.[30] As Marguerite S. Shaffer argues, "Just as Southerners and Midwesterners were engaged in inventing a shared public history in the aftermath of the Civil War . . . so Westerners sought to fuse their history and identity with that of the modern nation-state."[31] To prove their importance to the nation, Westerners often strove to present themselves and their states as similar, if not superior, to the East in terms of progress and civilization. Their civilizing discourse often represented Western residents as white, Protestant, traditionally gendered, and middle class in order to draw more white, Protestant settlers.[32]

Domesticating the West played an essential role in boosting the region to potential white settlers. As Westerners worked to attract more white people to the West, their boosterism proliferated so much between the 1870s and 1930s that most Americans and Europeans at the turn of the century had some familiarity with them.[33] Through their "embellished and effusive" accounts of life in the West, as David Wrobel describes them, boosters imagined the West into being, and shaped Eastern Americans' perceptions of the West. To appeal to Eastern and Midwestern residents, they portrayed uninhabited Western land as possessing economic and agricultural opportunities, substantial infrastructure, and numerous commercial advantages. The boosters' West was composed of settled, white communities that were safe and abundantly cultured. While small and agrarian towns were still evolving into industrial cities, Western promoters often publicized a new and modern West before it arrived.[34] Both Robinson and Rankin were elected in the midst of a homesteading boom, and they joined the effort to resist the "cowboy country" image of the West and attract more settlers by depicting their region as a civilized, modern, and desirable place to live.[35] As they were invited to speak to large audiences around the East, they used their platform to redefine and domesticate the meaning of the West.

ROBINSON'S DEFENSE OF COLORADO

When Robinson was invited East in 1913 to champion woman suffrage and recount her experiences in public office, she spent much of her time on stage defending the reputation of Colorado. Her performances were usually advertised in advance as informational lectures on women in politics. Before she spoke in New York, the *Daily News* announced that Robinson "has come to New York to tell skeptical seekers after the ballot just how it feels to sit with an upper circle of lawmakers."[36] Following her performances, however, the newspapers reported that she used her platform to "defend" Western women's voting rights and "Ridicule Anti-Suffrage Arguments."[37] In New York City, she heard that antis were claiming that Colorado was preparing to eliminate woman suffrage because Western women did not want the vote. She refuted this claim and assured New York's Equal Suffrage League that "there is nothing in the talk of dissatisfaction with Women Suffrage in the West and a desire to take away the franchise from the women. There is just as much truth in their trying to take the franchise from the women as that they are trying to take it from men because they are bald-headed or because they wear side whiskers."[38] After her 1913 Eastern speaking tour was over, she told the *Rocky Mountain News*, "Everywhere I am sorry to say, I found many wrong ideas prevalent about Colorado. Much of my time was devoted to nailing lies concerning our state. Strange and weird things are told and believed about the political corruption in Denver, and the things that the women have not accomplished through having the ballot."[39] When Robinson returned to the East for another lecture tour in 1915, she was explicit about her purpose of defending Colorado. The *Weekly Ignacio Chieftain* announced that "Senator Helen R. Robinson Goes East . . . to refute the charges made against women legislators and voters of the state."[40] While on her 1915 tour, she told her New York City audience, "I am tired of these constant slurs . . . I am tired of being used as an anti-suffrage argument." The *New York Times* reported that "while she is helping the women here [in New Jersey and New York] she is also trying to put down the incessant criticisms of the suffrage States by Eastern people."[41] When the *Summit New Jersey Herald* published false claims from antis that Senator Robinson had "introduced in the Colorado senate a bill to reestablish race track gambling in the state," she traveled to New Jersey to "brave the lion in his den."[42] She went on a lecture tour through New Jersey "in favor of votes for women," and filed a lawsuit for $5,000 against the New Jersey paper. Robinson's defense of women legislators and women voters involved defending her own reputation, as well as the West's.

Robinson discredited the slander against Colorado by revealing the sources of the slurs. Some of the claims about Western suffrage, she maintained, were made by people who had been paid to make them. As she told the *New York Times*, "It is very easy for someone to come from the East and to get a one-sided story, especially if he comes by contract."[43] Other lies, she insisted, were made by people who had never been west. When Robinson spoke to Pennsylvania councilmen in Pittsburgh, she "declared that Eastern antisuffragists who are basing many of their 'alleged arguments' on the failure of women's suffrage in Colorado are obliged to confess when confronted with the fact, that they have never visited Colorado."[44] Robinson also named men who had tried and failed to succeed in the state's politics—and then blamed their losses on women's votes—as the source of some of the lies: "You will find plenty of defeated candidates after an election who will say that Woman Suffrage is not a success and they will gladly say so in an interview. We court investigation and criticism; we only object to plain in fantasy lies."[45]

Repeatedly, Robinson countered and undermined the numerous claims about Western woman suffrage promulgated by Eastern antis by insisting on their physical attractiveness, as well as their mothering and housekeeping abilities and morality at the polls and in the bars. The most common antisuffrage claim she addressed was the argument that suffrage had masculinized Western women. She told an audience in New York, "Those stories of the women voters making themselves up in the image of men are not true. Neither do the women who vote or the office holders have faces like vinegar jugs. And we do not spend our time drinking cocktails and highballs or stuffing ballot boxes." She insisted that woman suffragists could also be attractive: "I wish you could see my daughter. She's a good looker. She is intelligent and very much interested in suffrage, only she says that she is going to Washington."[46] After Eastern newspapers published a statement made by Colorado senator John Hecker claiming that "the women of Denver drank twenty times more highballs than men," Robinson "denounced the quoted statement as an insult to the women of Colorado, and threatened to move the expulsion of Hecker from the Senate if it should be repeated."[47] The *Denver Express* reported that "Mrs. Robinson rose to a question of personal privilege this morning and leveled her oratorical guns against Senator Hecker."[48] Before the Colorado senate, Robinson protested, "If the senator from the First garners his information from the murk and slime of such places he has no right to spread such information over the records of his honorable body. He has no right to use it as a means of libeling my sisters and your wives and daughters. He has no right thus to spread broadcast such a wanton upon the womanhood of Colorado."[49]

Robinson also countered claims about the West's primitive legislation and political ignorance by imagining Colorado's legislation as more advanced than the East's and constructing the West as temporally ahead of the East in their movement toward civilization. In 1915, she told a New York audience, "We have a more human Legislature in Colorado than in the non-suffrage States . . . In New Jersey's canning factories the workers may keep at their work as long as flesh and blood will stand it. In Colorado we have an eight-hour day for the workers in the canneries. Colorado women stand as a unit for humane laws." Robinson's publicizing of Colorado's "humane" legislation addressed Eastern antis' claims about the Western states, advertised Colorado's progressive politics, and affirmed Colorado women's feminine and positive influence on public policy. Her promotion of their legislation positioned Colorado and the state's progressive legislation as the model of reform for Eastern states to model, flipping the perception that the East was more advanced than the West. "The last Colorado General Assembly passed an Industrial Disputes act which has already prevented one strike that threatened Denver . . . This is the most *advanced* industrial legislation commission. This is the most *advanced* industrial legislation now in force in any State in the Union. It is time other States stopped pointing their fingers at Colorado and began to think of *following* her example."[50] Her portrayal of the legislation envisioned their progressive politics, emphasizing the West's industrial and political reform, as evidence that the region moved toward civilization at the same pace and time as the East, if not ahead of the East. Instead of constructing the West as temporally behind the

East like the antis did, Robinson used rhetorical mobility to construct Colorado's movement toward modernity as ahead of the East.

Like Robinson, Rankin used the public's preoccupation with her status as the first woman in Congress to focus on the state that elected her. Rankin's Eastern lecture tour began with a speech at Carnegie Hall in New York City where she addressed a crowd of more than three thousand on the topic of "Democracy and Government."[51] She was introduced by Carrie Chapman Catt, who read a letter from Theodore Roosevelt congratulating Rankin and applauding the Republican Party that had elected her.[52] Although most of her audience attended her lecture "out of curiosity" to see what a congresswoman looked like or to celebrate her election as a sign of suffragists' nearing success, Rankin spent most of her speech talking about her home state of Montana. The *New York Tribune* reported, "like every other real Westerner you've ever met, or ever will, she launched straight into a eulogy of the Golden West." The Manhattan listeners gasped, looked dazed, and exchanged bewildered glances as Rankin boasted the many merits of Western life.[53]

Rankin began her speech by saying, "Perhaps some of you came here tonight hoping to learn something of the state that would send a woman to Congress; you may have the impression that there is something rather unusual about a state that will select a woman to be its representative in national affairs. I will put you at ease at once by assuring you that Montana is unusual. I am very proud of my native state."[54] The *New York Tribune* paraphrased the message of Rankin's opening statement as, "Montana is an unusual state—that's why it elected a woman to Congress."[55] She continued by recounting her childhood memory of the moment she heard "the news that Montana had been admitted into the Union. I remember being quite impressed with the idea that we then lived in a state. I am still thrilled by the consciousness that I live in Montana, that Montana belongs to me and I to Montana."[56] As she took advantage of her spotlight, she attributed her political success to her home state and used her election and Western women's voting rights to envision the West as a region of civilization, modernity, and progress. Although Rankin did not directly call out antis' claims about the West as Robinson did, Rankin's Western boosterism frequently proved these claims to be untrue of Montana. Instead of merely defending the meaning of Montana, Rankin went a step further than Robinson and boosted Montana as an ideal promised land for potential settlers and investors, drawing on the popular rhetoric of Western boosterism.

Like many other Western boosters, Rankin lauded Montana as an agricultural promised land for white homesteaders and settlers, a land of plenty with numerous resources for producing food and financial growth. Before her audience in Carnegie Hall, she boasted, "Last year Montana produced enough wheat to make 18 loaves of bread for every man, woman and child in the United States—33 million eight hundred thousand bushels." According to Rankin, life in Montana was easy with food widely available: "Recent government reports show that Montana farmers grow almost one and a half times as many bushels of potatoes to the acre as the average farmer in the United States." Assuring her audience that the state's produce was abundant in both quantity and quality, she added, "Montana has won the world's prize for the quality of her flax" and "We win world prizes for our apples, we raise small fruits and vegetables."[57] Her descriptions of the state's exceptional agricultural advantages featured Montana as the "garden of the world," which Wrobel explains was common in promotional material about the West.[58] At the turn of the century, Americans viewed gardens as "one of the highest forms of civilization and Americanization" because "gardens represent[ed] nature (with its redemptive potential) tamed and made productive."[59] Rankin's imagined "Montana as Garden of the World" promised agricultural and economic success for future settlers and depicted Montana as tamed and productive.

Rankin even directly compared Montana's resources to those of other Western states to prove the its superiority to her New York audience and solidify its place as garden of the nation. She claimed, "We have as much agricultural land as the state of Iowa or as Illinois. You are familiar with these states as agricultural states. Some day you will have to readjust your attitude toward Montana." Her comparisons shaped Easterners' understanding of the most fertile Western states as she reported, "Our per acre value of wheat is equal to that of Minnesota and South Dakota put together."[60] She elevated Montana's agricultural opportunities over other states and positioned Montana as a superior option for potential settlers.

Rankin disputed the antis' temporal construction of the West as dislocated from the East in part by boosting Montana's modern technology and machinery. For her Manhattan audience, she depicted the ease of modern life in Montana: "Many women have electrified kitchens. It is the unusual small town which does not boast of electricity. . . . We have water power enough in our state to cook every meal that is eaten, to do the hard work and heat every home." With these technological advancements, Rankin maintained that life in Montana was as comfortable as in New York City. Due to their great resources of natural gas, even in their most severe winter, "the inhabitants in the progressive town of Havre in the northern part of the state suffered no inconvenience for they simply lit the gas. No one had to get up in the cold to shovel coal, not even the janitor." This new machinery and technology provided Montanans a life of relative luxury, and according to Rankin, it was all powered by Montana's waterfalls, which produced enough electrical horsepower to "turn the wheels of machinery and light the passages of mines thousands of feet underground in one of the biggest mining camps in the world."[61] Alan Trachtenberg explains that turn-of-the-century Americans viewed machines as "instruments of a distinctively American progress" and modern technology was humanity's civilizing force.[62] In contrast to Montana's pioneer past, Rankin's Montana of the present was civilized and modern, a place of technology, machines, and progress.

Rankin featured Montana reaching modernity and civilization just as fast as the East by celebrating the West's luxuries and technology like Montana's modern railroad. Trachtenberg argues that of all of the technology and machinery revered at the turn of the century, the railroad was "the age's symbol of mechanization and of economic and political change."[63] The railroad symbolized the pinnacle of human progress at the turn of the century. Rankin noted that "Some of the reports of my election in the eastern papers said that I campaigned on horseback."[64] She clarified, however, that "as a matter of fact, I traveled on trains and automobiles. I took one trip of 400 miles across the Rockies on an electrified train." Proving that Montana had made more technological progress than Easterners may have expected, she praised Montana's new kinds of travel, "We are amazed and delighted that we can reach almost every point by train or automobile. . . . The last Saturday night in the Primary I spoke at Roundup, then went to bed in a comfortable sleeper and arrived at my home 380 miles distant in time for Sunday dinner."[65] Her stories of her train travel portrayed living in modern Montana as a civilized life of comfort.

Rankin boasted of Montana's temporal advancement by emphasizing its political success at implementing direct democracy, which countered antis' arguments about the Western suffrage states' political ignorance and immaturity. She described Montana's successes in direct legislation, including the initiative, the referendum, the Australian ballot, the direct primaries, the presidential primary law, woman suffrage, the absent voters law, the corrupt practices act, and the preferential vote for US senators.[66] These policies were part of the direct democracy movement of the early twentieth century that aimed to empower citizens to vote on, propose, or terminate legislation and elected officials themselves as a means of checking the power and influence of corporations on political leaders.[67] More Western states successfully implemented direct legislation than Eastern states, and Montana was the third US state to adopt the initiative and referendum.[68] Rankin declared that Montana's direct primary law was only disliked by "self-appointed political bosses or . . . the henchmen of some special privilege." She championed Montana's corrupt practices act, which had "prevent[ed] the soliciting of votes in any manner." When explaining the advantages of Montana's absentee ballot, she reported there was a Montana woman voter who "was spending the winter in Florida but this did not interfere with her using an absent voter ballot. For the first time every railroad worker and every other worker who was forced to be away on Election Day had the same privilege as those at home." She boasted that in Montana, these direct democracy policies had "brought about a closer, more direct relationship between the voter and the government. Better laws have resulted; civic spirit has been stimulated."[69] Rankin imagined the West's political processes as active, democratic, and intelligent.

Featuring the state's agricultural, technological, and political advancements supported Rankin's argument that Montana's past as a wild, uncultivated, frontier state was over. They were not stuck in the primitive frontier past, but had already arrived in the nation's modern future, just waiting for the rest of the country to catch up. Before her Carnegie Hall audience, she recalled that formerly, "The land was free, each one had the opportunity to wrest from nature his economic needs. . . . [But now] our public lands are about gone and with their enclosure the last of the free land of the nation is gone." Her comparison depicted the frontier days of open land as a thing of the past. For Rankin, the West was not a place to be settled, but a place that had been settled. Democracy had been created, technology had arrived, and citizens had created their ideal state of progressive politics. Therefore, her Montana had something to teach Easterners. The rest of the country could learn from Montana's advanced technology, politics, and citizens. Rankin told Easterners of the "educated, refined young women" who had moved to the West. White women's presence in the West was often read as a sign of civilization, as they were believed to bring with them the stabilizing influence of morality and family. Rankin's Montana women were also educated and refined. She impressed upon her audience the worldliness of Montana citizens who had come "from every state in the Union from every country in the world."[70] Montana residents were educated, had come from diverse places, and had experience with cultures and ideas from around the globe. The East would do well to pay attention to Montana's well-informed and world-wise residents, who made up their advanced, civilized, and settled West.

Enacting the West's Civilization with White Femininity

Given the common perception in the East that suffragists were unattractive, politicians were masculine, and Westerners were woolly, Eastern audiences expected Robinson and Rankin to appear ugly, masculine, and uncivilized.[71] The "inherently egotistical act" of running for office countered longstanding gender norms and expectations of women's altruistic nature.[72] Many Americans believed that women's political activity masculinized women and feminized men, and the press often depicted woman suffragists as "old maids" and "mannish."[73] Not only were Robinson and Rankin politicians, they were also from the West. Before meeting her, reporters had questioned Rankin's femininity because she was political and she was from Montana. A reporter for the *San Francisco Chronicle* wondered whether Rankin would be a "wild and woolly feminist" who "packs a 44 six-shooter and trims her skirts with chaps and fur."[74] The reporter from New York's *Evening Telegram* noted that he did not expect her to be feminine given "the fact that she comes from Missoula, a place of about 18,000 inhabitants, of which probably not a corporal's guard of persons hereabout ever have heard, but which is located in the western part of Montana. In the entire State there are 177,000 voters."[75]

Yet Eastern press coverage of both politicians indicated that the reporters and public were caught off guard by Robinson and Rankin's femininity. During Robinson's 1913 Eastern tour, the *Republican*'s headline announced that "Colorado's 'Lady Senator' Jars East Because She's No Freak."[76] After returning home from her Eastern tour, she confessed, "I feel no vain pride in my success because I feel that most of it was due to my having been advertised as a sort of curiosity or freak. Most of those who came to hear me came to see what sort of creature a woman senator was, and I know I disappointed them because I wore petticoats and had unshorn hair." Colorado suffrage leaders were proud that "if the 'antis' of the East expected Senator Robinson to be any different from thousands of the other cultured women of the country they were mistaken."[77]

Rankin also surprised her Eastern audiences with her femininity as most media coverage of her addressed questions about whether she would be masculine.[78] The *Independent* promised that despite their expectations, "Miss Jeannette Rankin is no Amazon. She is a little woman—a girl."[79] Newspapers assured Americans that their first congresswoman was a "very 'feminine woman'" and a "womanly woman" who could dance, sew, cook, and care for children.[80] Presenting her as "an excellent cook" and "Good Bread Maker," the newspapers claimed that she could make a "wonderful lemon meringue pie" and "can cook for a fifty man logging crew without mussing up her hair."[81] The *New York Times*, *Seattle Times*, *Chicago Daily Tribune*, and *Los Angeles Times* all reported on her sewing abilities: "She makes her own hats, often builds her own gowns."[82] Newspapers promised that she "is interested in children more than anything else in the world" and "Her Principal Object Will Be to Work for Better Conditions for Babies and Children of US."[83] Robinson and Rankin presented themselves, and Western political women in general, as feminine, different from men, and civilized as a way to justify women's political activism. Since Americans believed that civilized cultures were marked by sexual differentiation, women's femininity and difference from men functioned as a marker of civilization.[84] By enacting their white femininity in the East, Robinson and Rankin asserted to their Eastern audiences that Western, political women were just as civilized as Eastern women.

ROBINSON'S PUBLIC HOUSEKEEPING ARGUMENTS

Robinson enacted her femininity and gender difference by presenting her political leadership as public housekeeping and identifying herself as "the housewife of the senate."[85] When she told the *Grand Traverse Herald* about her 1913 lecture tour in the East, she recalled, "I spoke not as a senator or politician, but as a housewife. I told what equal suffrage would mean to women as housewives and mothers, what relation the garbage can bore to the ballot, and I think I gave a side of the question never before presented there."[86] Likewise, in the 1914 speech she gave on "The Home and the Ballot Box" in Pittsfield, Massachusetts, she "announced that she was not going to talk as a politician, but as an old-fashioned woman who had found it to her interest and to our family's interest to attend to her job—the job of housewife—in the new-fashioned way."[87] Her political housekeeping arguments strategically associated her political activity with women's domestic roles and private sphere in the home, which epitomized the ideals of upper class, white femininity in the industrialized East.

Justifying political activity as public housekeeping was a common rhetorical strategy of women in positions of public and political leadership in the late nineteenth and early twentieth centuries.[88] Jane Addams justified running a city as "enlarged housekeeping," Bertha Knight Landes presented her mayorship of Seattle in the 1920s as "municipal housekeeping," Frances W. Munds of Arizona presented herself as the "state housekeeper" in 1914.[89] Other women who ran for office campaigned as state housekeepers, as when Anne Martin ran for the US Senate as Nevada's state housekeeper in 1918 and Alice Lorraine Daly campaigned for the governorship of South Dakota in 1922.[90] This metaphor reasoned that when women expanded their housekeeping skills to tasks outside their own home, they could help clean up their communities, cities, and states. Sometimes public housekeeping focused on cleaning physical messes, such as sanitation, water quality, children's playgrounds, or transportation, and other times they focused on moral and social issues, such as political corruption, vice, prostitution, prohibition, and education.[91] Public housekeeping arguments for woman suffrage and political involvement met industrial-era ideals that associated femininity with the private sphere. As industrialization had created a separation between public and private work places, gender ideals in the late nineteenth century suggested that while men should care for public matters outside of the home, women should care for private concerns in the home. The idea of public housekeeping legitimized women's public work in their communities by arguing that it helped them be better mothers and homemakers.[92]

Robinson used the public housekeeping metaphor to figure her political leadership, and Colorado's voting women, as feminine. She critiqued the perception that suffrage interfered with women's ability to care for their homes and instead argued that women must vote to protect their homes. In 1913, she acknowledged, "We still meet, occasionally, men and women left over from yesterday who persist in the moth-eaten assertion that the home must suffer if now and then a woman takes a ballot in her hands instead of a broom; and yet there are beautiful, well ordered and inspiring homes in America where the mothers and grandmothers have been handling the ballot for 44 years."[93] She vividly dispelled the idea that voting interfered with housekeeping. *Wellesley College News* reported, "Senator Robinson then went on to tell the average length of time it takes a woman to vote and showed how after she had deposited her yearly vote in the ballot box, she had 364 days, twenty-three hours and forty minutes for her home and other duties."[94] Her humorous descriptions of the reality of Western women's voting practices offered proof that voting did not keep Western women from caring for their homes and children, or fulfilling their feminine roles.

Rather than an impediment to women's work in the home, Robinson used the public housekeeping metaphor to define women's political participation as a central component to keeping house. She explained to New York women that "a great deal of your housekeeping is done in the City Council, behind which is the State Legislature. How about the streets and the garbage cans and so many things which have direct connection with the home life?"[95] To her Massachusetts audience, she equated voting with keeping house: "I do half my housekeeping at the ballot box." She explained that housekeeping tasks like garbage disposal and getting milk and water for the home "were once questions of individual housekeeping. They are now matters of collective housekeeping."[96] In New York City, Robinson urged women to "go into politics . . . to protect the home."[97] Like Frances Willard and the Women's Christian Temperance Union, she featured women's public organizing as "home protection."[98] To Robinson, the motivation for woman suffrage was to help "women to preserve the home . . . from the dangers that more threaten it."[99] She insisted, "There is not a tiny arch of the home circle that is not touched with politics. To keep the home inviolate you must go into politics."[100] In 1914, she explained in Massachusetts, "Politics, for example, has come from the outside to the inside. Public sanitation is a question of politics; so is the question of clean streets. What, then, is the use of having a vacuum cleaner inside the house if there is not a vote without to settle the question of clean streets, since we cannot keep our houses clean unless our streets are clean." She even questioned unpolitical women's ability to care for their children when she asked, "How then, can a home-making woman face her conscience if she does not seek the ballot? If she does not seek to do her share in making her city a better place for her children and other women's children to dwell in?"[101] Robinson constructed political participation as necessary for women to fulfill their roles as homemakers and, in the process, depicted Western women who voted as feminine and fulfilling their domestic duty to protect the home.

Robinson also justified her political leadership according to her femininity and difference from men. She constructed herself and other women as capable of participating in politics and maintaining their femininity and difference from men. Politics did not threaten women's femininity. For Robinson, femininity was what made women needed in politics: "They say of a woman sometimes that 'She thinks like a man' . . . They think it is a compliment, but I never could see the reason why. A woman like that is not essentially the kind of a woman needed for political work. To have a man at one desk in the Legislature and a woman at another does not mean simply that the vote is going to be doubled."[102] Her public housekeeping arguments and domestic justifications for women's political participation were rooted in beliefs about men and women's differences: the idea that women had unique and feminine perspectives compared to men in positions of political leadership.[103] Her public housekeeping rhetoric and performance of gender difference reflected on the civilized West that she represented.

RANKIN'S DOMESTIC IDEOLOGY

Although Rankin did not regularly present herself as a public housekeeper, she often drew on domestic ideology to justify women's voting rights and political participation. Like Robinson, Rankin reasoned that women should have the vote so they would be better equipped to care for their homes and children. She made these arguments during the Montana suffrage campaign and as an elected official.[104] She wrote in the *Boston Traveller*:

> In the past women have been told to go to their homes to care for their children. Today, however, we realize that caring for children means more than washing their faces and feeding them and sending them to school. We realize that it means more than caring for each woman's individual child; that it involves assuming responsibility for the children of the nation and looking ahead to the time when they will become integral factors in the life of the nation.[105]

She depicted American women as responsible for caring both for their own children in their homes and for the nation's children through their political activity, feminizing the act of voting as a motherly and domestic act.

Rankin also justified women's presence in Congress by highlighting the impact Congress had on children and the lack of attention the national legislature paid children at the time. In her Carnegie Hall speech, she insisted that children "be represented not only at the polls . . . but in legislative halls and in our national government and international conferences."[106] In the *Boston Traveller*, she pointed to the national legislature's "direct bearing upon the home and upon the child . . . It is easy to see that every law that is passed in the United States deals directly or indirectly with the environment of the child."[107] She underlined the need for experts on children in Congress with the following narrative in the *New York Sunday American*:

> Several years ago during a session of Congress $300,000 was appropriated for the study of fodder for hogs. At the same session $30,000 was appropriated for a study of the needs of the nation's children. . . . It would seem that in the eyes of Congress the hogs of the nation are ten times more important than [children] . . . We have plenty of men in

Congress who devote their attention to the tariff, the hogs, irrigation projects, rivers and harbor labor, the farmer, etc, etc. But, until now, we haven't had a woman in our National Legislature to do for the nation's precious asset, its children, what the men have been doing for the hogs.[108]

Rankin's example underscored the disproportionate attention given to some areas compared to congressional attention to the nation's children. She carved out a niche for women members of Congress and transformed the act of serving in Congress from a masculine and political act into an opportunity to care for children and domestic matters, both seen as feminine responsibilities.

Using this depiction of governance as the enactment of feminine responsibilities, Rankin argued that women were needed in Congress because there were some legislative issues that could only be solved by women. In an interview with the *New York Sunday American* published shortly after her election, she reasoned, "There is certain needful social and economic legislation which will come only through the demands of our women. I believe, too, that these demands will not receive the attention they merit until they are pressed by women who are members of our State and National Legislatures—not merely members of committees who appear at hearings."[109] She held up women's differences to show "that the whole country desperately needed" their presence in Congress because women were uniquely suited to address issues related to women and children.[110] She told the *New York Sunday American*, "there is needed legislation which can best be handled by women."[111]

Another tactic Rankin employed to justify women's political activity was to imagine women as feminine and distinct from men. In her Carnegie Hall address, she argued that women should have the vote "because they are women and have a different viewpoint to express."[112] She told the *Evening Telegram*, "There Would Be No Food Gambling if Women Were in Congress" and that the "Nation Needs Feminine Minds to Solve Home Problems."[113] Rankin drew on expediency arguments as she appealed to the popular belief that women's minds were different from men's and were especially suited for solving problems related to the home.[114] She implied that women's difference from men gave them something unique to contribute to political life. She explained, "It would not take long for food and other problems relating to the home to be solved if women were in a position everywhere to make their influence felt with their votes for it is in the homes that their chief interest lies, and these would receive their first protection."[115] Echoing Willard, Addams, and Robinson, Rankin argued that political activity would allow women to better protect their home, a responsibility that already fell to women as the homemakers.[116] Through her words and her performance, she reaffirmed gender difference and justified women's political activity according their motherly expertise. She performed an embodiment of this claim, assuring the public that although she was elected to political office and represented a Western suffrage state, she was still feminine and domestic. In the process, she repositioned herself as less threatening to traditional gender norms and articulated the possibility for Western women to protest, vote, and enter office while also maintaining traditional ideals of femininity and civilization.[117]

Rankin's justification for women's participation in government rested on the belief that women were better at caring for children than men and that this was women's responsibility. According to her statement in the *New York Sunday American*, women were best equipped for issues related to children because "subjects like the welfare of our children and the welfare of our homes" are "subjects to which thinking women have for years devoted their energies."[118] As she claimed women's expertise on children, she simultaneously charged women with the responsibility of childcare. She clarified in her Carnegie Hall speech: "It is not fair to ask the men to do their work and women's work too and it is certainly women's work to care for the children."[119] Her appeal to the belief that it was women's unique responsibility to care for children used this domestic ideology as a rationale for women's political activity.

In this vein, Rankin used her experience in caring for children to assert her own readiness for political office. Although she was not a mother herself, she emphasized her experience as an asset that made her a distinctive and important government actor. She told the *Seattle Times*, "My work and study in the Children's Home Society gave me a good insight into the needs of babies, children and young adults, and it is for them that I shall work especially. My experience in politics ought to help me to do this with a goodly measure of success."[120] Rankin drew on her experience with both politics and children to defend her qualifications for office. When she told the *Chicago Daily Tribune* why she was "Entitled to the Floor," she explained, "I had something to do with a children's home society in Washington and I know the needs of the youngsters."[121] She maintained that she was best able to represent the children of the nation because she was a woman, had a "feminine mind," and had experience caring for children. Her femininity helped reconcile her political participation with gender norms of the time.

EMBODYING WHITE FEMININITY
THROUGH APPEARANCE AND DRESS

Perhaps Robinson's and Rankin's most vivid method of countering the perception that Western women were uncivilized or masculinized by political activity was by performing their white femininity and civility through their appearances. The way women dressed was a major rhetorical strategy in developing their ethos and ability to be heard by larger audiences.[122] Dressing appropriately signified women's belonging, propriety, and social status. Although dress was often a means of disciplining women, it also provided women speakers a medium for resisting and negotiating those restrictions. Women "enlisted 'feminine' dress as a powerful rhetorical symbol" and visual sign of their credibility.[123] Robinson communicated her cultivation and performed her femininity through her appearance, her scent, and her tone of voice (see figure 21). During her 1913 Eastern lecture tour, when Robinson delivered more than sixty speeches throughout five states, the *New York Times* described her "as attractively gowned in a blue suit and hat to match."[124]After her first lecture tour in the East, the *Grand Traverse Herald* declared that "the east is now convinced that there can be such a 'lady senator' who sometimes

uses smelling salts, wears frocks of the kind recommended by the best fashion magazines and speaks in the tone of a 'perfect lady.'"[125] A reporter in Rhode Island was impressed that Robinson retained her femininity, despite being political: "Although a State Senator and 'in politics,' Mrs. Robinson is still very much a woman . . . There is very little of the masculine about her . . . She is of average height and not too slender. There are no hard lines about her lips and the only light that shines in her eyes is the light of womanly zeal . . . Her voice is full of possibilities—clear, rich, quiet and controlled."[126]

Figure 21. Helen Ring Robinson photographed while attending the forty-fifth annual NAWSA convention in Washington, DC. "Women at the Suffrage Convention in Washington," *New York Times*, December 14, 1913.

Figure 22. Miss Jeannette Rankin of Montana speaking from the balcony of the National American Woman Suffrage Association, Monday, April 2, 1917. C.T. Chapman, Kensington, MD.

Rankin also dressed according to Eastern ideals of upper-class femininity (see figure 22). Before Rankin traveled to the Northeast, Wellington paid to have a New York clothing store prepare dresses for her lecture tour.[127] At Carnegie Hall she wore a $200 dress of white satin and pink chiffon that she later described as "very elegant."[128] Her dress was "cut rather short to show her ankles and trim little feet . . . The sleeves were long, but her slim, white throat was bare and her hair was dressed in a soft and becoming fashion."[129] She also had "her white satin cloak lay over the back of the chair, and her white satin pumpers were small and dainty."[130] Rankin's fashionable appearance was not lost on her New York audience: nearly every newspaper reporter commented on her feminine and stylish attire. The *New York City Herald* predicted, "The

House of Representatives is going to enjoy something of a sartorial treat when Miss Rankin arrives."[131] The *New York Tribune* described her as "a debutante on her way to the coming-out party of women into the class of real people."[132] While this description infantilized this thirty-five-year-old adult politician as a "young woman" and compared her to a teenage "debutante" at her coming out party, it also noted that Rankin was presenting herself to the "polite society" of the East in socially acceptable and sophisticated ways.

As the newspaper reporters commented on Rankin's clothing and womanliness, they often contrasted her appearance to other suffragists. The *Evening Telegram* commented that by dressing in "the latest feminine modes and in taste," she appeared to be "the last person who would be picked out as one of the nation's leading exponents of the cause of equal rights."[133] The *New York City Herald* also emphasized her fashion sense and attractiveness before comparing her to other reformers in Carnegie Hall that night: "In striking contrast to the young woman who has arrived, politically, were seen groups of matriarchal looking suffragists seated in boxes draped with their suffrage colors."[134] And the *Evening Telegram* noted that "what is most noticeable about [Rankin] is that she does not ape the mannish airs of many of her sister co-workers, and instead of wearing a vest, high collar and a Windsor tie she dresses in the latest feminine modes and in taste."[135] Similarly, the *Los Angeles Times'* feature story also clarified that Rankin was "not an old-school 'woman's rights' agitator of the comic cartoons of a generation ago—with hair whacked tight over her ears and done in a French pea behind her ears. Instead she is a dainty bit of femininity who is quite as popular in a ballroom as at a political meeting."[136] Her feminine performance articulated the possibility that women could participate in politics *and* reside in the West without being masculinized or barbarized.

In addition to the ways Rankin's feminine performance lent credibility to her suffrage campaigning, it also proved she was not a gun-shooting, horse-riding Western woman—an image that many Montana boosters attempted to shed in favor of a modern image. Instead, Rankin performed the epitome of East Coast femininity by presenting herself as

fit for an elite East Coast society event. Her fashionable femininity bol-
stered and enacted her claims that Montana was civilized and socially
advanced. Her performance implied that if such a feminine and sophisticated woman was raised in represented Montana, then future settlers
could also move West and enjoy lives of culture and civilization.[137] Most
Western boosters were men, so having a well-dressed, upper-class white
woman make these booster claims made a stronger argument for the
state's progress.[138]

Conclusion

Following Robinson's public defense of Colorado women, the women
employees of the Colorado State House sent her a bouquet of flowers with the message, "From your sisters whom you have so ably defended."[139] The Women's Senatorial League also adopted a "resolution
praising Mrs. Robinson for her defense of the women of the state."[140]
The *Denver Post* noted that Robinson and other "Colorado women have
brought fame and honor to themselves and to their state by going into
other states where the suffrage cause hangs in the balance and dedicating
their talents and practical experience to the women struggling for the
ballot."[141] She was popular with more than just Colorado women. The *St.
Louis Star* described her as "lovable" and the most "notable housewife" in
Denver.[142] But, as Robinson's biographer argues, "Helen was more than
'lovable'; she was amazingly effective in her first year," passing her bills
with the help of her majority party. She did not run for re-election, but
after her senatorial term, she continued her work for woman suffrage
and wrote a second book, *Preparing Women for Citizenship*, which focused
on educating and preparing women to be informed voters. In 1916, she
endorsed President Wilson's re-election and campaigned for him in the
East and West, in a departure from the suffrage strategy of the National
Woman's Party. She also supported the state-by-state suffrage strategy,
rather than pursuing a federal amendment, and encouraged the national
suffrage organizations to do the same. Nevertheless, when the suffrage

amendment passed through Congress in 1919, she joined in the campaigning efforts to persuade states to ratify the Nineteenth Amendment, even visiting Connecticut to help the cause there. In 1918, she ran for Colorado lieutenant governor but did not get enough votes to be placed on the Democratic primary ballot.[143] She also continued her leadership in the Denver Woman's Press Club and continued writing on issues of public affairs, reform, and women's rights.

After Rankin finished her Carnegie Hall speech, the *New York Tribune* reported that she was recalled for "as many curtain calls as a prima donna."[144] Within a month of her Carnegie Hall address, she arrived in Washington to take her seat in the House on the opening day of session. That morning, suffragists held a breakfast for her in which "Mrs. Catt sat on her right hand and Miss Alice Paul sat on her left."[145] After the breakfast, "her entrance to the house was signalized by uproarious cheering and applause." She received another round of applause when her name was called on the roll. The papers reported that when "she replied: 'Present,' . . . The ovation continued until she rose from her seat and bowed."[146] Within the week, Rankin told the *New York Times* that she hoped "to put in as [her] first bill the Susan B. Anthony nationwide woman suffrage amendment."[147] Although she would not speak on woman suffrage in the House until January of the following year, within her first week she cast her vote in opposition to the United States' entrance into World War I.[148] As the United States entered World War I and the progressive movements came to a halt, the direct democracy movement also lost its momentum and in the end, became a "regionalized phenomenon tied to the specific political cultures of the American West."[149] Overall, Rankin's and Robinson's rhetorical choices lent credibility to suffragists across the nation while dispelling the most commonly deployed arguments against suffrage.[150] Their work led to an increasing acceptance of woman suffrage, and their effective political activity opened the door for women's participation in American government.

Like the other suffrage discourse examined in this book, the meaning of the West functioned as a rhetorical resource for Robinson's and Rankin's suffrage advocacy. Yet they also used the regional rhetoric to change the image of the West into a resource that better suited their advocacy goals and their communities. Contrary to the woolly West rhetoric of the antis, Robinson and Rankin domesticated the region as a settled, civilized, and temporally advanced part of the nation that should be valued, respected, and imitated. Robinson defended the West against the antis' accusations of wooliness, and Rankin boosted it as a land of agricultural plenty, advanced technology, and progressive reform. Both women featured Western women's femininity and difference from men in their arguments about women's participation in politics and in their own dress and appearance. While they championed women's political abilities, they did so in ways that maintained beliefs about men and women's differences and traditional ideals of femininity valued in the industrialized East. These performances of traditional femininity reconciled women's political participation with the masculine perceptions of politics and depicted their political leadership as less threatening to traditional gender norms. Both suffragists and Westerners benefited from Robinson's and Rankin's domesticated images of the West. Suffragists wanted Americans to perceive the region as civilized to prove that woman suffrage did not harm society or women, and Westerners wanted it to appear civilized to draw more settlers and prove its significance to the nation.

Robinson's and Rankin's performances also differed from the portrayal Duniway employed as a part of suffrage advocacy. Robinson and Rankin contested Duniway's traditional image of the West as a mythic frontier, and instead encouraged Americans to view the West as modern and advanced. Their appearance and style also diverged from Duniway's, who performed her difference from Easterners by enacting the Western heroine in her speaking style, manner, and content. In contrast, Robinson and Rankin appeared as proper and refined as their Eastern counterparts, performing their civilization and similarity to Easterners through their words and appearance. Furthermore, while Duniway relied on natural rights and earned rights arguments for woman suffrage, Robinson's public housekeeping arguments and Rankin's emphasis on women's unique differences from men were much more similar to expediency arguments of the time. The differences between Duniway's frontier West and Robinson and Rankin's progressive West illustrate the distinct historical contexts of the activists. Duniway's speeches at the end of the nineteenth century were well suited for the time period of the "closing" frontier, when the frontier myth was well circulated by Frederick Turner, Roosevelt, and the Wild West shows. But in the second decade of the twentieth century, many Westerners were trying to discard their cowboy country image and remake it into the promised land they needed and wanted it to be.

Similar to Duniway, the suffrage maps, and the antis, Robinson and Rankin featured the West as distinct from the East. Robinson's and Rankin's rhetoric were most similar to that of the suffrage maps, which also featured the West as more civilized than the East. But Robinson and Rankin did not go so far as to depict the East as the new suffrage frontier, or to appropriate the rhetoric of continental expansion, like the suffrage maps did. Those regional rhetorics of civilization and continental expansion, however, were enacted by Western suffragists' transcontinental automobile touring.

CHAPTER 5

Embodying the West

THE WOMEN VOTERS' ENVOYS'
TRANSCONTINENTAL CAR TRAVEL, 1915

———— • ◆ • ————

On September 16, 1915, four white women left San Francisco by car and drove to Washington, DC, to present a petition for women's voting rights to President Woodrow Wilson. At a time when unfinished roads made transcontinental car travel so difficult and such a novelty that they received national press coverage, this trip was a significant undertaking. The women claimed that their petition for national voting rights was signed by five hundred thousand Western women voters and was half a mile long. Their "Great Demand" asked President Wilson to endorse the Susan B. Anthony amendment, a federal amendment to the US Constitution to ensure that citizens' right to vote would "not be denied or abridged by the United States or by any State on account of sex." The *Day Book* announced that the suffrage car was "racing" the petition to the White House "over the Sierra and Rocky Mountains, across the Great American desert, through Iowa prairies, and Kansas mud holes."[1] Between San Francisco and Washington, the

Figure 23. Suffrage envoy Sara Bard Field (*left*), her driver Maria Kindberg (*center*), and machinist Ingeborg Kindstedt (*right*) during their cross-country journey to present their suffrage petition to Congress, September–December 1915.

pilgrims stopped in towns and cities across the country to hold publicity events, speak on woman suffrage, and collect more signatures for their petition (see figure 23). When the women reached New York City, the *Suffragist* reported, Fifth Avenue "rubbed its eyes . . . when the weather beaten automobile, bearing the slogan, 'On to Congress!' . . . blazed a path of purple and gold down the great thoroughfare."[2] When the suffragists arrived in Washington, they presented their petition to Congress and to Wilson as material evidence of Western women's political power. This cross-country performance functioned as regional rhetoric that contested the meanings of the West and East and exploited them for persuasive power.

As the envoys rallied women voters, gained publicity for their cause, and secured the support of politicians they met along the way, they appropriated multiple meanings of the automobile and transcontinental travel for rhetorical power. I argue that the Western envoys' transcontinental trip performed a modern mythic journey that enacted the rhetorics of the frontier myth and continental expansion to bring women's voting rights to the East. The car trip leveraged the meaning of transcontinental car travel, the early twentieth century's form of pioneering, as the next technology for experiencing the US wilderness as the new frontier. Yet the suffrage envoys' pioneer journey imagined the US East as the new mythic frontier to conquer for women's voting rights and the US West as civilized. This chapter illuminates the way the envoys' cross-country road trip of 1915 personified the modern frontier heroine, enacted a civilizing mission to the Eastern suffrage frontier, and presented tangible evidence of Western women's electoral power. The trip inverted Abigail Scott Duniway's frontier myth and suggested that by enduring the struggles of the Eastern frontier and proving themselves to be exceptional frontier heroines, the envoys earned the support and enactment of a federal suffrage amendment granting voting rights to Eastern women. The envoys' car trip also enacted a civilizing mission to the East that, like the imagery of the suffrage maps, used an inversed rhetoric of continental expansion and Manifest Destiny to suggest that they were bringing the civilizing practice of woman suffrage across the continent and were destined to succeed. By physically enacting these regional rhetorics, the envoys' arrival in the East performed their determination to use their political power to win a federal amendment to the Constitution, and provided Wilson and members of Congress with visual evidence of Western women's ability and resolve to influence national politics.

The envoys began their trip at the three-day Woman Voters Convention held in San Francisco in 1915. This convention and the road trip were planned by the Congressional Union for Woman Suffrage (cuws) that broke from the National American Woman Suffrage Association (nawsa). Rather than continuing the traditional state-by-state campaign method that the nawsa favored, the cuws promoted their gathering as the first convention of women voters to focus on passing a federal amendment to the Constitution.[3] The convention coincided with the end of the Panama Pacific International Exposition, the 1915 world's fair that

Figure 24. The Congressional Union's Freedom Booth at the Panama Pacific Exposition, where Western voters could sign the petition for the federal amendment, 1915.

celebrated the West, the completion of the Panama Canal, and the power of modern technology to connect and unify the nation.[4] During the exposition, suffragists draped their giant petition over a table at their exhibit—their "freedom booth"—and invited fairgoers to sign it before they took it east (see figure 24).[5] Then the Woman Voters Convention elected two Western women as envoys to take their demand for a federal amendment to Washington. Stillion Southard argues that by having enfranchised women elect the delegates, the suffragists constructed the CUWS as a political party and the envoys as elected officials. Although the CUWS had sent petitions and delegates to Washington before, this time the envoys represented four million Western women voters. Their party was now a formidable voice in national politics.[6]

The convention ended with a dramatic and emotional pageant to celebrate and anoint the envoys as they embarked upon their journey.

Ten thousand men and women gathered to commission four women to take their petition to Washington. The ceremony included a suffrage tableaux, a massed choir, ornamented costumes, and colorful flags. After singing the "Song of Free Women," the attendees accompanied the envoys to their Overland car decorated with suffrage streamers. The delegates drove out of the exposition gates amidst the "wild cheering of the crowd," and the *Suffragist* described their exit as "ending the most dramatic and significant convention that has probably ever been held in the history of world."[7]

The four traveling messengers included two official envoys, one driver, and one mechanic. Sara Bard Field (1882–1974) and Frances Jolliffe (1873–1935) served as the envoys.[8] Field was from Oregon and acted as the trip leader by making most of the public appearances and speeches. The papers described her as attractive, vivacious, charming, young, brown-eyed, slender, and little but brave.[9] She had been an active suffrage leader and lecturer in Oregon for years, and participated in the Nevada state suffrage campaign before she moved to San Francisco and became involved in the cuws. An experienced writer and a talented speaker that audiences enjoyed and received positively, Field served as the primary spokesperson and most prominent member of the group at their publicity events. Jolliffe was a wealthy socialite from San Francisco active in Democratic politics and an enthusiastic supporter of President Wilson. Soon after they departed from the convention, Jolliffe backed out of most of the car trip once she realized the difficulties of the demanding journey and told the papers that she was in poor health. But she completed most of the trip by train, rejoining the travelers for public appearances in the East and newspaper stories along the way.[10]

Maria Kindberg drove the car, and Ingeborg Kindstedt acted as the mechanic. Kindberg and Kindstedt were in their sixties and were naturalized American citizens who had emigrated from Sweden. They were both active suffragists and members of the cuws who lived in Providence, Rhode Island. The women had come to the exposition by way of the Panama Canal, and when they heard of the cuws's desire to send Western envoys to Washington, they volunteered to buy the car and drive it home.[11] Although they performed invaluable roles in the group, they were often kept on the sidelines at public events because they did not fit the image of suffragists that the cuws was constructing—young, modern, and attractive.[12] The envoys' trip was designed to symbolize Western women voters bringing voting rights to disenfranchised women in the East; the driver and mechanic's Swedish accents, Eastern residences, and lack of voting rights made them imperfect representatives of Western women voters. Although the press sometimes sought out Kindberg and Kindstedt for interviews and featured them in news stories, Field and Jolliffe made most of the envoys' public statements and served as the official Western women delegates.

Between San Francisco and Washington, the envoys traveled the Lincoln Highway and other interstate roads through Sacramento, Reno, Salt Lake City, Laramie, Cheyenne, Denver, Colorado Springs, Emporia, Kansas City, Lincoln, Omaha, Des Moines, Chicago, Indianapolis, Dayton, Detroit, Rochester, Boston, Providence, New Haven, New York City, Newark, Philadelphia, Wilmington, and Baltimore. At each event, they met with local politicians and sought their support for the federal amendment. Mabel Vernon, of Wilmington, Delaware, organized the events and traveled ahead of them by train.[13] She set up welcoming rallies for the envoys in each town and worked as their campaign manager and advance agent. She arranged publicity and news coverage by keeping in communication with the cuws headquarters in Washington, setting up press interviews, arranging for speaking opportunities in each town, and scheduling their meetings with local politicians.[14] The envoys prepared for their public entrances by decorating their car with streamers, cuws flags, and a banner that read, "We Demand an Amendment to the United States Constitution Enfranchising Women" (see figure 25).[15]

They often held events on the steps of state capitols and city halls where Field would speak about the federal amendment (see figure 26). Local politicians who supported the amendment would welcome the women, sign their petition, and promise to support the amendment in Congress or write letters of endorsement, including Nevada's Representative Curry, Utah's Representative Howell, Wyoming's Senator

Figure 25. Women Voters' Envoys, October 1915. Maria Kindberg in the driver's seat, Ingeborg Kindstedt standing, Sara Bard Field in the backseat on the left, and Bertha W. Fowler, Colorado state chair of the Congressional Union, in the backseat on the right. Colorado Springs, Colorado.

Warren, Colorado's Representative Hillard, Denver's Mayor McKeason, Omaha's Mayor Dolman, Iowa's Senator Cummins and Representative Dowell, Chicago's Mayor Thompson, Ohio's Governor Willis, and New York's Governor Whitman.[16] Others were more lukewarm in their support. Representative Champ Clark of Colorado told them he would not support the amendment when it came up in Congress, but he "shall certainly not oppose its passage otherwise."[17] Some of the politicians supported woman suffrage but did not think a federal amendment was necessary, such as Lincoln's Mayor Bryan, who was "undecided as to the method, [but] in sympathy with the principal [sic]," and Missouri's Senator Cummins, who thought the "method of adding an amendment to the constitution [was] too hard [and] a gigantic task for the women."[18]

Photo courtesy the National Woman's Party Photograph Collection.

Figure 26. Women voters' envoys welcomed at event in Colorado, October 1915. *Left to right*: Colorado governor George Carlson, Mabel Vernon, Sara Bard Field, Ingeborg Kindstedt, unidentified woman, and Mrs. Lucius Cuthbert speaking on the right.

Sara Bard Field responded to these comments by reasoning, "If men really want to save women from waste of strength, money, and from insults they should advocate the national amendment. They do not realize what it means to go through the state campaigns and there are thirty seven states yet to be won." Only Governor Morehead of Nebraska refused to write a letter or sign the petition, even though he supported the amendment, because the policy had not yet been adopted in Nebraska.[19]

To understand this months-long performance, I draw on newspaper coverage of the envoys and contextual research on the meaning of the automobile and transcontinental travel in the early twentieth century.[20] I examine the car trip as a modern frontier journey for woman suffrage and an enactment of continental expansion as the suffragists brought the civilization of woman suffrage to the East. Their cross-country embodied performance envisioned the West as civilized and the East as the new frontier of women's voting rights. Before the 1915 car trip, suffragists performed the power and civilization of the Western suffrage states with a variety of dramatic, yet more local ways in the early twentieth century: parades, pageants, and tableaus.

Embodying the Western Suffrage States in Parades, Pageants, and Tableaus

Like driving from California to Washington, suffragists performed many embodied advocacy tactics: pickets, illegal voting, train tours, pilgrimages, parades, pageants, and tableaus.[21] Women used some of these performances to vividly participate in public life, present their arguments to larger audiences, elicit media attention, and perform their organizational skills through an attractive and creative medium. Parades have been a celebratory ritual for Americans since the Revolutionary Era, and suffragists began exploiting them at least as early as 1908.[22] The parades conveyed the suffragists' determination, agency, and political power. They impressed their audiences with their size and beauty, and communicated with attractive and colorful banners, signs, symbols, floats, and gowns.[23] Suffragists also adopted the performances of pageants and tableaus, which both have long histories as mediums of entertainment and civic engagement, and were especially popular during the last decades of the suffrage movement.[24] Usually performed outside, at a public event or civic holiday, pageants presented a narrative, or a series of short stories with large and colorful movement, costumes, and limited sound and dialogue. Some pageants included tableaus or "living pictures," which featured performers frozen in place for several minutes to portray a still picture of an important historical moment.[25] Although suffrage parades were controversial, drew critique, and were at times met with violent mobs, the parades, pageants, and tableaus drew large audiences and national publicity and allowed suffragists to enter and perform their organizational skills in public spaces.[26] In these public performances, suffragists often dressed up as the Western suffrage states or decorated their cars or parade floats as symbols of women's voting rights within the United States.[27]

I argue that in addition to projecting the movement's power, determination, and agency, the suffrage parades, pageants, and tableaus functioned as regional rhetoric that reimagined the meaning of the West and the East with costumed white bodies, decorated cars, or elaborate parade floats that promoted the existence of women's voting rights. Parade participants often dressed up as the Western suffrage states by wearing white or yellow, and sometimes carried ribbons, signs, or shields with the name of the suffrage states across the front.[28] In the 1913 suffrage parade in Washington, a parade float included "9 women dressed in white representing 'light,' and others walking around dressed in black, representing the 39 States which have no suffrage."[29] Similarly, an open-air suffrage tableau in St. Louis in 1916 featured a Goddess of Liberty figure holding a torch high above her head and surrounded by thirteen white women dressed in white to represent their equal voting rights in the eleven equal suffrage states, Alaska Territory, and presidential suffrage in Illinois (see figure 27). Performers dressed in gray to symbolize states with partial suffrage, and others dressed in black to represent the states with no suffrage rights for women.[30] Their embodied symbols appeared so similar to the suffrage maps that the *Philadelphia North-American* called a 1915 parade in Philadelphia "*a living map* of the United States, with the suffrage states designated by the yellow and white gowns of the marchers."[31] Like the suffrage maps, these performances depicted the Western suffrage states as civilized with the light-dark metaphor, whiteness, and traditional femininity. The 1912 suffrage parade down Fifth Avenue in New York City represented the western suffrage states with "four victory floats . . . drawn by snow-white horses [and] six golden chariots."[32] The chariot drivers wore "white classic costumes," and Mrs. Laidlaw ensured that "the chariot horses [were] pure white, no makeshifts, and no spots."[33] The white and gold imagery associated woman suffrage with whiteness, purity, traditional femininity, and civilization.

Figure 27. Open-air tableau on the steps of the Saint Louis Art Museum, 1916.

In contrast to the white suffrage states, the white women who represented the non-suffrage states dressed in black and wore "slave" costumes. In a 1915 Central Park tableau, the performers representing the non-suffrage states wore black clothing, shackles on their hands, and "cried out for freedom" to perform their role as "slave states."[34] When suffragists marched down Michigan Avenue in 1916 to agitate the Republican National Convention, twelve white women wearing white and the names of the suffrage states led "a detachment of thirty-six other girls dressed in gray, with their hands manacled and a ball and chain, in the shape of a toy balloon, attached to their ankles by a cord, symbolizing the States where women do not have the right to vote."[35] To represent the "slave states" in the 1916 tableau in Central Park, women wore "real clanking chains, commonly used to suspend hammocks" to "bind the unenfranchised states" (see figure 28).[36] Through their costumes, suffragists performed women's lack of political rights, and featured the non-suffrage states as barbaric and primitive, since many Americans in the Progressive Era viewed the institution of enslavement as a "relic of

Figure 28. Suffrage states represented in tableau near Central Park, New York City, 1915.

barbarism." The "slave" metaphor was commonly used by women's rights advocates, even as it grossly misrepresented and whitewashed the experience of people who were enslaved, which differed categorically from white women's lack of voting rights.[37] Their performance of the "slave" metaphor also dramatically enacted Eastern women's limited power and agency, and represented the East as less advanced than the West.

In addition to using light and whiteness, these performances employed attractive white bodies to represent the Western suffrage states. Enacting the sex differences believed to mark civilization, the parade planners chose traditionally gendered men and women to embody the Western suffrage states. The *New York Times* described the thousands of men and women marching in the 1912 New York City parade as "a line, miles long, of well-dressed, intelligent women," and "the majority [of the men were] young, husky fellows, who marched as haughtily as their sisters and carried high the yellow pennants of the cause."[38] A 1913 suffrage pageant in Manhattan attempted to represent all states of the Union with a man and woman, and they strategized that "the nine most beauteous

couples will be the nine states where women vote."[39] They often chose
less attractive women to portray the non-suffrage states as uncivilized in
tableaus. For the 1916 tableau in Central Park, they had women embody
"the Enfranchised States, the Slave States, [and] the Semi-Enfranchised
States."[40] The *New York Sun* reported that the suffragists planned so "the
tallest and most beautiful suffragists will be the voting States," and the
non-suffrage states would be represented by those who were not "top-
notchers physically."[41] Like the suffrage maps, these parades, pageants,
and tableaus visualized Western women's voting rights as civilized with
light, whiteness, and femininity, and in the process, they challenged
the traditional meanings of the West and East for suffrage. Eventually,
suffragists expanded and amplified these performances into a transcontinental, multi-month car trip, which began and ended with extravagant
pageants in San Francisco and Washington. Yet, as the car trip embodied Western women's voting rights, its mobility also enacted Western
women bringing their voting rights to the East through transcontinental
travel.

Transcontinental Motoring as Advocacy Tool and Modern-Day Pioneering

Beginning in the 1910s, suffragists frequently incorporated automobiles
into their public advocacy. Automobiles symbolized independence,
freedom, and individualism. To sell more cars to women, manufacturers advertised women motorists as autonomous, modern, and sophisticated.[42] Likewise, suffragists used the automobile's glamourous image of
feminine freedom to portray their movement's modernity. In addition
to its rhetorical value, the automobile also made it more feasible for suffragists to reach audiences with their message. In the West, where car
ownership was more common than in the rest of the country, suffragists
embraced the automobile for their campaigning earlier than their peers
in the East because it was the easiest and fastest way to reach voters who
were more dispersed than in the East. Eastern suffragists were hesitant to

use cars in their public events because car ownership was most accessible to the upper class and reinforced suffragists' image as elitist. But eventually, they too embraced it for its efficient transportation and symbolic value. In the 1911 California campaign, the College Suffrage League of Northern California reached audiences and got their attention by using the car as a speaking platform.[43] Illinois suffragists believed that using the automobile helped them win their state campaign for presidential suffrage in 1913.[44] Suffragists around the country used cars in parades, as speaking platforms, and as a means of attracting attention. The automobile also provided protection for advocates facing crowds of hostile audiences.[45] In 1913, Alice Paul and the CUWS organized a national petition campaign that ended in Washington with an automobile parade of eighty cars motoring down Pennsylvania Avenue toward the Capitol. Historian Georgine Clarsen argues that women motorists became so strongly associated with woman suffrage, audiences often assumed that any group of women drivers traveling together were suffragists.[46]

Of all the kinds of driving available to women, transcontinental car travel received the most publicity. Automobile manufacturers famously promoted women's transcontinental touring to advertise the reliability of their vehicles around the country. Companies used these trips to convince consumers that their automobiles were comfortable for women and easy enough for anyone to drive. They also sponsored women motorists to complete the long-distance trips to ensure abundant publicity since, as historian Virginia Scharff explains, driving across the country was seen as a test of masculine fortitude, which made the idea of women driving such long distances a spectacular stunt.[47] In 1909, the Maxwell Car Company sponsored Alice Huyler Ramsey, the president of the Women's Motoring Club of New York, to drive her party of four women from New York to San Francisco. The car company advertised the women as the first all-women group to travel the continent by car, six years after the first trip made by men had been completed. In 1915, Kissel Motor Car Company sponsored silent film star Anita King's "Koast to Koast" tour, which left San Francisco for New York on the Lincoln Highway, stopping at one hundred Paramount Theatres along the way to speak on filmmaking.[48] Just weeks later, the suffrage envoys also left San Francisco for Washington, DC, on the Lincoln Highway. Their trip resembled King's tour to such an extent that King's tour likely served as a template for the suffragists. The newspaper coverage of these trips associated women travelers with adventurousness, sophistication, and modernity, which made transcontinental travel an ideal vehicle for suffragists to exploit in their advocacy.

Yet in addition to serving the purposes of automobile advertisers and suffrage advocates, transcontinental travel was also associated with pioneering and westward migration. The first people to drive across the country from coast to coast exhibited fearlessness and tenacity because Americans did not know yet whether such a feat was possible.[49] In the 1910s, transcontinental travel evolved into a popular tourist activity. Automobile tourists who took these trips were described as modern pioneers, partly because long-distance highways were rare and difficult to travel. Historian Marguerite S. Shaffer explains that transcontinental travel required "braving rough, unmarked roads and unpredictable machines to escape the confines of urban industrial society and revitalize themselves on the open road."[50] In 1915, many of the transcontinental highways were incomplete. Although the roads were called "highways," they were actually an assemblage of unpaved local roads that often functioned more as a continuous progression of mud holes.[51] When Emily Post traveled on the Lincoln Highway in 1915 to attend the San Francisco Exposition, she described the Lincoln Highway as "a meandering dirt road that became half a foot of mud after a day or two of rain."[52]

The highways used for transcontinental travel were constructed along, and subsequently named after, the old trails that Western pioneers traveled as they emigrated west, further contributing to their association with pioneering. The National Old Trails Road, a highway that ran from coast to coast, was constructed over old trails that had been essential to western migration: Daniel Boone's "Lick Road," which he used to visit his family; the Santa Fe Trail, which pioneers traveled to settle the Southwest; and the Oregon Trail, which was used to reach the Pacific Northwest.[53] The builders of the Old Trails Road explained that they built the highway where the old trails "were stamped out by Nature's engineers—the buffalo, the elk and the deer . . . followed by the Indians and later by the pioneer who blazed and broadened them into wagon roads, over which traveled opportunity, civilization, religions and romance."[54] Promoters of the Old Trails Road maintained that the highways manifested the nation's history of continental expansion and pioneering.[55] Elizabeth B. Gentry, the chair of the Old Trails Road Committee in Missouri, argued in 1912 that the highway would "perpetuate the pioneer history" and "conserve the ideals of the Nation by building a National highway over the trails of the pioneer."[56]

The Lincoln Highway, which the suffrage envoys traveled for the Western portion of their trip, was designed as the first coast-to-coast highway from San Francisco to New York, and it was planned to be completed in time for the 1915 exposition in San Francisco. The Lincoln Highway also followed historic pioneer trails: the Salt Lake Trail, the Cherokee Trail, and the path of the Pony Express and Overland Stage Line. The *Official Guide to the Lincoln Highway* told of the many pioneers and frontiersmen who had traveled the highway's path, including Buffalo Bill Cody, the Donner Party pioneers who perished trying to reach California, the Forty-Niners who emigrated to California, and the historic expeditions of John Fremont, Howard Stansbury, and Frederick Lander. Highway builder and promoter Arthur Pardington argued that by traveling the Lincoln Highway, the most famous transcontinental highway, the tourist was able to "trace the footsteps of the pioneer and follow the path of the frontier as it moved ever westward."[57] Eastern tourists could experience the "memories of early days," such as the bravery of stage drivers and Indian fighters, and the thrilling adventures of the hardy men who formed the vanguard of civilization in laying the Union Pacific.[58] The *Official Guide to the Lincoln Highway* suggested that traveling on the Lincoln Highway "was about escaping the routines and restrictions associated with the overly civilized qualities of the Pullman Palace car and European travel. It was about directly experiencing the people, the places, and the history that made America unique."[59] Shaffer argues that motoring and highway advocates used the imagery and language of the old pioneer trails to suggest "that in escaping the restraints of urban industrial society, in vicariously reenacting a sanitized pioneer past, and in seeing America firsthand along the Lincoln Highway, automobile tourists became better Americans."[60]

Highway builders promoted the development and improvement of highways by construing automobile travel as a way to connect to United States' heroic history of frontiering and a means of becoming better Americans. Promoters of national highways, like the Daughters of the American Revolution, suggested that driving these highways allowed Americans to leave the city, assume the autonomy and adventurousness of the frontier journey, and in the process, simulate the nineteenth-century pioneers' experience and enact their American character.[61] As the *American Motorist* claimed, touring the national highways provided the best way to see Western scenery, meet people of the West, and fully experience "what difficulties confronted its pioneers, when they claimed this land as their own."[62] Their claims were similar to Frederick Jackson Turner's argument that it was through the process of escaping civilization and experiencing the American wilderness that Europeans shed their European manners and adopted the individualistic and democratic lifestyle that defined American character. Transcontinental car travel became a new way for Americans to experience and access the frontier, even when the land was no longer open for physical settlement.

There were so many similarities between transcontinental travel and pioneering that some travelers compared their cars to the covered wagons that had carried their owners into the frontier. After Caroline Poole's transcontinental car trip in 1913, she wrote *A Modern Prairie Schooner on the Transcontinental Trail: The Story of a Motor Trip.*[63] In this book, Poole nicknamed her car Schooner Sallie, invoking the "prairie schooner," a term for a covered wagon. She recalled that "when packed and stowed with our equipment and ready for the long adventure she was in truth the modern replica of the historic Prairie Schooner of the early days."[64] Although the Western tourist industry focused most on promoting pioneer reconstructions, or "What-it-was-like-in the-Old Day's" trips for younger and urban clients, pioneers themselves were also a market for Western journeys. Western residents who had settled there decades before also traveled by car to reenact and reminisce about their pioneering pasts. Reenacting from the comfort of a modern car seemed to emphasize how much more difficult it was. They contrasted the difficulties of their first trip with the ease of twentieth-century travel; the juxtaposition of these trips gave pioneers pride and most importantly allowed them to boast that they had successfully completed the journey with many more difficulties and obstacles.[65]

The Suffrage Envoys' Modern Frontier Journey

By travelling across the country through a mode so closely associated with pioneering and westward migration, the envoys enacted a modern frontier journey. In an updated context and transposed form, their transcontinental car trip invoked the traditional frontier myth and deployed it for women's voting rights. The envoys and their press often imagined the overland travelers as modern-day pioneers, and portrayed the three thousand–mile journey according to frontier mythology. A Baltimore reporter narrated the suffragists' trip like a Western dime novel: "The prairies, the Rockies infested with 'Injuns' and coyotes, impenetrable forests, valleys, streams and rivers have had no terrors for four women in an automobile who are traveling hitherward from San Francisco."[66] Similarly, the *Washington Herald* featured the envoys as frontier heroines that would be remembered in history:

> Schoolboys of the present generation read the thrilling tales of how pioneers of the 'D. Boone. He Killed a Bear' type, hewed and chopped and swam and climbed their way westward. Suffragists assert that in the primers and 'readers' they are to give the children there will be the record of how four women chugged, speeded, shocked, and skidded their way eastward over mountains and plains through the sand marshes, with a six cylinder for their charger and an automobile tool kit as a sort of modern crusader's spears.[67]

Figure 29. Women voters' envoys with their "On to Congress" sign displayed on their car, 1915.

These newspapers described the envoys' journey as adventurous, difficult, and as exceptional as the trek of the mythic frontier heroes.

On their epic journey, the envoys personified independent frontier heroines who had earned their status by leaving the comforts of home, enduring the struggles of the frontier, being tested in the uncharted wilderness, and triumphing over the land and people of the West.[68] The envoys left the comforts of San Francisco to journey through the suffrage movement's new mythic frontier: the East. Instead of traveling in a covered wagon marked with the "Westward, ho!" sign of pioneer settlers, the suffragists rode in a "weather beaten automobile, bearing the slogan, 'On to Congress!'" (see figure 29).[69] Rather than setting up camp or circling their wagons at night, the envoys "slept at night in oil lamp frontier hotels."[70] Still, like nineteenth-century pioneers, the envoys traveled overland on old trails and struggled through their long and demanding journey on rough and unmarked roads.[71] They took the Lincoln Highway at least as far as Omaha before varying their route some to reach other cities beyond the highway, including Indianapolis, Dayton, Rochester, and other cities north of New York.

Although the suffrage envoys' mythic frontier was the settled East, their testing ground was still featured as wild, dangerous, and difficult, a means of proving the heroines' strength and courage. Vernon told a reporter in Kansas City that "in order to reach Cheyenne, Wyoming, to keep an appointment with the governor of the state, the young women followed a mountain road in a snowstorm, a journey men drivers were afraid to attempt. . . . It will be an easy stunt to speak for suffrage from a downtown street corner in comparison to finding a lost mountain trail." The *Kansas City Post* agreed that "street speaking in Kansas City will be tame to them after the Western experiences . . . [they] have undergone."[72] The *Lincoln Nebraska Journal* reported the "numerous hardships [the envoys] experienced on their trip, including a night in the desert in Nevada," a "blinding snowstorm" in Wyoming, and an "all night vigil in the Kansas mud." But "despite this, [the envoys had] no intention of shortening the trip a bit," for they were not deterred by their challenges as they showcased their heroic mettle.[73]

The rigors of their trip served as trials to prove the women's strength, ability, and determination. The *Boston Post* reported that when attempting to drive through the "blinding snowstorm" in Wyoming to make a speaking event, the envoys "met three motor parties returning to town . . . [who] advised against the trip, telling them they surely would be lost, but that 'grit' necessary in a case like that asserted itself and they went through the storm to the next town, glad of the trip for the novelty, as well as testing their mounts to its utmost."[74] The envoys verified their exceptional bravery in the face of a storm and in their willingness to risk their safety for the suffrage cause. Similarly, on their way to Emporia, Kansas, their car got "stuck in the mud" and since they "ha[d] no man along to do the swearing . . . it was a woman's job to get them out." The *Emporia Gazette* reported that "it was sheer strength and moral courage that got them through." After "wad[ing] in the mud up to their hose supporters" and "greasing themselves up, they looked like the last survivors of the battle of the Marne." The *Emporia Gazette* claimed that afterward, the "Three Lone, Lorn, Weemin" were "three of the muddiest, maddest women who ever got out of a motor" when they "piled from an Overland car at midnight . . . and sneaked into the Mitway Hotel."[75]

These stories of frontier challenges attested to the envoys' exceptional endurance and grit.

Their stories from the road often emphasized the women's ability to get by on their own, like the independent frontier hero, without help from men. An exemplary case is the story Field related of their experiences with "car trouble . . . about ten miles from town out in the wilds of Nevada." The *Des Moines Register* reported that when the envoys discovered that "someone had stolen the tools," Kindstedt, the driver, "did not say anything but she pulled the car apart, took out something and made a jack of it, raised the car, repaired the damage and replaced the something and the car went on." In contrast, Field recalled, "I have made campaign tours in Oregon when the man driver would wait on the road until an automobilist would arrive to help him out." She surmised from the incident that, "It just goes to show what women can do."[76] Kindberg, their mechanic, told audiences in New York, "When we were in the mountains, I would change the tires myself. . . . [and] yes, we bare [*sic*] all the expense ourselves, my partner and I."[77] The envoys' narrative featured their heroic independence with their auto repair and expenses, as these women showed that they did not need the help of men.

On the suffragists' Eastern frontier, the dangers were not wild bears and American Indians, but the white men they met on their trip who always seemed to create more challenges for them. The women repeated over and over again to reporters the story of the "only misadventure" of the trip, which was all the fault of a man because it happened "during the only time they were accompanied by a man."[78] When they were traveling through the deserts of Arizona, Kindberg was so "overcome by fatigue" that she could not drive any longer.[79] So, they "hired a guide, who declared positively that he knew the way. When finally they bumped into a signpost after wandering for hours over the country, imagine their consternation upon finding themselves forty-five miles out of the way."[80] After "he lost them," the *Washington Herald* reported, they "were late for a speaking engagement and that ended their reliance on any mere man."[81] Field concluded from that experience, "It seems to me it was intended that women should do this work by themselves and we have taken this as a warning so to do."[82] The envoys swore to the *New York Tribune*, "When we were by ourselves we never got lost. We didn't run over so much as a chicken."[83] Getting help from men only seemed to make their trip harder. The heroines were in the best hands when they took care of themselves.

They especially had to avoid men who worked in garages or maintained the roads. Motorists often claimed that farther east many of the roads were deliberately kept as quagmires so that local farmers could make money from helping motorists out of the mud.[84] And the suffragists met plenty of these men. Kindberg told the *Nebraska State Journal*, "We were warned to provide red pepper to protect ourselves against dangerous men . . . but the only protection we have needed has been for our pocketbooks. We have been held up in every garage for the payments of nine or ten dollars for a night, with the additional loss often of having our tools and other property stolen from the car."[85] But as frontier heroes before them accomplished extraordinary feats that were remembered in exaggerated tall tales, the envoys often found a way to outsmart their adversaries, or talk them into supporting women's voting rights. They often recounted a story about the time that "their motor [got] stuck in the mud," and a farmer agreed to pull them out if they paid him five dollars. Then when the farmer's "mule got stuck in the mud" as well, they "pulled him out" and "charged the farmer $5 for that."[86] This favorite story of the envoys implied that they were equally able as men to use the open road for gain. Another kind of man they came across on their trip were cowboys. The envoys told the *Boston Herald* of a night they were "searching for the right route to take" when "they found at the roadside two sleeping figures, rolled up in blankets, with revolvers at their hips. Horrid men were there—cowpunchers." Yet, they reported that they even got the cowpunchers to sign their petition for the federal amendment.[87]

The envoys testified to the many difficulties they overcame on their frontier journey as evidence of their exceptional endurance. Traditional frontier heroes completed their cosmogonic cycle by writing home to pass on their knowledge to those they left behind. Like Duniway and other Western pioneers, Field kept a journal of their travels and the difficulties the group faced on their journey, which she shared widely in the

Western and Eastern newspapers. The *Washington Herald* published an excerpt of one of her letters home about the challenges they faced: "We get up at 6 a.m., jolt, bounce and shake over a hundred miles of awful roads, land weary to the breaking point and with sore lips and cheeks at a coal oil hotel where the roof leaks and where spiders and other bugs visit one. We eat a supper veiled in mystery as to just what it is and then to bed. If the lumpy, mumpy thing we lie on can be so called."[88] In their public appearances, they rehearsed their frontier difficulties for their audiences. When they arrived in upstate New York, the *Rochester Chronicle* reported, "A curious crowd gathered to see them and [the envoys] told of their mishaps."[89] The envoys and the newspapers narrated the many difficulties the envoys encountered on their trip as evidence of their mythic trek.

By personifying frontier heroines, their appearance in the East provided material evidence of their grit and determination. The *Nebraska State Journal* noted the toll the travel had taken on "the ladies" whose "faces were tanned and weather-beaten."[90] In Caledonia, New York, the *Rochester Chronicle* described the "three travel stained and tired, yet dauntless women, [who] autoed into the village."[91] The envoys' weathered skin and travel-worn appearance verified their journey and the difficulties they had endured while exposed to the elements. According to the *Baltimore News*, after arriving in Maryland the envoys were "tanned and ruddy, but none the worse for the experience of crossing a continent."[92] When they arrived in New York City, the image of their "grimy and battered" car with the "mud-stained banner" corroborated their tales of adventure.[93] Their travel-worn bodies and automobile bore visual evidence that these women had endured and triumphed over many struggles on their journey to the Eastern frontier.

Eastern audiences seemed to celebrate the envoys' trip as an endurance of hardship and evidence of their courage, ability, and heroic nature (see figures 30 and 31). In Delaware, Wilmington's Mayor Price welcomed the envoys and declared, "You ladies who have crossed our continent and have endured the hardships of the trip on your way to Washington have proven beyond a doubt your earnestness and faith in the cause that you have so ardently espoused."[94] In Philadelphia, Mayor

Figure 30. Suffrage envoys from San Francisco greeted in New Jersey on their way to Washington, DC, to present a petition to Congress containing more than five hundred thousand signatures, 1915.

Figure 31. Maria Kindberg driving, Ingeborg Kindstedt in passenger seat, and Sara Bard Field in the back.

Blankenburg told the envoys, "You have shown courage in marching through this bad weather. And the long trip which you three ventured to take shows courage and the ability to do man's work when occasion requires." Alva Belmont, a leading member and funder of the cuws, agreed that after coming "over mountains, down into mines, through the desert, into the forests, across the prairies, [the envoys] come as heroes, whose deeds and adventures will be recorded by future historians, as those of the present record the ride of Paul Revere."[95] Some Easterners read the envoys' transcontinental travel as an indication of their physical strength and size. When the messengers arrived in Albany, Governor Whitman "seemed amazed that a woman had driven the car all the way from San Francisco, and was equally amazed at the size of the women. 'I thought you would be six feet tall,' said he."[96] When the envoys arrived in New York City, the *New York Tribune* recognized Kindstedt and Kindberg as "the heroines of the hour," and "everybody wanted to see the woman who had done the driving, and she was glad to tell her adventures to all." The *Tribune* highlighted the differences between the women who had traveled from the West and their New York audience as the *Tribune* noted that the women "in rough fur coats and warm caps, were a strange contrast to the velvets and flowers of their Fifth Avenue hostesses."[97] For these women had been changed on their journey, and as frontier heroines, they were visibly distinct from their Eastern counterparts. As modern frontier heroines, whose fortitude had been tested and verified, their performance invoked the meritocracy of the frontier myth to imply that they were owed the federal amendment for national women's voting rights.

The Envoys' Civilizing Mission

In addition to enacting the frontier myth, the envoys' car trip also appropriated the rhetoric of continental expansion, which imagined the East in need of the West's civilizing. The envoys and their news coverage featured the cross-country trip as a mission to bring the light and civilization of woman suffrage to the "dark lands" of suffragists' frontier

wilderness. In the *San Francisco Bulletin*, Belmont depicted the envoys'
trip as a "Suffrage Mission," and described how the speakers in the
commissioning ceremony of the Woman Voters' "bade the two suffrage
envoys godspeed and told them of the import of their mission."[98] Like
European-American settlement of North America, the envoys' mission
to the East was sometimes imagined as an "errand into the wilderness."
Seventeenth-century Puritans imagined their religious mission in the
North American wilderness as an "errand" from God and used biblical
language to compare the New England mission to John the Baptist's
mission into the wilderness to prepare the way for Jesus Christ ("Make
straight the way of the Lord").[99] Likewise, during the envoys' departure
pageant, the actress Miss Margaret Anglin dedicated the suffragists' mission to Washington with the biblical language used to describe the New
England errand: "Remember, you are a voice of one crying to Congress
and to the President, 'Make straight the paths of justice for women.' You
are to be the mouthpiece of the West speaking to the government for the
women of the nation and, in a most profoundly true sense, for the womanhood of the world."[100] The *New Haven Register* also described the suffragists' trip as their errand, and when the envoys arrived in Washington,
DC, Field declared "that her wonderful *errand* was accomplished."[101] Like
the Puritans in the wilderness of New England, the suffragists aimed
to subdue and civilize the wilderness. The envoys' suffrage mission was
to civilize the Eastern wilderness and prepare the way for their divine
message: a demand for national voting rights.

The suffragists used the light and dark imagery of civilization and
Manifest Destiny to represent the envoys' civilizing mission. The send-
off pageant in San Francisco was held outside at night, so it was dark, but
lit by the "giant tower gate flaming aloft in the white light" and "bright
masses of women" with lights and "orange lanterns [that] swayed in the
breeze." The women carried their lights while "forming in procession
to escort the envoys to the gates of the Exposition" where their Overland car was waiting for the departure. The *Suffragist* reported, "and then
came the envoys, delegated by woman voters to carry the torch of liberty
through the dark lands and keep it burning." The envoys were bringing

the light of liberty, civilization, and woman suffrage into the darkened wilderness of the East. They sang "Song of Free Women," written by Field and sung to the tune of "Marseillaise," with lyrics that described their trip east with language reminiscent of Manifest Destiny. The song described the envoys as "white-robed, advancing, through night's dark portal to the dawn . . . Eastward from the West they move."[102] The song's chorus repeated, "We are women clad in new power. We seek the weak. We hear their plea. We march to set our sisters free." Another verse of the song assured their "weak" Eastern sisters, "we come. We come at last . . . Trust thou our might. Thou, too, shall walk in light." When the envoys arrived in Philadelphia months later, the Eastern suffragists held a reception for the envoys at the Ritz-Carlton where Belmont said to the audience, "Our guests today have carried the torch of liberty across the American continent," and they recognized the envoys for bringing the light of women's freedom to the East.[103]

The envoys also featured their car trip as conquest of the Eastern non-suffrage territory with war language, repeatedly depicting the West as safe and the East as enemy territory. In San Francisco, the *Suffragist* called the envoys "crusaders," and Jolliffe declared, "We are only two women, but we go armed with the fighting strength of four million."[104] Belmont's special edition of the *San Francisco Bulletin* also described the women at the Woman Voters Convention as "women who felt they were fighting for holy war," and asserted that "the convention brought out the fact that women, when aroused to the importance, will stand together in fighting solidarity."[105] The "Song of Free Women" declared, "We are women strong for women warring."[106] In New York City, Belmont declared her hope that the envoys' trip and petition would "convince [Congress] that, like the fighting nations of Europe, we intend to continue the struggle as long as they compel us to do so."[107] The newspaper coverage of the envoys also used militaristic language to describe the envoys. The *Kansas City Post* called Mabel Vernon "the advance guard of a small suffrage army which intends to take Kansas City for the 'votes for women' cause." In response to one of their questions, Vernon told the *Post* that "an invading army never betrays its military secrets."[108]

The *Philadelphia Record* described the envoys' event in Philadelphia as an "affair very like the triumphal entry of a conqueror."[109] The imagery of battles and territorial conquest positioned the East as the enemy to be conquered. The *Washington Herald* featured the East as "enemies [*sic*] country" and the "strongholds of anti-suffrage sentiment."[110] In contrast, the *San Francisco Bulletin*'s conquest language imagined California as "the political stronghold of women."[111] The *Emporia Gazette* predicted that once the envoys left the suffrage territory of the first half of their trip and arrived in their first non-suffrage territory of Missouri, Field would "face her first hostile crowd" in Kansas City.[112]

Like the discourse of Manifest Destiny and many civilizing missions, suffragists justified their conquest of the East as benevolent and helpful. Civilizing missions were often rationalized as helping indigenous groups who Europeans believed could not civilize themselves. European Americans justified taking land from American Indians and forcing them to abandon their lifestyle in order to "civilize" them and help them become more like European Americans.[113] Similarly, Field emphasized the way Western women were attempting to help women in the East, because disenfranchised women could not help themselves. In the *San Francisco Bulletin*, the Western suffragists declared that the "express purpose" of the convention was "for aiding their disenfranchised sisters."[114] In Boston, Field declared, "at the first call from the East, the 4,000,000 women voters of the West have risen as a unit on behalf of their sisters whom they have never even seen."[115] In New York City, the envoys appeared at a Congressional Union event held at Sherry's Ballroom, one of the ritziest restaurants in Manhattan, attended by about five hundred women. Jolliffe told the guests, "'I am glad to come East, to tell the women how ready we voters are to help them.'"[116] Then Field spoke, and the *New York Tribune* reported, "A tired little woman in a travel-worn brown suit stood in the glitter of Sherry's ballroom yesterday afternoon and held out a tired little brown hand. 'We want to help you, we voting women of the West,' she pleaded. 'Will you let us? Will you take our hand and help us in our fight for the Federal Amendment?'" The *Tribune* summarized Field's message as conveying that "Field had come all the way from San

Francisco by automobile to hold out that hand to the women of the East. For it, she said, she had shivered in the Rocky Mountain passes, starved in the Nevada deserts and spent a long night in a Kansas mud hole."[117] The language of benevolence celebrated women who helped other women and positioned the West as politically powerful, thus allowing Western suffragists to use their voting power to help their weak and dependent sisters in the East.

To justify the work of Western women, the envoys' civilizing mission featured Eastern women as uncivilized, "enslaved," or in need of Western women's voting power. During the Woman Voters Convention, the *San Francisco Bulletin* explained that to Western women, "Their Eastern disenfranchised sisters seemed like denizens of darkest Africa. To listen to them still arguing on the right to vote, what which they now accepted as the air is breathed, seemed ridiculous and even laughable."[118] They adopted the racial hierarchy of civilization discourse to depict disfranchised Eastern women as less civilized than Western women. The envoys' trip was presented as an effort to save the weak, "enslaved" Eastern women, much like the "Song of Free Women" described women in the East as weak, pleading, crying, and imploring for the West's help on bended knee. At the convention, Jolliffe said, "We are going through the states where women are enslaved in the factories and the mills, where they work long, back-aching hours, and cannot register their protest in any way."[119] Belmont told the Woman Voters Convention, "The western woman with the power of her ballot will give her enslaved sister justice and freedom."[120] The *Bulletin* depicted the West as the East's savior and reported that Eastern women at the convention "looked to California with hope in their eyes [and] expectations their hearts."[121] The envoys often pleaded with other Western women to help win the vote for women in the East. Field told a reception of Colorado women at Antlers Hotel "of the need of workers in the East for independence. It is a Macedonian cry we western women are hearing—'Come over into our land and help us.'"[122] As the suffragists urged Western women to help Eastern women get the right to vote, they often positioned Eastern women as weak and dependent on Western women.

The Envoys' Arrival in Washington as Material Evidence of Western Women's Political Power

On December 6, 1915, nearly three months after they departed from San Francisco, the envoys arrived in Washington and presented themselves and their petition to members of Congress and to President Wilson. The cuws timed the arrival in Washington to coincide with the first day of the new 64th Congress, when Representative Mondell of Wyoming would reintroduce the Susan B. Anthony amendment. A suffragist told the *Washington Herald* that they planned this event "with deep design" so that "every Congressman who watched the performance, who saw the group of dignified women from all parts of the country making their way to Congress on the first day of its assemblage would have that picture as one of the first and most lasting impressions of this sixty-fourth Congress."[123] Their Washington reception included as much pageantry and fanfare as their departure in San Francisco. The ceremonial presentation of the petition included one thousand marching women with flags and banners, a brass band, decorated cars, twelve women on horseback, and twelve girls in liberty caps to represent the twelve enfranchised states (see figures 32 and 33).[124] The *New Haven Register* described the performance as an "impressive sight" with purple and yellow flags, banners, robes, chrysanthemums, bows, pennants, and bunting.[125] About a hundred members of Congress met the envoys on the Capitol steps to receive the petition (figure 34). The women rolled out a portion of the huge petition to show some of the many signatures of Western voters, and Field claimed that "the petition spread out at full length would extend for more than four miles."[126] Field and Jolliffe spoke to Senator Sutherland of Utah and Representative Mondell and asked to speak on the floor of the House. Their request was not granted, but Sutherland and Mondell "assured the suffrage envoys that the dignity and importance of their mission, backed as it was by four million voting women, would receive the most serious attention of Congress."[127]

After the presentation of their petition to Congress, the envoys and the parade continued their march to the White House to meet with

Figure 32. Procession of two thousand women, including the envoys and other Western women voters, marching to the US Capitol to present their petition to a deputation from Congress, December 1915.

Figure 33. The envoys arriving at the Capitol steps in the car they drove across the country, December 1915.

Figure 34. Parade of envoys from San Francisco arriving at Capitol, December 6, 1915.

President Wilson who agreed to receive the envoys and other invited guests. The women asked Wilson to look at their petition with the signatures of so many Western voters and consider endorsing the national suffrage amendment in his message to Congress. Wilson looked at the petition "with interest," but was "sorry to say that it is too late to take under consideration your request that I embody this in my message." He explained that his speech had already been completed and sent to the newspapers, and he preferred to address only "one subject at a time for fear that two subjects might compete with one another for prominence." Yet he acknowledged that "nothing could be more impressive than the presentation of such a request in such numbers and backed by such influences as undoubtedly stand back of you." He also promised to "always have an open mind," and to "confer in the most serious way with my colleagues in regard to what is the right thing to do at this time concerning this great matter."[128]

The suffragists interpreted Wilson's response positively. Field said that his "remarks were most encouraging. He showed a desire to concili-ate. His attitude was of genuine interest, not merely one of just being willing to hear us."[129] Kealty Claggett, a Washington suffragist, told the *Washington Herald*, "The President was in one of his best moods. I heard him speak on many occasions and on many subjects but I was never more favorably impressed . . . This time he gave us the impression that he would give us more substantial support."[130] And Mrs. Lowenburg said, "President Wilson was very friendly . . . He said he realized there was a great influence behind our movement. This was the first time he has ever given us this kind of a response and we have every reason to feel exul-tant." The *New York Sun* reported that after meeting with Wilson, "suffrage leaders issued statements saying the President's utterances showed that he was not against, if he was not for, the proposed amendment to the Constitution and intimat[ed] that they expect to secure his support."[131]

Suffragists' public statements suggested that the envoys' trip and presentation of their appeal in Washington were effective. The *Washington Post* reported, "the women were confident that their latest pilgrimage to the White House had been the most fruitful of all."[132] When a reporter for the *Washington Herald* asked Claggett whether she thought the trip was "a means toward real persuasion?" she responded, "Indeed I do. Men do not like to be argued with. They do not like to quarrel with women. In a demonstration like this we show them our enthusiasm and our confi-dence, we put that spirit into a spectacle that they can see for themselves, and it cannot fail to have a favorable impression."[133]

Although the envoys did not speak on the floor of the House as they requested, they did speak before the House Judiciary Committee, the Democratic National Committee, and the Republican National Com-mittee, and were able to convey the power the West had to shape future elections.[134] At the Republican National Committee, Jolliffe "roused the committee to laughter and applause when she said, 'We have the last word, gentlemen, because we have the votes . . . Sadly you are wrecked out [in the West]. Here is your chance—the votes of 4,000,000 women." Field added in her message that the enfranchised women in the West "will remember at election time the action of the parties for or against the suffrage measure."[135] Several months after the envoys arrived in Washington, she reflected on their trip and recounted, "The only thing those men in Washington care about is voters, and when we showed them the votes behind us, they were afraid not to listen. Even President Wilson changed his mind when he saw the strength behind us." She also said, "A very prominent Republican said to me after the demonstration, 'This thing has put suffrage on the national map. It has now become a party issue. Congress is afraid of it. . . . They are afraid of the western women if they vote against it. They realize that this is a presidential year and that the western suffrage states control 91 electoral votes—the balance of power."[136] The envoys communicated that Western women were a political force and that they would use their power in future elections to hurt politicians who did not support the federal amendment.

The suffragist envoys' transcontinental feat made Western women's political power apparent to Eastern suffragists and politicians. Instead of mailing letters and requests for federal suffrage, the Western envoys showed up in person after crossing the continent by car with material evidence of half a million voters' support for the federal amendment. By physically representing the Western women voters through their presence and petition, they demonstrated the electoral influence Western women had accumulated and constituted themselves as a political force for politicians to respect and heed. As Belmont commented on their "monster petition" in New York City, "Suffrage petitions have been submitted to Congress from time immemorial, but none that was backed by the strength of four million votes."[137] For in the following election year, women would be able to vote for president in twelve states and would represent ninety-one votes in the Electoral College, which was dramatically more than in 1912, when women could only vote in six states, representing thirty-seven Electoral College votes. Field explained that the petition provided tangible evidence to support the cuws's claim that "there are enough women voters in this country to elect the president." She warned that "President Wilson may well take this into account. . . . There are 4,000,000 voting women today. They have something to say politically and they will say it. They can swing the election."[138] The envoys' presence and trip concretely reminded politicians in the West and the East "what it will mean to alienate four million voters."[139]

The envoys also encouraged Eastern suffragists in their own efforts. After Wilson's reception of the envoys, Lowenburg declared to the *New York Sun*, "My eyes were opened by the attitude of the women of the West. I believe we made a brilliant move by going west and securing the help of the Western women."[140] Ida Husted Harper told the *Washington Times* that the "most impressive and historic scene" to occur on the Capitol steps was "of three little women voters from three states in the far West appealing for political liberty of their millions of disenfranchised sisters."[141] Claggett told the *Washington Herald* that when "we who marched down Pennsylvania avenue with our colors waving in the wind could not help but feel that those who watched us caught something of the spirit of enthusiasm and determination of those Western women."[142] That week the Congressional Union held their national convention, which included reports and speeches by Field and many women from Western states. In her welcoming address, Mrs. Nina Allender declared, "The coming of the women of the West to aid us here in the East in our struggle for enfranchisement is one of the most inspiring things that has ever developed in suffrage work."[143] And when the envoys appeared at a fundraiser in the Belasco Theater to tell the story of their transcontinental trip, four thousand dollars were raised in twenty-five minutes, which the *Washington Herald* author believed "showed in the most striking manner their firm belief that the promise of the women voters of the West to wield their political power in behalf of the unfranchised women of the East will make this Federal campaign the last."

Conclusion

Like the suffrage speeches, maps, and writing of other suffragists, Field and her suffragist companions exploited the meaning of the West as a symbol of women's political freedom and power. Their trip leveraged the new meanings of the West and East to advocate for suffrage—images of the East as the new mythic frontier and the West as a place of civilization, progress, and women's freedom. Like the suffrage maps and the speeches of Rankin and Robinson, the envoys' trip also envisioned the Western suffrage states as more civilized and powerful than the East. The envoys concretely enacted the physical process of bringing suffrage east, similar to the way Western pioneers traveled overland to the West. The performance of transcontinental travel embodied twentieth-century pioneering, which allowed the envoys to appropriate and reverse the rhetorics of continental expansion and the frontier myth.

The envoys' modern pioneering enacted and reversed the traditional frontier mythology as they performed the role of the frontier heroines and exploited the frontier myth for women's voting rights. Like Duniway's frontier myth that justified woman suffrage, the envoys' trip implied that by enduring their struggle on the frontier and completing their rite of passage, they had earned equal voting rights for women. Even Congress and President Wilson recognized that their feat at the very least deserved a public presentation of their petition and demand. In an important departure from Duniway, the envoys' trip invoked frontier mythology not only for the voting rights of Western women who had completed the frontier trek, but also for the disfranchised women of the East. The petition filled with Western women's signatures visualized Western women's political capacity to influence national politics, and the envoys' superior grit enacted Western women voters' determination to use their political power for national women's voting rights. The envoys survived the many difficulties they faced on their journey, enacted their independence and freedom, and proved themselves as exceptional heroines who had earned a federal amendment for women's voting rights. They also physically demonstrated their determination to win those rights for women. The envoys' triumph communicated their intention and ability to win national women's voting rights was a powerful force to be reckoned with.

Performing an inverted form of continental expansion rhetoric for suffrage asserted the power and ability of Western women and their suffrage cause. The depiction of the envoys as a civilizing mission, destined by God to succeed, implied the rightness of their cause and the inevitability of their success. They suggested that women's voting rights were destined to succeed in the East, just as the United States' continental expansion had succeeded in the West. Like Robinson and Rankin, the envoys and the cuws equated woman suffrage with civilization and maintained the West's superior civilization and deserving status as a model for the East to emulate. The envoys' civilizing mission also positioned Eastern women as helpless and dependent on Western women. Like Duniway, the envoys imagined Eastern women as weaker than Western women. But whereas Duniway associated this weakness with their life of ease in the civilized East, having not been tested on the frontier, the envoys saw them as weak because the East had not yet been civilized by women's voting rights. The envoys' arrival in the East provided material evidence of Western women's political power, shrewdness, and ability to use their votes to win national woman suffrage.

Like the suffrage maps, the envoys' trip appropriated and reversed the imagery of Manifest Destiny, and performed the process of the civilization and progress of woman suffrage moving east. In the process, the trip implied that the federal amendment was inevitable and equated women's voting rights with civilization and progress. In addition to presenting a compelling embodied argument to Congress and President Wilson, the trip effectively raised enthusiasm and secured political support for the federal amendment across the country. Their trip constituted Western women as politically powerful and encouraged Eastern suffragists that their suffrage success was fast approaching, as Western women would undoubtedly use their votes to ensure national women's voting rights in the 1916 election.

Afterword

———— • • ————

J ust days after the presidential election of 1916, as the nation waited to learn that the incumbent Woodrow Wilson had defeated Charles Hughes to secure his office, the *Woman's Journal* reviewed the election cycle and declared that the "new principle" in national politics was that "the spirit of the West has proved the dominant factor." The *Woman's Journal* asserted, "One fact is definitely established—the States where women vote have been the decisive factors. For the first time in the history of the country the political power of the States west of the Missouri River has successfully rivaled that of the industrial States of the East."[1] What was different in 1916 that had not been true of other presidential elections was that the Western states held enough electoral votes to sway the election. The *Woman's Journal* explained, "Until the year 1916, any candidate who carried New York, Pennsylvania, Indiana, Michigan, and Illinois has been sure of election." But this year, the states that held

Figure 35. Rollin Kirby, "Pauline Revere," *New York World*, November 9, 1916.

electoral power included "California, Oregon, Nevada, Wyoming, Kansas, Idaho, New Mexico, North Dakota and Minnesota."

Newspapers around the country similarly declared the power of the West in the 1916 presidential election.[2] The *Boston Globe* pronounced, "Political power has taken Horace Greeley's advice with a vengeance, gone West and grown up with the country. As late as 1896 the belfry on City Hall in New York was the pivot of presidential elections. In two decades the center of gravity has shifted out beyond Chicago." The *New York World* agreed that "the issue [of the election] rested wholly with the West, and that the West would determine whether President Wilson was defeated or re-elected." The *New York Evening Post*, during the days after the election, commented, "Whoever has carried the election, the United States stands today in the presence of something like a political revolution. It glares at one from the map. The scepter of power is passing to the West in conjunction with the South and Southwest." To visualize their claim, the *New York World* published "Pauline Revere," a political cartoon that symbolized Western women's voting power with a Paul Revere figure riding in from the West with the election results (see figure 35). The Revere image was modified to appear like the Pony Express representing the West and feminized with the name Pauline to indicate women's vote. Instead of the news of an impending British invasion, Pauline Revere brought the election results from the West, suggesting that Western women had determined the election.[3]

For suffragists, the West's rising political power was especially promising, since most of those Western states now included women in their electorate. Suffragists frequently claimed that the twelve suffrage states included four million women voters and ninety-one electoral votes—one fifth of the total electoral votes and one third of the votes necessary to elect a president who supported a national suffrage amendment.[4] Women's influence had increased since the 1912 election, when two million could vote in six states, representing thirty-seven votes in the Electoral College. The growing power of the suffrage states gave women the exciting opportunity to influence the election of the president, twenty-two US senators, and forty US representatives.[5]

Political cartoons also visualized Western women's opportunity to sway the presidential election. The *Saturday Evening Post* visualized women's dominance in national politics as "a new ringmaster" (see figure 36). The cartoon represented the suffrage movement as a white woman with the strength and power of four million women voters to use as a whip to make the major political parties support women's right to vote. Fredrikke S. Palmer, the *Woman's Journal*'s cartoonist and art director, visualized the Democratic donkey and Republican elephant eyeing the Western suffrage states on the map and considering their electoral power as a "tempting morsel" for their campaign (see figure 37). These images asserted Western women's potential to shape the election.

The West's influence on national politics in 1916 was key to suffragists' political strategy as the cuws worked to mobilize Western women's vote to secure a national amendment to the Constitution. The cuws organized Western women voters to form the Woman's Party, which was briefly called the Woman's Party of Western Voters. The Woman's Party replaced the cuws chapters in the Western suffrage states, and the cuws continued

Reprinted in *Suffragist*, September 2, 1916.

Figure 36. Herbert Johnson, "A New Ringmaster," *Saturday Evening Post*, 1916.

Figure 37. Fredrikke S. Palmer, "A Tempting Morsel," *Woman's Journal*, May 20, 1916.

their work in the non-suffrage states. Alice Paul, the leader of the CUWS, reasoned that if women voters organized as an independent party and voted as a block, they could make a larger impact with their votes than if they divided their votes to help their own parties. Most political parties worked to elect their party candidate to office, but the Woman's Party focused instead on targeting whichever party was in power, since the party in power had blocked the passage of the federal amendment. They identified themselves as nonpartisan, but since the Democrats were in power, they worked to defeat the Democratic candidates running for election that year, even the ones who had supported the amendment. Since Hughes publicly endorsed the federal suffrage amendment in 1916, but Wilson did not support it until 1918, they campaigned against Wilson's re-election. They viewed this strategy as holding the Democrats responsible for their failure to enact the federal amendment.

For their political strategy to work, the CUWS had to convince Western women to comply. As Charles Beard wrote in the *New Republic* in the summer of 1916, "That a very small percentage of the women voters of the West can decide the fate of the presidential and congressional elections is a fact . . . [The Woman's Party] is aware that it cannot now swing the entire mass of women voters, it also knows that it does not have to swing more than a few thousand in each state."[6] So leading up to the 1916 election, the CUWS traveled around the West to organize its state branches in every suffrage state and present their appeal to Western women voters through three main strategies: the Suffrage Special, the launch of the Woman's Party, and a campaign against President Wilson in the weeks leading up to the election.

In the spring of 1916, the CUWS sent women envoys from the East "to appeal to the voting women of the West" with the Suffrage Special: twenty-three Eastern members of the CUWS traveled across the continent on a four-week tour to raise support for the federal amendment. But this time the envoys traveled by train, in a railroad car dedicated entirely to the CUWS. And instead of taking their message to Wilson or Congress, they directed their appeal to Western women voters. When the CUWS advertised the official "Farewell to the Women Envoys to the West" at

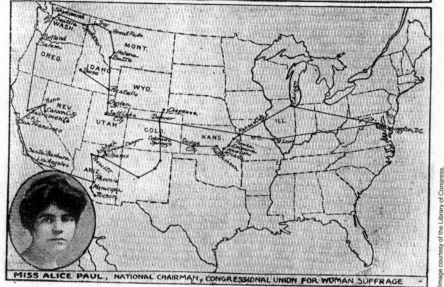

Figure 38. Map showing the route of the "Suffrage Special" to appeal to Western women voters, 1916.

Union Station, they described the envoys: "They go bearing petitions of appeal from thousands of societies in the East, to the enfranchised women of the West asking them to put their political strength back of the immediate passage of the Susan B. Anthony Amendment for Woman Suffrage."[7] When the Suffrage Special left Washington, DC, for their Western tour, five thousand suffragists gathered to send off the women envoys to the West.[8] Lucy Burns led the expedition and the twenty-three travelers included Alva Belmont and Harriot Stanton Blatch. The *Suffragist* claimed that "never has a crusade for political liberty been undertaken by a more distinguished group, representing an unenfranchised class, than that which left Washington this week to ask for help from the free women of the West."[9]

The Suffrage Special visited and held demonstrations in Illinois, Kansas, Wyoming, Colorado, New Mexico, Arizona, California,

Nevada, Oregon, Washington, Montana, Idaho, Utah, and Missouri before returning to Washington, DC (see figure 38). The CUWS members in the Western states organized welcoming receptions and meetings for the traveling envoys, and often arranged for Western political officials like mayors and governors to participate and publicly endorse the federal amendment. At their first event in Chicago, Florence Kelly explained to their audience that "at last we are turning from the men in the East who do not understand to the women in the West who will understand."[10] The envoys invited Western women voters to join them in June for a convention in Chicago that would launch the Woman's Party and work to pass the federal suffrage amendment. When the Suffrage Special arrived in Maricopa, Arizona, a reporter described, someone in the crowd that met the train "gruffly demanded" of the porter, "What are they coming out here for? Don't they know that women vote out West, now?" The porter replied "Of co'se. That's why they's comin' here. This is where the powah am!"[11] Before returning to Washington, the Suffrage Special stopped at the 1916 Woman Voters' Conference that was held in Salt Lake City in May that year, and attended by women delegates from all of the suffrage states. The delegates of the voting West pledged to prioritize the federal amendment that election year and strategized to use Western women's vote as a "united voice of the disfranchised east and the enfranchised west."[12]

In June 1916, the CUWS formally launched the Woman's Party at a three-day convention at the Blackstone Theater in Chicago (see figure 39). The packed theater listened to speakers like Helen Keller and Maud Younger, and elected Western women like Anne Martin of Nevada to lead the Woman's Party so that "the task of further organizing women voters of the west behind the Susan B. Anthony amendment was for the first time definitely taken over by western women."[13] Belmont read aloud the convention call that "appeal[ed] to the four million enfranchised women of the West, urging them to do all in their power to press for the immediate passage of the national suffrage amendment."[14] The convention, which the *Suffragist* later described as the "most historic event" of 1916, gathered thousands of women around the country and created a

Figure 39. Opening Session of the Woman's Party Convention that launched the formation of the Woman's Party, Blackstone Theater, Chicago, June 5, 1916.

"full fledged woman's political party," which mimicked many political strategies of third-parties.[15] Before the convention's end, the Woman's Party formally resolved to support Republican candidate for president, Charles Hughes, because of his public endorsement of the federal amendment.

From August until the November election, the Woman's Party focused on campaigning against the Democratic Party in the twelve suffrage states (see figure 40). In the weeks before the presidential election, the CUWS toured the West to urge Westerners to vote against Wilson and the Democratic congressional candidates to protest their failure to endorse a federal amendment. Inez Milholland, one of the most beloved and famous Eastern suffragists, served as the "Flying Envoy," as she toured twelve thousand miles in the suffrage states by car to appeal to Western voters to support the suffrage issue by voting against

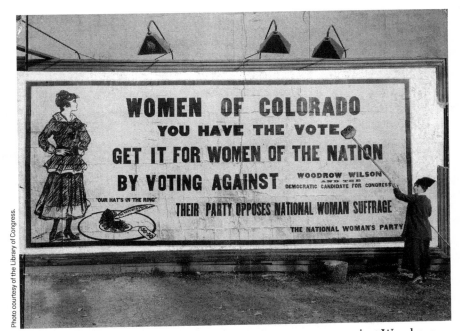

Figure 40. Suffrage billboard urging Western women to vote against Woodrow Wilson and the Democratic Party, Denver, 1916.

Wilson. During this trip, Milholland fell sick while speaking for the federal amendment and died soon after the tour, which was a rallying cry for many suffragists. Although Milholland was well loved, plenty of Western Democrats described the Eastern suffragists' Western tours as interference and did not appreciate being told how to vote. On October 19, 1916, the Woman's Party silently protested outside of the Chicago auditorium where Wilson was speaking. Their protest angered Western Democrats and a mob of Western men attacked the silent protesters and took their signs. Many Western women were loyal Democrats or pacifists who supported Wilson's success at keeping the United States out of the war during his first term in office. Western representatives and voters largely agreed with the administration's progressive legislation, reform measures, and maintenance of peace, so the Woman's Party's campaign was controversial and met with resistance.[16]

The West's significance for national politics was emphasized by that year's close election. Because Wilson's victory was so narrow, the nation had to wait several days for the returns from the West Coast to come in. The earliest returns, from the states in the Northeast, showed Hughes winning. It was not until Friday morning that enough of the Western votes had been counted to show that he had won the Electoral College.[17] Wilson eventually secured California's thirteen electoral votes by a victory of 0.38%, which won him the election. The election was so close that several thousand more votes (out of over a million) for Hughes in California would have swung the election. Although Hughes won most of the Northeastern states, Wilson took most of the West and South. Days after the election, the *New York Times* declared:

> The complexion of the national political map underwent marked transformation in last Tuesday's election . . . New political zones were established. New York, the Eastern States, and the Middle West, once the deciding block in Presidential elections, were wiped out by the Far West and part of the Middle West casting their lot with the solid South . . . There is no overlooking the fact that the Far West has thrown its lot in with the solid South, and no longer seems to be dependent on the East.[18]

The West's election of Wilson underscored the region's political power and independence, and defied the Woman's Party's numerous campaigns.

The Western suffrage states' support of Wilson, who won every suffrage state except Oregon, was largely seen as a defeat for the Woman's Party and the CUWS, and many claimed that it was Western women that kept Wilson in office. The *New York Times* reported that "political observers here are asserting that the dominating votes of women (in support of Wilson) in California, Washington, and other States may set the suffrage movement back twenty-five years."[19] But of the suffrage states, Wilson only won fifty-seven electoral votes, compared to the sixty-nine he won in 1912, so the Woman's Party counted that as a victory. The Woman's

Party also maintained that even with the loss, they had "succeeded in making the national enfranchisement of women one of the dominant issues in the campaign throughout suffrage territory." At the end of 1916, the cuws reviewed the year and maintained in the *Suffragist* that 1916 had "been the year of greatest activity and greatest accomplishment since the cuws began its active fight for the passage of the federal suffrage amendment." Furthermore, they believed that their work had effectively made "astute politicians realize that the women of the nation are now able to make a political demand which must be heeded." They had successfully "visualize[d] to Congressmen, to political leaders, and the general public the existence of the woman voter and her interest in national suffrage."[20]

After 1916, woman suffrage discourse shifted away from the West. In 1917, New York's suffrage campaign succeeded, and once New York women were enfranchised, woman suffrage was no longer solely a Western phenomenon. That same year, the Woman's Party merged with the cuws to form the National Woman's Party (nwp). Western women voters were active in both the nwp and the National American Woman Suffrage Association (nawsa), but both organizations focused less on the Western suffrage states and more on persuading Wilson and Congress. The nwp and the nawsa advocated the passage of the federal amendment through different strategies. Carrie Chapman Catt's "Winning Plan" for the nawsa focused mostly on the federal amendment but also supported some of the important state campaigns. While the nawsa continued to use more moderate and conservative advocacy strategies, the nwp continued their militant campaign by picketing President Wilson in front of the White House.

The federal amendment was finally achieved as public opinion turned. Wilson publicly endorsed it, Congress passed it, and the states finally ratified it. But each of these actions required extensive advocacy. The nwp's White House pickets became especially controversial after the United States entered World War I. They were met with arrests and time in prison. When the imprisoned protestors positioned themselves as political prisoners and went on hunger strikes, they were violently force-fed to prevent them from dying at the hands of the Wilson administration.

As the public learned about the way upper-class white women were being abused in prison, public sentiment pressured Wilson to publicly support the federal suffrage amendment on January 9, 1918. The day after his statement of support, the House of Representatives passed the amendment for the first time by one vote, but the Senate did not. To compel the Senate to pass the amendment, suffragists spent another year and a half lobbying their representatives in the West and the East, going on national speaking tours, protesting and picketing at the US Capitol, the Senate Office Building, and Lafayette Park in Washington, DC.[21] During this time, more protesting suffragists were attacked by police, arrested, and imprisoned. They again went on hunger strikes and were violently abused. They also ran another Western tour called the "Prison Special" to raise support for the federal amendment and encourage voters to tell their senators to endorse it. Suffragists who had been imprisoned went on this tour to tell Westerners about how they were treated in prison to increase their sympathy.[22] On June 4, 1919, the Senate passed the amendment, and it was approved by Congress.

Then the ratification campaign began. For over a year, suffragists campaigned for the required thirty-six state legislatures to meet and ratify the amendment by a three-fourths majority. Although all of the Western suffrage states eventually ratified the amendment, they did not do so as readily as suffragists had hoped. Suffragists again published suffrage maps to visualize which states had ratified the amendment with black and white (see figure 41). The regional pattern of Western suffrage states on the suffrage map did not appear on the ratification map. The *Remonstrance* called it the "Melancholy Map," because "from the suffrage point of view, the most depressing [feature of the map] was the prevailing funereal hue over the Western suffrage states. It was assumed by the suffragists that the states which had woman suffrage through state laws would tumble over each other in their haste to spread suffrage through ratification of the amendment. Nothing of the sort."[23] The NAWSA and the NWP appealed to Western governors to call special ratifying sessions to ratify the federal amendment. The NWP also sent delegates to the Democratic and Republican Conventions to convince them to support

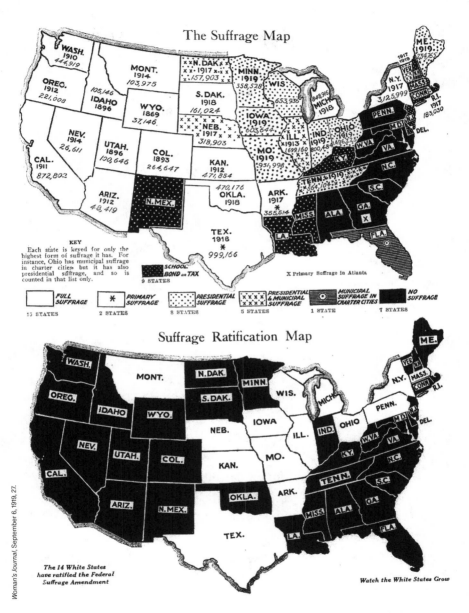

Figure 41. The suffrage map contrasted with the ratification map three months into the ratification campaign.

ratification and put a woman suffrage plank in their party platform, and succeeded with the Democrats. In March of 1920, Washington ratified the amendment and became the thirty-fifth state to do so, and the last Western suffrage state. Finally, Tennessee's state legislature narrowly ratified the amendment by one vote, giving suffragists their thirty-sixth state, and officially made the amendment law on August 26, 1920.

The West and the Woman Suffrage Movement

Woman suffragists successfully achieved the federal amendment to the Constitution through the militant strategies of the NWP and the traditional tactics of the NAWSA, both of which leveraged the power and meaning of the Western suffrage states in their advocacy around the nation. Western suffrage states played an important role in the national campaign and demonstrated the numerous ways suffragists strategically employed and reimagined the meaning of the West. Between Wyoming Territory's enfranchisement of women in 1869 and the 1916 presidential election, the Western suffrage states and the meaning of the West shaped the woman suffrage movement.

Suffragists strategically deployed the West as a rhetorical resource: they verbally evoked the meaning of the West in their speeches, writing, and publications; they visually appealed to the West in their posters, flags, maps, and cartoons; and they embodied the West in their parades, pageants, tableaus, and automobile touring. Furthermore, Americans debating women's voting rights strategically imagined the meaning of the Western suffrage states in a variety of ways: a mythic frontier for women's freedom; a civilized and imperial power; a wild and woolly region of primitivism; a domesticated model of American progress and democracy; and a civilized suffrage territory expanding to the new Eastern frontier.

Suffragists helped make women's voting rights matter through their preferred visions of the West. They capitalized on the Western suffrage states' existence to legitimize women's voting rights and champion their movement as powerful, growing, and successful. Furthermore, their use of region in protest appealed to Americans' fascination with the West as the region was shaped by the ideas of the mythic frontier, civilization, and continental expansion. As Americans grieved the exceptionalism that they believed the mythic frontier had provided, the suffrage movement's use of regional rhetoric gave Americans a new frontier to conquer for women's voting rights: the East. Suffragists positioned white women's voting rights as in line with national values that the mythic frontier often represented—the values of individualism, independence, bravery, and grit. The suffrage movement came to be represented by a region that many Americans revered, and invited Americans to imagine suffragists, at least for a time, as frontier heroines who had earned their right to vote, civilized the West, and were destined to succeed across the nation.

In the nineteenth century, Abigail Scott Duniway appealed to Americans' preoccupation with the changing West by employing the frontier myth to advocate women's voting rights. She mythologized the West as a place of freedom and equality for white women, and envisioned white Western women as frontier heroines who deserved the franchise. Her myth naturalized women's liberty in the West and maintained the masculine and white ideals of US citizenship and the frontier myth. Although it did not always include Eastern women, her frontier myth for women's rights continued to circulate in suffrage discourse into the twentieth century. In the early twentieth century, suffragists celebrated and promoted the Western suffrage states with visual images like flags and maps. The maps constituted suffrage advocates as successful and powerful as they also disrupted and employed the meaning of the West. As the maps of women's voting rights legitimized the existence of woman suffrage, they also visualized the Western suffrage states as powerful and civilized. Their regional patterns contested traditional meanings of the West as a frontier by depicting it as more civilized than the East. Over time, they allowed suffragists to deploy regional rhetorics like civilization, continental expansion, and Manifest Destiny to depict women's voting rights expanding eastward.

Antisuffragists dismissed the maps' claims about the Western suffrage states' significance with the rhetoric of the woolly West. They opposed women's voting rights by envisioning the West as uncultivated,
immature, and unevolved with the rhetoric of civilization and its racialized, gendered, classed, and mobility-based premises. Their regional
rhetoric appealed to many Easterners' ideals of the West as static and
halted in time, resistant to the civilizing forces of the rest of the nation.
But the antis' vision of the West as irrelevant, uncivilized, and temporally dislocated clashed with suffragists' efforts to tactically deploy the
meaning of the West and with Westerners' efforts to build their lives and
communities. To defend the image of the Western states from the smears
of Eastern antis, Jeannette Rankin and Helen Ring Robinson toured
the East disproving the antis' claims and boosting the many advances of
the progressive and modern West. These elected officials from Western
states used their political notoriety and traditional femininity to defend
the region against the antis' claims and featured it as a place of freedom,
progress, and civilization. They domesticated the image of the West and
women's participation in politics as progressive, civilized, and modern—
a model for the East to emulate.

As the West had become a well-known symbol of women's voting
rights, suffragists embodied the Western states in their parades, pageants, and tableaus. Suffragists eventually expanded these performances
into an adventurous transcontinental car trip. When Sara Bard Field
and her companions drove from San Francisco to Washington, DC,
with the giant petition from Western voters, they enacted and reversed
the rhetorics of the frontier myth and continental expansion to bring
woman suffrage to the East. By personifying modern frontier heroines,
the envoys suggested that they had earned the endorsement of a federal
suffrage amendment. Simultaneously, their appropriation of continental expansion rhetoric implied that they were destined to bring the
civilization of Western woman suffrage to the East. Their performance
vividly embodied the political power and determination of Western
women voters for President Wilson and members of Congress. In the
following campaign year of 1916, suffragists focused on wielding their

political power in the West to influence the presidential and congressional elections. As women appealed to Western women voters to use their voting power to support national women's voting rights, they often constructed Western women voters as the East's politically powerful saviors. Although the United States did not elect a president in 1916 who endorsed suffrage immediately, President Wilson eventually supported the federal amendment in the years to come. The eventual success of the woman suffrage movement took decades of work, numerous advocacy organizations, and thousands of committed activists and leaders. To win the Nineteenth Amendment to the Constitution, suffragists used many inspired agitation tactics, one of which was the leveraging and reimagining of the West.

Region in Protest

The West's role in the woman suffrage movement illuminates *region in protest* as another rhetorical strategy advocates have at their disposal: tactically leveraging or contesting the meaning of region. Activists can strategically evoke and reimagine region to advocate social change. Regional rhetoric can be a valuable persuasive resource for social movements because of its ability to connect disparate sites and places to each other and to particular histories, meanings, and politics. Since regions are rhetorics of relationships, region has the capacity to disrupt and re-envision the meaning of movements, politics, and places, and their relationship to each other. Challenging, shaping, and constructing the location or meaning of region can provide rhetorical power for protest, and provide advocates with an avenue for creating and expanding a social movement's networks, relationships, or rhetorical strategies.

The US suffrage movement illustrates how region can be employed by social movement activists in at least three ways. Advocates can deploy the traditional or dominant meaning of a region in social protest, like Duniway and other suffragists who invoked the traditional meaning of the West as a mythic frontier to justify women's voting rights. Activists can also contest and reimagine the meaning of a region that is connected to a social movement, as the suffrage maps, parades, pageants, and tableaus did, as well as the speeches of Robinson and Rankin. Protesters can also deploy a new and re-envisioned meaning of a region in social protest. As the West came to be identified with women's voting rights, and was regularly featured as more civilized than the East, suffragists invoked the new image of the civilized Western suffrage states and asserted that women's voting rights were expanding imperially and were destined to spread across the continent like Manifest Destiny.

Likewise, a social movement's opponents can also tactically appeal to that region by disputing or refuting the social movement's preferred visions of that region. Since no region has an authentic meaning but is always in the ongoing process of being invented, any region has multiple and competing definitions. Residents and outsiders often favor different meanings for a region, since they have different uses and purposes, and they attempt to strategically define, evoke, and describe a region according to their preferences. When a social movement attempts to employ and reimagine a region's meaning, it can be contested or resisted by opponents and by those who have vested interests in the meaning of that region. When suffragists employed region in protest, both antisuffragists and Eastern residents resisted their visions of the West. As woman suffragists exploited the meaning of the West, their preferred vision often aligned most closely with Westerners' ideal regional rhetoric. But antis also had at their disposal the wild and woolly rhetoric that was already widely used.

A region's meaning can also be shaped by its symbolic role in a social movement. The West was employed in debates over woman suffrage to such an extent that over time public discourse identified women's voting rights with the West. Eventually, the continued and varied ways the West was used in suffrage advocacy shaped the way that Americans discussed the West and the East. The rhetorical process of shaping the suffrage movement with the meaning of the West disrupted the meaning of the West in national public discourse—at least temporarily. Likewise, championing region in protest may simultaneously disrupt the meaning of the region in the process.

Region as a tool for social protest is not limited to large, domestic regions like the West, South, and East. Because any region's network of sites and relationship to meanings, politics, and histories are unstable, they are rhetorically malleable and available to be reimagined and deployed for persuasive purposes. There are smaller and newer regions that may be more persuasive and relevant for particular movements and moments in time. Silicon Valley, America's Heartland, the Rust Belt, Appalachia, the Great Plains, the Rocky Mountain West, and the Bible Belt are all regions that associate particular sites to each other and to particular histories, practices, politics, or values. Furthermore, there are countless transnational regions that have the capacity to be contested and redeployed for social change.

Finally, the rhetoricity of region in protest is historically contextual. Some regions are more rhetorically powerful at some moments in history than at others. The rhetoric of the West was most powerful for suffragists during the years shortly after Americans believed the frontier had closed, and they collectively competed to shape its meaning. Easterners' interest in the region grew as their nostalgia for the old West increased and descriptions of life in the frontier West were romanticized. At other moments in time, and for other movements and campaigns, other regions have and will be more central to American identity and more rhetorically powerful. Regions that are in the midst of change and transition may be more readily available to be deployed and re-envisioned for advocacy purposes because their region-making rhetorics will most likely be more prevalent in public discourse and therefore, more convenient rhetorical resources for social movements.

Region scholars have established that no map, performance, or speech can fully define or represent a particular region. Yet maps, performances, and speeches can be used to evoke and disrupt the meaning of a region as a persuasive strategy—especially when a region is particularly salient to popular culture at the time. In the early twentieth century, the cultural project of region-making the settled West was so ubiquitous in American public life that the West's region-making rhetorics made convenient rhetorical resources for women's rights activists to exploit. Furthermore, as Americans employed a variety of meanings of the West to understand, explain, advocate, and oppose women's voting rights, the meanings of the West and women's voting rights mutually influenced each other. During the early twentieth century, both the West and the woman suffrage movement matured, and in the process, the West played a significant role in the campaign for women's voting rights.

Notes

———— ·◆· ————

INTRODUCTION

1. "400,000 Cheer Suffrage March," *New York Times*, November 10, 1912, 1.
2. "400,000 Cheer Suffrage March," *New York Times*, November 10, 1912, 8.
3. "Torches in Hair to Guide Parade," *New York Times*, November 8, 1912, 7.
4. Although Western states fully enfranchised women before the Nineteenth Amendment was passed, their electorates still restricted women and men according to race, ethnicity, citizenship, literacy, property, and residency. Idaho, Washington, and Montana excluded most American Indians from their electorates. Wyoming, Washington, Oregon, Arizona, and California restricted their franchise to those who could demonstrate their ability to read and write in English. Utah, Oregon, and Arizona restricted some elections to property holders or property tax payers. Almost all Western states required residency for a particular number of months or years before being eligible to vote. Arizona, California, Colorado, Idaho, Kansas, Montana, and Oregon excluded inmates

of institutions. Many of these restrictions functionally disfranchised immigrants and black and brown women and men. Alexander Keyssar, *The Right to Vote: The Contested History of Democracy in the United States* (New York: Basic Books, 2000), 321–368.

5. I focus on the suffrage movement's regional rhetoric by building on the extensive scholarship on women's activism and public participation in the nineteenth and early twentieth centuries, including Karlyn Kohrs Campbell's recovery and analysis of early feminist advocacy and the foundational literature her work has inspired. More recent scholarship has begun examining the way women in the West, Midwest, and South appealed to regional cultures, ideals, and practices in their advocacy. Sara Hayden, Cindy Koenig Richards, and Casey Ryan Kelly have illuminated the ways that Western women creatively employed Western ideologies, heroes, and narratives to advocate for the vote, convince Western women of their agency, and create new roles for women. I extend their work to reveal that the West was also used to champion the right to vote around the country in both the West and the East. Instead of examining the way women adapted to audiences within specific regions, I highlight the ways suffragists invoked and reimagined the West in their national advocacy. Karlyn Kohrs Campbell, *Man Cannot Speak for Her*, vols. 1 and 2 (Westport, CT: Praeger Publishers, 1989); Martha M. Solomon, *A Voice of Their Own: The Woman Suffrage Press, 1840–1910* (Tuscaloosa: University of Alabama Press, 1991); Cheryl R. Jorgensen-Earp, *The Transfiguring Sword: The Just War of the Women's Social and Political Union* (Tuscaloosa: University of Alabama, 1997); Belinda A. Stillion Southard, *Militant Citizenship: Rhetorical Strategies of the National Woman's Party, 1913–1920* (College Station: Texas A&M University Press, 2011); Shirley Wilson Logan, *We Are Coming: The Persuasive Discourse of Nineteenth Century Black Women* (Carbondale: Southern Illinois University Press, 1999); Angela G. Ray, *The Lyceum and Public Culture in the Nineteenth-Century United States* (East Lansing: Michigan State University, 2005); Kristy Maddux, *Practicing Citizenship: Women's Rhetoric at the 1893 Chicago World's Fair* (University Park: Pennsylvania State University Press, 2019); Angela G. Ray and Paul Stob, *Thinking Together: Lecturing, Learning, and Difference in the*

Long Nineteenth Century (University Park: Pennsylvania State University Press, 2018); Bonnie J. Dow, "The Womanhood Rationale in the Woman Suffrage Rhetoric of Frances E. Willard," *Southern Communication Journal* 56 (1991): 298–307; Amy R. Slagell, "The Rhetorical Structure of Frances E. Willard's Campaign for Woman Suffrage, 1876–1896," *Rhetoric & Public Affairs* 4 (2001): 1–23; Angela G. Ray and Cindy Koenig Richards, "Inventing Citizens, Imagining Gender Justice: The Suffrage Rhetoric of Virginia and Francis Minor," *Quarterly Journal of Speech* 93 (2007): 375–402; Jennifer L. Borda, "Woman Suffrage in the Progressive Era: A Coming of Age," in *Rhetoric and Reform in the Progressive Era,* ed. J. Michael Hogan (East Lansing: Michigan State University Press, 2003), 339–386; Kristan Poirot, "(Un)making Sex, Making Race: Nineteenth-Century Liberalism, Difference, and the Rhetoric of Elizabeth Cady Stanton," *Quarterly Journal of Speech* 96 (2010): 185–208; Belinda A. Stillion Southard, "A Rhetoric of Inclusion and the Expansion of Movement Constituencies: Harriot Stanton Blatch and the Classed Politics of Woman Suffrage," *Rhetoric Society Quarterly* 44 (2014): 129–147; Belinda A. Stillion Southard, "A Rhetoric of Epistemic Privilege: Elizabeth Cady Stanton, Harriot Stanton Blatch, and the Educated Vote," *Advances in the History of Rhetoric* 17 (2014): 157–178; Meridith Styer, "Nineteenth Century Extemporaneous Speaking Culture: Susan B. Anthony's Extemporaneous Speaking for Woman Suffrage," *Women's Studies in Communication* 40 (2017): 401–418; Angela G. Ray, "What Hath She Wrought? Woman's Rights and the Nineteenth-Century Lyceum," *Rhetoric & Public Affairs* 9 (2006): 183–214; Randall Lake, "She Flies with Her Own Wings": The Collected Speeches of Abigail Scott Duniway (1834–1915), asduniway.org; Susan Zaeske, "'The South Arose as One Man': Gender and Sectionalism in Antislavery Petition Debates, 1835–1845," *Rhetoric & Public Affairs* 12 (2009): 341–368; Carmen Heider, "Suffrage, Self Determination, and the Woman's Christian Temperance Union in Nebraska, 1879–1882," *Rhetoric & Public Affairs* 8 (2005): 85–107; Casey Ryan Kelly, "Women's Rhetorical Agency in the American West: *The New Penelope,*" *Women's Studies in Communication* 32 (2009): 203–321; Sara Hayden, "Negotiating Femininity and Power in the Early Twentieth-Century West: Domestic Ideology and Feminine

Style in Jeannette Rankin's Suffrage Rhetoric," *Communication Studies* 50 (1999): 83–102; Cindy Koenig Richards, "Inventing Sacagawea: Public Women and the Transformative Potential of Epideictic Rhetoric," *Western Journal of Communication* 73 (2009): 1–22.

6. This narrative of the women's rights movement is so conventional that Lisa Tetrault argues it has achieved mythic status. Women's rights leaders constructed an origins myth for their movement—which Tetrault calls the "myth of Seneca Falls"—to celebrate the work they had accomplished, to give their movement meaning, and to instruct others on how to think and act. Lisa Tetrault, *The Myth of Seneca Falls: Memory and the Women's Suffrage Movement, 1848–1898* (Chapel Hill: University of North Carolina Press, 2014), 1–17.

7. During and shortly after the nation's founding, before voting rights had been codified, some women voted in US elections. Although some colonies, like Virginia, explicitly excluded women from voting, many colonies did not reference gender, so some propertied women in Massachusetts and New York voted and participated in elections. As the former colonies rewrote their new state constitutions, many followed traditional British law, which limited the franchise to white, male property owners. But New Jersey's constitution defined their voters as "all inhabitants" who owned property, including women, African Americans, and aliens. In 1807, however, to address accusations of voting fraud, New Jersey's legislature limited their franchise to "free, white male citizens." Although women petitioned the New Jersey legislature and declared the change illegal, they did not succeed. Following this disenfranchisement, women across the nation were prohibited from voting. When US women married, they legally lost their political identity and independence. The legal concept of coverture—that the husband and wife became a single entity—put a married woman's legal, political, financial, and property rights under her husband's authority. For more information, see Keyssar, *The Right to Vote*; Rebecca J. Mead, *How the Vote Was Won: Woman Suffrage in the Western United States, 1868–1914* (New York: New York University Press, 2004).

8. Angelina Grimke [Weld], "Address at Pennsylvania Hall, 1838," in *Man*

Cannot Speak for Her, vol. 2, *Key Texts of the Early Feminists*, ed. Karlyn Kohrs Campbell (Westport, CT: Praeger, 1989), 25–32; Stephen Browne, *Angelina Grimke: Rhetoric, Identity, and the Radical Imagination* (East Lansing: Michigan State University Press, 1999); Suzanne M. Daughton, "The Fine Texture of Enactment: Iconicity as Empowerment in Angelina Grimke's Pennsylvania Hall Address," *Women's Studies in Communication* 18 (1995): 19–43.

9. Campbell, *Man Cannot Speak for Her*, vol. 1, 9–10.

10. Barbara Welter, "The Cult of True Womanhood: 1820–1860," *American Quarterly* 18 (1966): 151–174; Nancy F. Cott, *The Bonds of Womanhood: "Woman's Sphere" in New England, 1780–1835* (New Haven, CT: Yale University Press, 1977); Eleanor Flexner and Ellen Fitzpatrick, *Century of Struggle: The Woman's Rights Movement in the United States* (Cambridge: Harvard University Press, 1996); Susan Zaeske, *Signatures of Citizenship: Petitioning, Antislavery, and Women's Political Identity* (Chapel Hill: University of North Carolina Press, 2003); Alisse Theodore, "'A Right to Speak on the Subject': The U.S. Women's Antiremoval Petition Campaign, 1829–1831," *Rhetoric & Public Affairs* 5 (2002): 601–624; Alisse Theodore, *Their Right to Speak: Women's Activism in the Indian and Slave Debates* (Cambridge, MA: Harvard University Press, 2005).

11. The majority of these women reformers were white, but some African American women were involved in these efforts, although they were not always included in the traditional narrative of the movement. Rosalyn Terborg-Penn, *African American Women Struggle for the Vote, 1850–1920* (Bloomington: Indiana University Press, 1998).

12. In the nineteenth century, woman suffrage was considered radical because it contradicted so many misconceptions about human biology, prevalent religious beliefs, legal principles, and popular social ideals. Common British and early American thought assumed that women were too delicate for political engagement. Physical delicacy and size were read as indicators that women were incapable of higher education and political activity, and their capacity to menstruate and bear children was used as justification that women were destined to be child bearers and mothers only. Religious objections included the belief held by many that

women voting contradicted God's ordained plan for men to be the head of the household. In the early nineteenth century, the ideal of republican motherhood celebrated women who contributed to the republic primarily by raising sons to be good citizens. Later in the nineteenth century, as industrialization and urbanization meant that men often worked outside of the home, ideals shifted again to categorize financial and political work as masculine and unfit for women. These social norms combined to idealize women who concerned themselves solely with domestic matters within the home. Keyssar, *The Right to Vote*; Aileen Kraditor, *The Ideas of the Woman Suffrage Movement, 1890–1920* (New York: Columbia University Press, 1962); Campbell, *Man Cannot Speak for Her*, vol. 1.

13. They also published women's rights newspapers, including the *Una* and the *Lily*, collected signatures on petitions for women's rights, and presented those petitions to state legislatures. They stopped holding conventions during the Civil War but began again afterward with even greater urgency since the newly ratified reconstruction amendments included the words "male inhabitants" and for the first time explicitly stated women's long-implied exclusion in the Constitution. The women's rights conventions resumed meeting in 1866, and Stanton and Anthony started taking lecture tours around the nation to speak publicly for women's rights.

14. The NWSA began publishing the *Revolution*, a women's rights newspaper based in New York. Stone and Beecher began publishing the *Woman's Journal*, another women's rights journal based in Boston.

15. Flexner and Fitzpatrick, *Century of Struggle*.

16. See Stillion Southard, *Militant Citizenship*.

17. Additionally, the Eastern suffrage organizations were the most well-funded and professional, which allowed them to extensively document their movement's history. The archives and histories they left allowed scholars of women's history, women's rhetoric, and social movements to study and analyze their organizations and provide scholarship on the history, oratory, and methods of woman suffrage advocacy in the Eastern region of the United States. Thus, most scholarship on the suffrage movement documents the organizational strategies, public oratory, and

persuasive writing of national suffrage leaders who resided in the East. This large body of literature includes Flexner and Fitzpatrick, *Century of Struggle*; Campbell, *Man Cannot Speak for Her*, vols. 1 and 2; Robert J. Dinkin, *Before Equal Suffrage: Women in Partisan Politics from Colonial Times to 1920* (Westport, CT: Greenwood Press, 1995); Margaret M. Finnegan, *Selling Suffrage: Consumer Culture and Votes for Women* (New York: Columbia University Press, 1999); Jennifer L. Borda, "The Woman Suffrage Parades of 1910–1913: Possibilities and Limitations of an Early Feminist Rhetorical Strategy," *Western Journal of Communication* 66 (2002): 25–53; Susan Schultz Huxman, "Perfecting the Rhetorical Vision of Woman's Rights: Elizabeth Cady Stanton, Anna Howard Shaw, and Carrie Chapman Catt," *Women's Studies in Communication* 23 (2000): 307–336; Lauren C. Santangelo, *Suffrage and the City: New York Women Battle for the Ballot* (Oxford: Oxford University Press, 2019); Johanna Neuman, *Gilded Suffragists: The New York Socialites Who Fought for Women's Right to Vote* (New York: New York University Press, 2017); Susan Goodier and Karen Pastorello, *Women Will Vote: Winning Suffrage in New York State* (Ithaca: Cornell University Press, 2017); Brooke Kroeger, *The Suffragents: How Women Used Men to Get the Vote* (Albany: State University of New York Press, 2017); Nathan Stormer, "Embodied Humanism: Performative Argument for Natural Rights in 'The Solitude of Self,'" *Argumentation and Advocacy* 36 (1999): 51–64; Ryan Skinnell, "Elizabeth Cady Stanton's 1854 'Address to the Legislature of New York' and the Paradox of Social Reform Rhetoric," *Rhetoric Review* 29 (2010): 129–144.

18. Carol Mattingly, scholar of nineteenth-century women's rhetoric, encourages scholars to look at figures in the suffrage movement other than Stanton and Anthony, and to study leadership in locales beyond the Northeast. Carol Mattingly, "Telling Evidence: Rethinking What Counts in Rhetoric," *Rhetoric Society Quarterly* 32 (2002): 99–108.

19. Keyssar, *The Right to Vote*, 107, 117, 340, 345.

20. Even after the Nineteenth Amendment was passed, this pattern in electoral politics continued. Texas and Wyoming put the first women state governors into office in 1925, Seattle elected the first woman mayor of a sizeable American city in 1926, and North Dakota made a woman the

speaker of its state House of Representatives in 1933. Michael P. Malone and Richard W. Etulain, *The American West: A Twentieth-Century History* (Lincoln: University of Nebraska Press, 1989), 61–62.

21. Scholars have offered numerous competing explanations for the regional pattern of Western suffrage victories, including men's economic and political motives, boosterism, and egalitarian gender roles in the West. Yet many have been persuaded, as I have been, by Rebecca Mead's argument that three primary reasons explain women's suffrage success in the West: fluid regional politics, women's innovative agitation tactics, and coalitions with other political and labor reform movements. Mead, *How the Vote Was Won*; Holly J. McCammon and Karen E. Campbell, "Winning the Vote in the West: The Political Successes of the State Suffrage Movements, 1866–1919," *Gender and Society* 15 (2001): 83–109; Beverly Beeton, "How the West Was Won for Woman Suffrage," in *One Woman, One Vote: Rediscovering the Woman Suffrage Movement*, ed. M. S. Wheeler (Syracuse, NY: New Sage Press, 1995), 99–116; Sandra Haarsager, *Organized Womanhood: Cultural Politics in the Pacific Northwest, 1840–1920* (Norman: University of Oklahoma Press, 1997); T. A. Larson, "Woman Suffrage in Western America," *Utah History Quarterly* 38 (1970): 7–10; Ruth Barnes Moynihan, *Rebel for Rights: Abigail Scott Duniway* (New Haven: Yale University Press, 1983); Jennifer M. Ross-Nazzal, *Winning the West for Women: The Life of Suffragist Emma Smith DeVoe* (Seattle: University of Washington Press, 2011); Heidi J. Osselaer, *Winning Their Place: Arizona Women in Politics, 1883–1950* (Tucson: University of Arizona Press, 2009); Karen M. Morin, "Political Culture and Suffrage in an Anglo-American Women's West," *Women's Rights Law Reporter* 19 (1997): 17–37; Carolyn Stefanco, "Networking on the Frontier: The Colorado Women's Suffrage Movement, 1876–1893," in *The Women's West*, ed. Susan Armitage and Elizabeth Jameson (Norman: University of Oklahoma Press, 1987), 265–276.

22. Beeton, "How the West Was Won"; Larson, "Woman Suffrage in Western America," 7–10; Morin, "Political Culture and Suffrage"; Mead, *How the Vote Was Won*, 2.

23. Mead, *How the Vote Was Won*, 43.

24. Marilyn S. Blackwell and Kristen T. Oertel, *Frontier Feminist: Clarina Howard Nichols and the Politics of Motherhood* (Lincoln: University Press of Kansas, 2010); Larson, "Woman Suffrage in Western America"; Morin, "Political Culture and Suffrage"; Mead, *How the Vote Was Won*, 2, 112; Beeton, "How the West Was Won"; Ross-Nazzal, *Winning the West for Women*; Abigail Scott Duniway, *Path Breaking: An Autobiographical History of the Equal Suffrage Movement in Pacific Coast States* (New York: Source Book Press, 1970); Osselaer, *Winning Their Place*, 20, 62; Solomon, *A Voice of Their Own*.

25. Populists also called for democratic reforms that became associated with the larger progressive movement like the initiative, the referendum, and popular election of political representatives. They advocated for an eight-hour working day, immigration restriction, and a graduated income tax in efforts to attract Easterners to their party. Richard White, *It's Your Misfortune and None of My Own: A New History of the American West* (Tulsa: University of Oklahoma Press, 1991), 370–373; Malone and Etulain, *The American West*, 3; Robert V. Hine and John Mack Faragher, *The American West: A New Interpretive History* (New Haven: Yale University Press, 2000), 350–351; Paul Stob, *Intellectual Populism: Democracy, Inquiry, and the People* (East Lansing: Michigan State University Press, 2020).

26. Women like Mary Elizabeth Lease took an active role in the agrarian protests by writing, speaking, and organizing for the Grange and the Farmers' Alliance. Deborah Fink, *Agrarian Women: Wives and Mothers in Rural Nebraska, 1880-1940* (Chapel Hill: University of North Carolina Press, 1992), 23; Thomas R. Burkholder, "Mary Clyens Lease," in *Women Public Speakers in the United States, 1800-1925*, ed. Karlyn Kohrs Campbell (Westport, CT: Greenwood Press, 1993), 111–124; Thomas R. Burkholder, "Kansas Populism, Woman Suffrage, and the Agrarian Myth: A Case Study in the Limits of Mythic Transcendence," *Communication Studies* 40 (1989): 292–307; Joan Jensen, *With These Hands: Women Working on the Land* (Old Westbury, NY: Feminist Press, 1981), 144.

27. Progressives sought to keep politics and business free from corruption and sustain the public good. Western progressives argued that direct democracy was the best means to empower "the people" to limit corporate power, resist monopolies, and decrease government

corruption. Direct democracy reforms primarily appeared in Western
states during the Progressive Era, beginning with South Dakota in
1898. Following the example of Switzerland's initiative and referendum,
twenty-two states adopted the referenda into their constitutions between
1898 and 1918. Direct democracy was popular because it appealed to
the numerous reform groups working in the 1890s: populism, woman
suffrage, prohibition, single tax, the American Federation of Labor,
labor unions, and farmers' organizations like the Grange. All of these
groups endorsed direct democracy "as a way to expand their repertoire
of political strategies" and as a means to achieving their various ends.
Linking all of these groups together gave them much more leverage as
they worked to advance their differing political agendas and submit them
"directly to the people." Nathaniel Persily, "The Peculiar Geography
of Direct Democracy: Why the Initiative, Referendum and Recall
Developed in the American West," *Michigan Law & Policy Review* 2 (1997):
40; Thomas Goebel, *A Government by the People: Direct Democracy in America,
1890–1940* (Chapel Hill: University of North Carolina Press, 2002), 5–6,
69, 75–79; Malone and Etulain, *The American West*, 55–56; James P. Young,
Reconsidering American Liberalism: The Troubled Odyssey of the Liberal Idea (Boulder,
CO: Perseus Books Group, 1996), 150–151; William Deverell, "Politics
and the Twentieth-Century American West," in *A Companion to the American
West*, ed. William Deverell (Malden, MA: Blackwell Publishing, 2004),
444.

28. The goal of direct democracy was to increase the power of "the people"
and the state, and thereby limit the power of monopolies and corporate
influence on governmental and political leaders. The initiative enabled
voters to pass laws directly by ballot, the referendum allowed voters to
directly repeal laws by ballot, and the recall allowed voters to directly
remove public officials through the ballot. These progressive reforms
assumed that if ordinary American citizens had more input and more
access to political participation, the government would have to respond
to popular will, and democracy would cure governmental corruption and
corporate power. Persily, "The Peculiar Geography of Direct Democracy,"
13; Goebel, *A Government by the People*, 4; Deverell, "Politics and the

Twentieth-Century American West," 446.

29. Mead, *How the Vote Was Won*, 2.

30. John Markoff, "Margins, Centers, and Democracy: The Paradigmatic History of Women's Suffrage," *Signs: Journal of Women in Culture and Society* 29 (2003): 108.

31. Sara L. Spurgeon, *Exploding the Western: Myths of Empire on the Postmodern Frontier* (College Station: Texas A&M University Press, 2005), 7; David M. Wrobel, *The End of American Exceptionalism: Frontier Anxiety from the Old West to the New Deal* (Lawrence: University Press of Kansas, 1993).

32. Census enumerators were directed to classify and exclude American Indians who were not taxed because they were "living on reservations under the care of Government agents or roaming individually or in bands over unsettled tracts of country." Yet enumerators were directed to include American Indians who "mingled with the white population, residing in white families, engaged as servants or laborers, or living in huts or wigwams on the outskirts of towns or settlements." In the 1870s and 1880s, the results of the census showed a clear vertical "frontier line" running north and south down the map of the United States showing where the settled land ended and the frontier began. But in 1890 the US census maps no longer had such a line. *Eleventh United States Census, 1890* (Washington, DC: Government Printing Office, 1892); Harold Simonson, "Introduction," *The Significance of the Frontier in American History*, by Frederick Jackson Turner (New York: Frederick Ungar, 1963), 1–24; US Census Bureau, "1890 Questionnaire," *Measuring America: The Decennial Censuses From 1790 to 2000* (Washington, DC: US Department of Commerce, 2002), 24.

33. Patricia Limerick, *Legacy of Conquest: The Unbroken Past of the American West* (New York: W. W. Norton & Company, Inc., 1987); White, *It's Your Misfortune*.

34. Wrobel, *The End of American Exceptionalism*, viii, 4.

35. Wrobel, *The End of American Exceptionalism*, 5; Alan Trachtenberg, *The Incorporation of America* (New York: Hill and Wang, 1982), 11.

36. Wrobel, *The End of American Exceptionalism*, 6–7; Thomas Jefferson, *Notes on the State of Virginia*, ed. W. Peden (New York: Norton, 1982), 164–165;

Benjamin Franklin, "Letter to Benjamin Vaughan, July 26, 1784," in *The Writings of Benjamin Franklin*, ed. Albert H. Smyth (New York: Macmillan Company, 1907); Richard Hofstadter, *The Age of Reform* (New York: Alfred A. Knopf, 1958); Burkholder, "Kansas Populism"; Henry Nash Smith, *Virgin Land: The American West as Symbol and Myth* (Cambridge, MA: Harvard University Press, 1950).

37. Wrobel, *The End of American Exceptionalism*, 4–5.
38. Frederick Jackson Turner, "The Significance of the Frontier in American History," (presentation, American Historical Association, Chicago, IL, 1893), 31; Frederick Jackson Turner, "The Significance of the Frontier in American History," in *Proceedings of the State Historical Society of Wisconsin*, ed. F. Mood (Madison, WI: The Society, 1894). Turner later published this paper as a book: Frederick Jackson Turner, *The Frontier in American History* (New York: Henry Holt and Company, 1920). Harold P. Simonson, *Beyond the Frontier: Writers, Western Regionalism and a Sense of Place* (Fort Worth: Texas Christian University Press, 1989), 16; Ronald Carpenter, "Frederick Jackson Turner and the Rhetorical Impact of the Frontier Thesis," *Quarterly Journal of Speech* 63 (1977): 117–129.
39. Wrobel, *The End of American Exceptionalism*, viii, 4.
40. Liza Nicholas, *Becoming Western: Stories of Culture and Identity in the Cowboy State* (Lincoln: University of Nebraska Press, 2006); Trachtenberg, *The Incorporation of America*, 23; Wrobel, *The End of American Exceptionalism*, 91–92; Spurgeon, *Exploding the Western*, 7; Robert G. Athearn, *The Mythic West in Twentieth-Century America* (Lawrence: University Press of Kansas, 1986), 24.
41. Trachtenberg, *The Incorporation of America*, 23–24; Turner, "The Significance of the Frontier in American History," (paper) 31.
42. Alexander Nemerov, *Frederick Remington and Turn-of-the-Century America* (New Haven, CT: Yale University Press, 1995), 43; Wrobel, *The End of American Exceptionalism*, 25, 41, 91–92; Nicholas, *Becoming Western*, 25–29; Owen Wister, *The Virginian; A Horseman of the Plains* (New York: Macmillan Company, 1902); Theodore Roosevelt, *The Winning of the West*, 4 vols. (New York: G. P. Putnam's Sons, 1889–1896); Trachtenberg, *The Incorporation of America*, 23; Spurgeon, *Exploding the Western*, 7; Athearn, *The Mythic West*, 24.
43. Nicholas argues that both Easterners and Westerners were champions

of civilization, but Westerners often wanted to civilize the region, while many Easterners enjoyed feeling more civilized in comparison to it. Nicholas, *Becoming Western*, 5, 22. See also Hine and Faragher, *The American West*, 348–349.

44. Turn-of-the-century civilization discourse asserted that the most evolved humans were white, upper-class Protestants who performed traditional gender roles. Based on a social Darwinian model of human progress, civilization was believed to be the highest level of evolution that a human could reach. Civilization discourse asserted that humans evolved from "simple savagery, through violent barbarism, to advanced and valuable civilization." This discourse was used for many disparate purposes, and it informs all of the regional rhetorics I examine in this book. Gail Bederman, *Manliness and Civilization: A Cultural History of Gender and Race in the United States, 1880-1917* (Chicago: University of Chicago Press, 1995), 25.

    I discuss the discourse of civilization throughout this book, focusing primarily on beliefs about civilization at the turn of the century. For further discussion of civilization discourse throughout US history, see Robert L. Ivie, "Savagery in Democracy's Empire," *Third World Quarterly* 26 (2005): 55–65; Robert L. Ivie, "Democracy, War, and Decivilizing Metaphors of American Insecurity," in *Metaphorical World Politics*, ed. Francis A. Beer and Christ'l De Landtsheer (East Lansing: Michigan State University Press, 2004), 75–90.

45. As a racial category, "white" is imprecise and had different meanings at different times. Westerners often defined white narrowly to include Anglo-Americans whose ancestors came from England and Northern Europe, and excluded those who were Irish, Italian, or recent immigrants. But members of these excluded groups eventually and more easily accessed the privileges of whiteness that were not extended to American Indians, Asians, or African Americans. Jason E. Pierce, *Making the White Man's West: Whiteness and the Creation of the American West* (Boulder: University Press of Colorado, 2016), 5; Wrobel, *Promised Lands*, 2, 176; Matthew Frye Jacobsen, *Whiteness of a Different Color: European Immigrants and the Alchemy of Race* (Cambridge, MA: Harvard University Press, 1998). See also Quintard Taylor, *In Search of the Racial Frontier: African Americans*

in the American West, 1528-1990 (New York: W. W. Norton, 1998); Shirley Ann Wilson Moore and Quintard Taylor, *African American Women Confront the West, 1600-2000* (Norman: University of Oklahoma Press, 2003); Vicki Ruiz, "Shaping Public Space/Enunciating Gender: A Multiracial Historiography of the Women's West, 1995–2000," *Frontiers: A Journal of Women Studies* 22 (2001): 22–25; Marta Effinger-Crichlow, *Staging Migrations toward an American West: From Ida B. Wells to Rhodessa Jones* (Boulder: University Press of Colorado, 2014).

46. George H Beasley, "The Great Inland Empire," *Sketch Book* 1 (March 1907), n. p.; Richard B. Roeder, "Montana Progressivism Sound and Fury—and One Small Tax Reform," *Montana: The Magazine of Western History* 20 (1970), 24; David M. Wrobel, *Promised Lands: Promotion, Memory, and the Creation of the American West* (Lawrence: University Press of Kansas, 2002), 2; Nicholas, *Becoming Western*; Marguerite S. Shaffer, *See America First: Tourism and National Identity, 1880-1940* (Washington, DC: Smithsonian Institution Press, 2001).

47. "What a Nurse, Teacher and Newspaper Women Learned about Suffrage," *Woman's Protest*, March 8, 1916, 11.

48. bell hooks, *Ain't I a Woman: Black Women and Feminism* (New York: Routledge, 2015); Terborg-Penn, *African American Women*; Aida Hurtado, *The Color of Privilege: Three Blasphemies on Race and Feminism* (Ann Arbor: University of Michigan Press, 1996); Catherine H. Palczewski, "The 1919 Prison Special: Constituting White Women's Citizenship," *Quarterly Journal of Speech* 102 (2016): 107–132; Maegan Parker, "Desiring Citizenship: A Rhetorical Analysis of the Wells/Willard Controversy," *Women's Studies in Communication* 31 (2008): 56–78; Kristin Hoganson, "'As Badly off as the Filipinos': U.S. Women's Suffragists and the Imperial Issue at the Turn of the Twentieth Century," *Journal of Women's History* 13 (2001): 9–33; Allison L. Sneider, *Suffragists in an Imperial Age: U.S. Expansion and the Woman Question, 1870-1929* (Oxford: Oxford University Press, 2008); Amy Kaplan, *The Anarchy of Empire in the Making of US Culture* (Boston: Harvard University Press, 2005); Campbell, *Man Cannot Speak for Her*, vol. 1; Angela Y. Davis, *Women, Race, and Class* (New York: Random House, 1981); Stillion Southard, *Militant Citizenship*; Zornitsa Keremidchieva, "The

Congressional Debates on the 19th Amendment: Jurisdictional Rhetoric and the Assemblage of the US Body Politic," *Quarterly Journal of Speech* 99 (2013): 51–73.

49. Allison Sneider argues that suffragists were successful in part because of the United States' expansiveness during the nineteenth century. Sneider, *Suffragists in an Imperial Age.*

50. Pierce, *Making the White Man's West*, ix, xvii.

51. Douglass Reichert Powell, *Critical Regionalism: Connecting Politics and Culture in the American Landscape* (Chapel Hill: University of North Carolina Press, 2007), 5; Gary J. Hausladen, "Introduction," in *Western Places, American Myths: How We Think About the West*, ed. Gary J. Hausladen (Reno: University of Nevada Press, 2003), 1–18.

52. Limerick defines "the West" as the "present day states of California, Oregon, Washington, Idaho, Utah, Nevada, Arizona, New Mexico, Colorado, Kansas, Nebraska, Oklahoma, Texas, Montana, Wyoming, North Dakota, and South Dakota and, more changeably, Iowa, Missouri, Arkansas, in Louisiana." Malone and Etulain define the West as all states that embrace "the 98th meridian, including their eastern portions, since state boundaries do not coincide with geographic boundaries and since it makes no sense to speak openly of the western and less populous portions of those states, states that are truly part of the West." Walter Nugent, "Where Is the American West? Report on a Survey," *Montana: The Magazine of Western History* 42 (1992), 2–23; Limerick, *Legacy of Conquest*, 26; Hine and Faragher, *The American West*, 10–11; Athearn, *The Mythic West*; Malone and Etulain, *The American West*, 9.

53. Some scholars define the boundaries of the West according to its distinguishing characteristic of aridity, in contrast to the humid plains east of the 98th meridian. But significant portions of Washington, Oregon, and California are not arid, so scholars also disagree about whether the West extends all the way to the Pacific Coast. Richard White also notes that defining the West according to aridity makes the West's current environment appear natural, obscuring the ways it has been shaped by the human beings who have used and abused it. White, *It's Your Misfortune*, 2.

54. John Walton Caughey, *The American West: Frontier and Region* (Los Angeles: The Ward Ritchie Press, 1969), 6; Hine and Faragher, *The American West,* 10–11.

55. Virginia Scharff, "Else Surely We Shall All Hang Separately: The Politics of Western Women's History," *Pacific Historical Review* (1992): 535–555; Joan M. Jensen and Darlis A. Miller, "The Gentle Tamers Revisited: New Approaches to the History of Women in the American West," *Pacific Historical Review* 49 (1980): 173–213; Hine and Faragher, *The American West,* 10–11.

56. See Eiichiro Azuma, *Between Two Empires: Race, History, and Transnationalism in Japanese America* (Oxford: Oxford University Press, 2004); Arnoldo De Leon, *Racial Frontiers: Africans, Chinese, and Mexicans in Western America, 1848–1890* (Albuquerque: University of New Mexico Press, 2002).

57. White, *It's Your Misfortune,* 4.

58. Limerick compares the United States' legacy of conquest and continental expansion to its legacy of enslavement. But she argues that while the subject of enslavement permanently shaped the nation and became the domain of serious scholars and the occasion for sober national reflection, the subject of conquest has long remained comfortably in the domain of mass entertainment and lighthearted national escapism. Just as the United States' legacy of enslavement shaped the collective memory of the South, its legacy of conquest shaped the collective memory of the US West and many of the rhetorics, histories, and meanings attached to the West. Limerick, *Legacy of Conquest,* 54.

59. Richard White defines the American West as "a product of conquest and of the mixing of diverse groups of peoples," and Patricia Limerick defines it as "a place undergoing conquest and never fully escaping its consequences." Other New Western Historians define it as a place where diverse groups met and were tied into the same history. Annette Kolodny and Sara Spurgeon have defined the frontier as "the meeting place between two or more cultures encountering each other for the first time, often in a landscape perceived as dangerous and unfamiliar to at least one of the cultures involved." New Western History refers to the revisionist Western history that has challenged the accuracy, ideology,

and ethnocentricity of Old Western History, which was founded on Turner's frontier thesis, the mythic West, and American exceptionalism. New Western Historians note that a frontier experience was not unique to the United States, and highlight the imperialist ideology of Old Western History that depicted the United States as progressing in culture, politics, and character the farther it moved the frontier line westward. White explains that Old Western History reads like a comedy with a happy ending for white pioneers, and New Western History reads like a tragedy for multiple groups of people. White, *It's Your Misfortune*, 4; Limerick, *Legacy of Conquest*, 26; Alan G. Bogue, "The Course of Western History's First Century," in *A New Significance: Re-Envisioning the History of the American West*, ed. Clyde A. Milner II (Oxford: Oxford University Press, 1996), 16; Hausladen, "Introduction," 3; Spurgeon, *Exploding the Western*, 6; Annette Kolodny, *The Land Before Her: Fantasy and Experience of the American Frontiers, 1630-1860* (Chapel Hill, NC: University of North Carolina Press, 1984); Sarah Deutsch, *No Separate Refuge* (Oxford: Oxford University Press, 1987); Patricia Nelson Limerick, Clyde A. Milner II, and Charles E. Rankin, eds., *Trails: Toward a New Western History* (Lawrence: University Press of Kansas, 1991).

60. Kenneth Frampton, *Modern Architecture: A Critical History*, 4th ed. (London: Thames & Hudson, 2007), 315; Powell, *Critical Regionalism*, 8, 21-23, 33; Jenny Rice, "From Architectonic to Tectonics: Introducing Regional Rhetorics," *Rhetoric Society Quarterly* 42 (2012): 210; Dave Tell, "The Meanings of Kansas: Rhetoric, Regions, and Counter Regions," *Rhetoric Society Quarterly* 42 (2012), 214-232; Carly S. Woods, Joshua P. Ewalt, and Sara J. Baker, "A Matter of Regionalism: Remembering Brandon Teena and Willa Cather at the Nebraska History Museum," *Quarterly Journal of Speech* 99 (2013): 341-363; Ronald W. Greene and Kevin Douglas Kuswa, "From the Arab Spring to Athens, from Occupy Wall Street to Moscow: Regional Accents and the Rhetorical Cartography of Power," *Rhetoric Society Quarterly* 42 (2012): 271-288.

61. Powell, *Critical Regionalism*, 5-6.

62. Powell, *Critical Regionalism*, 55-56.

63. Since any particular region has multiple potential definitions and

multiple groups attempting to define it, those definitions are continually in competition, as insiders and outsiders of a region often have different purposes and imagined meanings of those regions. Regional appeals are always attempting to prove, at the very least, "the validity of their own particular definitions." Regions do not just happen to be constructed, they are "self-consciously cultivated" and "always deliberately constructed." Powell explains that although region-making is usually "less instrumental than direct forms of social action," it is still "more deliberate than a passive social construction." Powell, *Critical Regionalism*, 8, 10, 21–25, 33; Frampton, *Modern Architecture*, 315.

64. Powell, *Critical Regionalism*, 18–19; Rice, "From Architectonic to Tectonics," 210.

65. Many times, the names, descriptions, and definitions of region are evoked for a particular purpose: to make political, cultural, or physical changes. Through their rhetorical construction, regions create relationships between places. Since regions are social inventions, their meanings and shifting boundaries are shaped by social, economic, political, and cultural activity. Powell, *Critical Regionalism*, 4, 5, 21, 55–56.

66. Powell, *Critical Regionalism*, 5; Tell, "The Meanings of Kansas."

67. Although Powell's language of region is not used by all of them, many Western scholars also view the West as shaped both by its material, geographic elements as well as its symbolic meanings, myths, and texts. Greg Dickinson, Brian Ott, and Eric Aoki argue that the region is both a "material, geographic" area, as well as "a textual construction—a set of memory images in the collective national imagination." Similarly, Alan Trachtenberg characterizes the Gilded Age West as simultaneously a "genuine historical fact," "land and minerals" that provided economic resources for the United States, and "an invention of cultural myth." Most famously, Henry Nash Smith popularized the understanding of the American West as a "symbol and myth," as well as a tangible land of plains and mountains. Even scholars who do not use Powell's vocabulary of regional rhetoric still recognize the simultaneous material and symbolic elements of the West. Greg Dickinson, Brian Ott, and Eric Aoki, "Spaces of Remembering and Forgetting: The Reverent Eye/I at

the Plains Indian Museum," *Communication and Critical/Cultural Studies* 3 (2006): 22–47; Trachtenberg, *The Incorporation of America*, 17; Smith, *Virgin Land*.

68. Powell, *Critical Regionalism*, 26.

69. Rice, "From Architectonic to Tectonics," 203.

70. Powell, *Critical Regionalism*, 26; Rice, "From Architectonic to Tectonics," 210.

71. Danielle Endres and Samantha Senda-Cook, "Location Matters: The Rhetoric of Place in Protest," *Quarterly Journal of Speech* 97 (2011).

72. Places are geographic locations that cannot be separated from their symbolic meaning. All places simultaneously have material and ideological elements. When Tim Cresswell defines place, he uses a church as an example. A church building is not a church unless it has both the material elements of walls and a roof and the religious belief system that provides meaning for worshipers. Without both the material and ideological elements, it would not be a church. As worshipers label, use, and visit the building as a place of worship, they give it meaning, a discursive process called "place-making." Place-making involves transforming material space into a place by giving it meaning through language and symbolic action. Like place, regions are also material and symbolic—shaped by the meanings and ideas humans assign to spaces—and created using language and symbols to give meaning to particular places. Tim Cresswell, *In Place/Out of Place: Geography, Ideology and Transgression* (Minneapolis: University of Minnesota Press, 1996). See also Keith H. Basso, *Wisdom Sits in Places: Landscape and Language Among the Western Apache* (Albuquerque: University of New Mexico Press, 1996), 5; Jessie Stewart and Greg Dickinson, "Enunciating Locality in the Postmodern Suburb: FlatIron Crossing and the Colorado Lifestyle," *Western Journal of Communication* 72 (2008): 280–307; Endres and Senda-Cook, "Location Matters"; Theresa Ann Donofrio, "Ground Zero and Place-Making Authority: The Conservative Metaphors in 9/11 Families' 'Take Back the Memorial' Rhetoric," *Western Journal of Communication* 74 (2010): 150–169; Thomas F. Gieryn, "A Space for Place in Sociology," *Annual Review of Sociology* 26 (2000): 463–96; Henri Lefebvre, *The Production of Space*, trans.

Donald Nicholson Smith (Malden, MA: Blackwell Press, 1974); Lefebvre, *The Production of Space*; Michel de Certeau, *The Practice of Everyday Life*, trans. Steven Rendall (Berkeley: University of California Press, 1984); Raymie McKerrow, 'Space and Time in the Postmodern Polity,' *Western Journal of Communication* 63 (1999): 271–290; Thomas J. St. Antoine, "Making Heaven Out of Hell: New Urbanism and the Refutation of Suburban Spaces," *Southern Communication Journal* 72 (2007): 127–144; Doreen Massey, *For Space* (London: Sage Publications, 2005); Donovan Conley and Greg Dickinson, "Space, Matter, Mediation, and the Prospects of Democracy," *Critical Studies in Media Communication* 27 (2010): 1–7; Sonja Modesti, "Home Sweet Home: Tattoo Parlors as Postmodern Spaces of Agency," *Western Journal of Communication* 72 (2008): 197–212; E. Cram, "Queer Geographies and the Rhetoric of Orientation," *Quarterly Journal of Speech* 106 (2019): 98–115; Joan Faber McAlister, "Ten Propositions for Communication Scholars Studying Space and Place," *Women's Studies in Communication* 39 (2016): 113–121; Kundai Chirindo, "Rhetorical Places: From Classical Topologies to Prospects for Post-Westphalian Spatialities," *Women's Studies in Communication* 39 (2016): 127–131.

73. Powell, *Critical Regionalism*, 4, 67.

74. Rice, "From Architectonics to Tectonics," 206.

75. My arguments and analytical approach share similarities with scholarship that critically examines white women's writing about migrating to, traveling around, and living in the West in the nineteenth century. Scholars have studied their constructions of the West in nineteenth- and early twentieth-century novels, letters, diaries, promotional literature, captivity narratives, travel accounts, political advocacy, and participation in public ceremonies. Some have found that when white women wrote in and about the West, they drew on a rhetoric of Western expansion as they depicted the land as a place to be colonized, and discussed people of other races and classes as subjects to be dominated. Like these scholars, I also illuminate the way white women imagined and constructed the West for their purposes and find some similar themes of domestication, continental expansion, and racial hierarchy. However, none of this scholarship examines the woman suffrage movement.

Martha M. Allen, *Traveling West: 19th Century Women on the Overland Routes* (El Paso: Texas Western Press, 1987); Susan J. Rosowski, *Birthing a Nation: Gender, Creativity, and the West in American Literature* (Lincoln: University of Nebraska Press, 1999); Brigitte Georgi-Findlay, *The Frontiers of Women's Writing: Women's Narratives and the Rhetoric of Western Expansion* (Tucson: University of Arizona Press, 1996); Karen M. Morin, *Frontiers of Femininity: A New Historical Geography of the Nineteenth-Century American West* (Syracuse, NY: Syracuse University Press, 2008); Susan Armitage and Elizabeth Jameson, eds., *Writing the Range: Race, Class, and Culture in the Women's West* (Norman: University of Oklahoma Press, 1997); Kolodny, *The Land Before Her*.

76. Thomas B. Farrell, "Sizing Things Up: Colloquial Reflection as Practical Wisdom," *Argumentation* 12 (1998): 1.

77. I use the methods of a rhetorical critic to examine the public discourse of and about the suffrage movement and how this discourse interacted with its historical context. I analyze the persuasive texts that women's rights advocates used to champion their cause—speeches, public essays, flags, maps, parades, tableaus, and one well-publicized, cross-country car trip—as well as public discourse about the suffrage movement and the West that appeared in newspapers and antisuffrage publications. I pay particular attention to suffrage discourses that used the Western suffrage states and their meanings in the national imaginary to do persuasive work for and against women's voting rights. Each chapter of this book examines a specific kind of regional rhetoric that suffragists or antisuffragists used to imagine the West as a region: the frontier myth, civilization, continental expansion, the woolly West, and Western boosterism. The case studies are organized thematically. Since the various regional rhetorics were used simultaneously, each chapter focuses on one particular kind of regional rhetoric that influenced the suffrage movement.

Chapter 1. Mythologizing the West:
Abigail Scott Duniway's Mythic Frontier, 1884–1905

1. The original quote used a different spelling and appears in the text as "created something of a furore." Also, the author notes in this article that they are recalling a convention they attended two years previously. "Woman Suffrage," *Sunday Morning Oregonian*, February 28, 1886.

2. "Woman Suffrage," *Sunday Morning Oregonian*, February 28, 1886.

3. "Woman Suffrage," *Sunday Morning Oregonian*, February 28, 1886.

4. Randall Lake, "'She Flies with Her Own Wings': The Collected Speeches of Abigail Scott Duniway (1834–1915)," asduniway.org/home/.

5. Eleanor Flexner and Ellen Fitzpatrick, *Century of Struggle: The Woman's Rights Movement in the United States* (Cambridge, MA: Harvard University Press, 1996), 152.

6. Ruth Barnes Moynihan, *Rebel for Rights: Abigail Scott Duniway* (New Haven: Yale University Press, 1983), 93.

7. Ida Husted Harper, *The Life and Work of Susan B. Anthony*, vol. 1 (Indianapolis: Bowen-Merrill Co., 1899), 399–400.

8. Harper, *The Life and Work of Susan B. Anthony*, 391.

9. Abigail Scott Duniway, *Path Breaking: An Autobiographical History of the Equal Suffrage Movement in Pacific Coast States* (New York: Source Book Press, 1970), 46.

10. Moynihan, *Rebel for Rights*, 83.

11. Jean M. Ward and Elaine A. Maveety, eds., *Yours for Liberty: Selections from Abigail Scott Duniway's Suffrage Newspaper* (Corvalis: Oregon State University Press, 2000); Sheree Keith, "Abigail Scott Duniway: The Rhetoric of Intervention and the New Northwest," *Texas Speech Communication Journal* 30 (2006): 146–157; Ruth Barnes Moynihan, "Abigail Scott Duniway: Mother of Woman Suffrage in the Pacific Northwest," in *Grit and Grace: Eleven Women Who Shaped the American West*, ed. Glenda Riley and Richard W. Etulain (Golden, CO: Fulcrum Publishing, 1997), 174–197.

12. Mary Ashton Rice Livermore and Frances Elizabeth Willard, eds., *American Women: Fifteen Hundred Biographies with over 1,400 Portraits; A Comprehensive Encyclopedia of the Lives and Achievements of American Women During the Nineteenth Century*, vol. 1 (New York: Mast, Crowell, & Kirkpatrick,

1897), 264.

13. Duniway's involvement in suffrage began in the NWSA and continued in the NAWSA. Flexner and Fitzpatrick, *Century of Struggle*.

14. Sandra Haarsager, *Organized Womanhood: Cultural Politics in the Pacific Northwest, 1840-1920* (Norman: University of Oklahoma Press, 1977); Moynihan, "Abigail Scott Duniway," 174.

15. Lucy Stone, "One Faithful Worker," *Woman's Journal*, 1886, 4.

16. Livermore and Willard, *American Women*, 264.

17. James Oliver Robertson, *American Myth, American Reality* (New York: Hill and Wang, 1980).

18. Drawn from a society's real and imagined history, myths include not only what happened in the past, but also what was said to have happened in the past. Thus, while they are often molded from history, they simultaneously shape it. Janice Hocker Rushing and Thomas S. Frentz, "The Rhetoric of the 'Rocky': A Social Value Model of Criticism," *Western Journal of Speech Communication* 42 (1978): 63–72; Richard Slotkin, *Gunfighter Nation: The Myth of the Frontier in Twentieth-Century America* (New York: Atheneum, 1992); Richard Slotkin, *Regeneration through Violence: The Mythology of the American Frontier, 1600-1860* (Middletown, CT: Wesleyan University Press, 1973); Northrop Frye, "Literature and Myth," in *Relations of Literary Study*, ed. J. Thorpe (New York: Modern Language Association of America, 1966), 27–55.

19. Of all of our myths, the frontier myth remains among the oldest and most characteristically American. Considered the exemplar of American stories, the Western frontier myth significantly influenced the creation of American character, consciousness, and spirit. Slotkin, *Gunfighter Nation*, 10; Brigitte Georgi-Findlay, *The Frontiers of Women's Writing: Women's Narratives and the Rhetoric of Western Expansion* (Tucson: University of Arizona Press, 1996), 6; Robert V. Hine and John Mack Faragher, *The American West: A New Interpretive History* (New Haven: Yale University Press, 2000), 321; Harold P. Simonson, *Beyond the Frontier: Writers, Western Regionalism and a Sense of Place* (Fort Worth: Texas Christian University Press, 1989), 1.

20. Although the traditional frontier myth elevated white men as frontier heroes, it had so much cultural power that even men who were excluded

from it harnessed it for their own purposes. Dan Moos's research
illustrates that the imperialist and racist mythologies of the West
were also used by the very people they were meant to subjugate. He
demonstrates that although African American, American Indian, and
Mormon men were by definition not frontiersmen, some commandeered
the roles of pioneer, cowboy, or "noble" savage to prove their connection
to the West and, therefore, their belonging to the American nation. Dan
Moos, *Outside America: Race, Ethnicity, and the Role of the American West in National
Belonging* (Lebanon, NH: Dartmouth College Press, 2005).

21. For Turner, Western expansion had decreased America's dependence on
England and promoted "the formation of a composite nationality for the
American people." Turner's rationale for his thesis drew on the traditional
frontier myth as he explained that the frontier was the "most rapid and
effective Americanization." He described how the European colonist
arrived in the wilderness as "a European in dress, industries, tools,
modes of travel, and thought . . . and the frontier . . . environment [wa]s
at first too strong for the man." Turner's account of the frontiersman's
transformation from European to American follows the plot of the
frontier myth: "[The frontier] takes [the European] from the railroad car
and puts him in the birch canoe. It strips off the garments of civilization
and arrays him in the hunting shirt and the moccasin. It puts him in
the log cabin of the Cherokee and Iroquois and . . . Before long . . . he
shouts the war cry and takes the scalp in orthodox Indian fashion." He
proclaimed that as the European frontiersman "transforms the wilderness
. . . the outcome is not the old Europe . . . Here is a new product that is
American." The new American exemplified the qualities of the masculine
frontier hero, which he described as "coarseness and strength combined
with acuteness and inquisitiveness; that practical, inventive turn of
mind . . . that dominant individualism, working for good and for evil,
and withal that buoyancy and exuberance which comes with freedom."
Frederick Jackson Turner, *The Frontier in American History* (New York: Henry
Holt and Company, 1920), 3–4.

22. The frontier myth is also at work in many mediated contexts. John
Jordan, "Kennedy's Romantic Moon and Its Rhetorical Legacy for Space

Exploration," *Rhetoric & Public Affairs* 6 (2003): 209–231; Zoe Hess Carney and Mary E. Stuckey, "The World as the American Frontier: Racialized Presidential War Rhetoric," *Southern Communication Journal* 80 (2015): 163–188; Leah Ceccarelli, *On the Frontier of Science: An American Rhetoric of Exploration and Exploitation* (East Lansing: Michigan State University Press, 2013); Janice H. Rushing, "Mythic Evolution of 'The New Frontier' in Mass Mediated Rhetoric," *Critical Studies in Mass Communication* 3 (1986): 265; Hillary A. Jones, "'Them as Feel the Need to Be Free': Reworking the Frontier Myth," *Southern Communication Journal* 76 (2011): 230–247; Stephen M. Underhill, "Urban Jungle, Ferguson: Rhetorical Homology and Institutional Critique," *Quarterly Journal of Speech* 102 (2016): 396–417; Casey Ryan Kelly and Ryan Neville-Shepard, "Virgin Lands: Gender, Nature, and the Frontier Myth in David Magnusson's *Purity*," *Women's Studies in Communication* 43 (2020): 1–22; Nicolas C. Hernandez, Cristi C. Horton, Danielle Endres, and Tarla Rai Peterson, "The Frontier Myth in U.S. Offshore Wind Energy Communication," *Frontiers in Communication* 4 (2019): 1–12; Stephen M. Underhill, *The Manufacture of Consent: J. Edgar Hoover and the Rhetorical Rise of the FBI* (East Lansing: Michigan State University Press, 2020).

23. Frederick Jackson Turner, "The Significance of the Frontier in American History," (presentation, American Historical Association, Chicago, IL, 1893).

24. John F. Kasson, *Houdini, Tarzan, and the Perfect Man: The White Male Body and the Challenge of Modernity in America* (New York: Hill and Wang, 2001), 181; Alan Trachtenberg, *The Incorporation of America* (New York: Hill and Wang, 1982), 23.

25. The Boone and Crockett Club worked to preserve the spirit of the frontier by commemorating the "old race of Rocky Mountain hunters and trappers, of reckless, dauntless Indian fighters." Theodore Roosevelt, *Ranch Life and the Hunting Trail* (New York: The Century Co., 1911), 81. Roosevelt promoted the cowboy character in politics with his best-selling book, *The Winning of the West*, and in 1893, he reminisced in *Century Magazine* about his times spent with the "hard-working, brave, resolute, and truthful" pioneers "in Cowboy Land." Theodore Roosevelt, *The Winning*

of the West: An Account of the Exploration and Settlement of Our Country from the Alleghanies to the Pacific (New York: G. P. Putnam's Sons, 1917); Theodore Roosevelt, "In Cowboy-Land," *Century Illustrated Monthly Magazine* 46 (1893), 276–284.

26. In 1902, Wister wrote one of the most famous cowboy novels, *The Virginian*, about a cultured white man from the East who went west and learned to be masculine and tough from a Wyoming cowboy. Owen Wister, *The Virginian: A Horseman of the Plains* (New York: The Macmillan Company, 1902); Owen Wister, "The Evolution of the Cow-Puncher," *Harper's Monthly Magazine*, September 1895; Frederic Remington, *The Fall of the Cowboy*, painting, 1895, Amon Carter Museum of American Art, Fort Worth, TX.

27. The symbol of the frontiersman persists today as a distinguishing feature of hegemonic masculinity. Western scholar Richard Bartlett characterized the masculinity of the frontier "as obvious as the sun in the daytime." Feminist author Susan Faludi maintains that a frontier to be claimed remains one of the "time tested tenets of . . . the national male paradigm." Nick Trujillo, "Hegemonic Masculinity on the Mound: Media Representations of Nolan Ryan and American Sports Culture," *Critical Studies in Mass Communication* 8 (1991): 290–308; Susan Faludi, *Stiffed* (New York: Perennial, 1999), 26; Richard Bartlett, *The New Country: A Social History of the American Frontier, 1776–1890* (New York: Oxford University Press, 1974), 343.

28. Susan Armitage, "Through Women's Eyes: A New View of the West," in *The Women's West*, ed. Susan Armitage and Elizabeth Jameson (Norman: University of Oklahoma Press, 1987), 9.

29. Susan Lee Johnson argues that the "overdetermined maleness of the West," along with its "overblown rhetoric of white masculinity" needs to be marked as such so that we can begin to understand the lives of those who were not white men in the American West. Johnson calls for scholars to ask "what studying gender can do for the history of the West and what studying the West can do for the politics of gender." Susan Lee Johnson, "'A Memory Sweet to Soldiers': The Significance of Gender in the History of the 'American West,'" *Western Historical Quarterly* 14 (1993):

90–93. Faludi, *Stiffed*, 26; Trujillo, "Hegemonic Masculinity on the Mound."

30. Annette Kolodny, *The Land Before Her: Fantasy and Experience of the American Frontiers, 1630–1860* (Chapel Hill, NC: University of North Carolina Press, 1984).

31. Laura McCall, "Introduction," in *Across the Great Divide: Cultures of Manhood in the American West*, ed. Matthew Basso, Laura McCall, and Dee Garceau (New York: Routledge, 2001), 5; Georgi-Findlay, *The Frontiers of Women's Writing*, ix, 6.

32. Theodore Roosevelt employed the frontier myth to persuade the American people to improve the status of immigrants in American culture and link progress to conservation of the environment. His essay on "The Manly Virtues and Practical Politics" established physical and moral strength as "manly virtues," and promised in *The Winning of the West* that men could best gain these virtues on the American frontier. The American public widely accepted his explicitly masculine politics, and feminist scholars have argued that his emphasis on "manly virtues" created an obstacle for the public's acceptance of women in political roles. Thus, he likely further contributed to the already established masculine notions of the frontier hero, just as he did to politics. Leroy G. Dorsey, *We Are All Americans, Pure and Simple: Theodore Roosevelt and the Myth of Americanism* (Tuscaloosa: University of Alabama Press, 2007); Theodore Roosevelt, *The Winning of the West: An Account of the Exploration and Settlement of our Country from the Alleghanies to the Pacific*, in *The Works of Theodore Roosevelt* (New York: Charles Scribner's Sons, 1926); Leroy G. Dorsey, "The Frontier Myth in Presidential Rhetoric: Theodore Roosevelt's Campaign for Conservation," *Western Journal of Communication* 59 (1995): 1–19; H. W. Brands, "Politics as Performance Art: The Body English of Theodore Roosevelt," in *The Presidency and Rhetorical Leadership*, ed. Leroy Dorsey (College Station: Texas A & M University Press, 2002), 115–128; "Mr. Roosevelt Sees a Cowboy Festival," *New York Times*, April 26, 1903, 1; "President Calls for a Larger Navy," *New York Times*, May 23, 1903, 2; "The President Talks on the Philippines," *New York Times*, April 8, 1903, 3; Theodore Roosevelt, "The Manly Virtues and Practical Politics," *Forum*,

July 1894, 552, 555; Roosevelt, *The Winning of the West*, Rebecca Edwards, *Angels in the Machinery: Gender in American Party Politics from the Civil War to the Progressive Era* (New York: Oxford University Press, 1997).

33. Suzanne M. Daughton, "The Fine Texture of Enactment: Iconicity as Empowerment in Angelina Grimke's Pennsylvania Hall Address," *Women's Studies in Communication* 18 (1995): 19–43; Karlyn Kohrs Campbell, "Enactment as a Rhetorical Strategy in *The Year of Living Dangerously*," *Central States Speech Journal* 39 (1988): 258–268.

34. Duniway included edited versions of some these speeches in her autobiography, and the speeches were also printed in local newspapers or saved as speech manuscripts in her papers. Abigail Scott Duniway papers, 1852–1992 (Collection 232 B). University of Oregon Libraries, Special Collections and University Archives, Eugene, Oregon. Randall Lake has also made Duniway's extensive rhetorical corpus available online. Lake has authenticated her speeches by meticulously collecting, comparing, editing, and publishing all the known versions of Duniway's speeches. Randall Lake, "She Flies with Her Own Wings": The Collected Speeches of Abigail Scott Duniway, asduniway.org.

35. Duniway addressed the US Senate Select Committee on Woman Suffrage in 1884 in Washington, DC. The speech was included in the *Congressional Record* and was also published in her paper, the *New Northwest*. Mrs. Duniway, speaking before the Select Committee on Woman Suffrage, US Senate, on March 7, 1884. 49th Cong., 2nd sess., *Congressional Record* 18, pt. 1 (January 25, 1887): 996; "Remarks by Mrs. Duniway," *New Northwest*, April 24, 1884. An authenticated text of the speech is available at Abigail Scott Duniway, "U.S. Senate Select Committee on Woman Suffrage—March 7, 1884," "She Flies with Her Own Wings": The Collected Speeches of Abigail Scott Duniway, asduniway.org/u-s-senate-select-committee-on-woman-suffrage-march-7-1884/.

36. Duniway delivered "The Pacific Northwest" before the Congress of Women at the World's Columbian Exposition in Chicago in 1893. Abigail Scott Duniway, "The Pacific Northwest, Address Delivered before the World's Congress of Women at the Columbian Exposition, June 1st,

1893," speech manuscript in Abigail S. Duniway Papers, University of Oregon Libraries, Special Collections and University Archives, Eugene, Oregon. An authenticated text of the speech is available at Abigail Scott Duniway, "The Pacific Northwest—June 1, 1893," "She Flies with Her Own Wings": The Collected Speeches of Abigail Scott Duniway, asduniway.org/"the-pacific-northwest"-june-1-1893/.

37. Duniway addressed the NWSA at their sixteenth national convention in 1884, Washington, DC. Her speech was delivered at the opening session of the convention, which met at Lincoln Hall. An incomplete version of the speech is included in Duniway's papers. Abigail Scott Duniway Papers, Scrapbook 2, University of Oregon Libraries, Special Collections and University Archives, Eugene, Oregon. An authenticated text of the speech is available at Abigail Scott Duniway, "National Woman Suffrage Association Convention—March 4, 1884," "She Flies with Her Own Wings": The Collected Speeches of Abigail Scott Duniway, asduniway. org/national-woman-suffrage-association-convention-march-4-1884/.

38. Duniway delivered "Ballots and Bullets" on January 23, 1889 at the twenty-first NWSA convention in Washington, DC, and she included it in her autobiography, *Path Breaking*. "Ballots and Bullets" was reprinted seventeen years after she delivered the speech in the *Morning Oregonian*. "Mrs. Duniway, Equal Suffrage and W.C.T.U.," *Morning Oregonian*, September 9, 1906, 33. An authenticated text of the speech, which marks the discrepancies between the two speeches, can be accessed at Abigail Scott Duniway, "'Ballots and Bullets'—January 23, 1889," "She Flies with Her Own Wings": The Collected Speeches of Abigail Scott Duniway, asduniway.org/"ballots-and-bullets"-circa-january-21-23-1889/.

39. Duniway delivered "How to Win the Ballot" at the NAWSA's convention in Grand Rapids, Michigan, on May 2, 1899. "How to Win the Ballot: Mrs. Duniway's Address to the Women Suffragists," *Morning Oregonian*, May 3, 1899, 2. An authenticated version of the speech is available at Abigail Scott Duniway, "'How to Win the Ballot'—May 2, 1899," "She Flies with Her Own Wings": The Collected Speeches of Abigail Scott Duniway, asduniway.org/"how-to-win-the-ballot"-may-2-1899/.

40. Duniway delivered "Success in Sight" at the NAWSA's convention

in Washington, DC, on February 12, 1900. She published it in her autobiography, and it was published in in the *Oregonian* the day after her speech. "Her Eightieth Birthday: Celebration of Susan B. Anthony's Four-Score Years," *Morning Oregonian*, February 13, 1900, 5. An authenticated version of the speech is available at Abigail Scott Duniway, "'Success in Sight'—February 12, 1900," "She Flies with Her Own Wings": The Collected Speeches of Abigail Scott Duniway, asduniway. org/"success-in-sight"-february-12-1900/.

41. Duniway delivered "Equal Rights for All" at the Idaho Constitutional Convention in Boise City on July 17, 1889. "Equal Rights for All" was published in two parts: "Woman suffrage: An enthusiastic advocate of the subject," *Idaho Weekly Statesmen*, July 19, 1889, 1, and "Woman Suffrage," *Idaho Weekly Statesmen*, July 20, 1889, 1, 4. An authenticated text of the speech is available at Abigail Scott Duniway, "Equal Rights for All—July 17, 1889," "She Flies with Her Own Wings": The Collected Speeches of Abigail Scott Duniway, asduniway.org/"equal-rights-for-all"-july-17-1889/.

42. Duniway addressed the Oregon State Equal Suffrage Association at her home in Portland on November 20, 1897. Oregon State Equal Suffrage Association, November 20, 1897, speech transcript, Abigail Scott Duniway Papers, Scrapbook 1. University of Oregon Libraries, Special Collections and University Archives, Eugene, Oregon. An authenticated text of the speech is available at Abigail Scott Duniway, "Oregon State Equal Suffrage Association—November 20, 1897," "She Flies with Her Own Wings": The Collected Speeches of Abigail Scott Duniway, http://asduniway.org/oregon-state-equal-suffrage-association-november-20-1897/.

43. Duniway delivered "Woman in Oregon History" in Salem, Oregon, at the fortieth anniversary celebration of Oregon's admission to statehood on February 14, 1899. Duniway included this speech in her autobiography, *Path Breaking*, and it was published in the *Oregonian* the following day: "Admission Day Observed at Salem: Governor Geer Presided—Principal Addresses were by George H. Williams, W. P. Lord, L. B. Cox and Mrs. Duniway," *Morning Oregonian*, February 15, 1899, 9. An

authenticated text of the speech is available at Abigail Scott Duniway, "Woman in Oregon History—February 14, 1899," "She Flies with Her Own Wings": The Collected Speeches of Abigail Scott Duniway, asduniway.org/"woman-in-oregon-history"-february-14-1899/.

44. Duniway delivered "Eminent Women I have Met" at the Oregon Federation of Women's Club Convention, which was held in Pendleton, Oregon, just a few days before the state voted on an equal suffrage amendment. This speech is included in Duniway's Papers and was published in the *Morning Oregonian*. "Oregon Women's Clubs," *Morning Oregonian*, June 2, 1900, 5. An authenticated text of the speech is available at Abigail Scott Duniway, "Eminent Women I Have Met—June 1, 1900," "She Flies with Her Own Wings": The Collected Speeches of Abigail Scott Duniway, asduniway.org/"eminent-women-i-have-met"-june-1-1900/.

45. Duniway delivered "The Pioneer Mother" at the Lewis and Clark Exposition held in Portland in 1905. This speech was delivered at the ceremony held for the unveiling of the statue of Sacagawea. Abigail Scott Duniway, "The Pioneer Mother—July 6, 1905," "She Flies with Her Own Wings": The Collected Speeches of Abigail Scott Duniway, asduniway. org/"the-pioneer-mother"-july-6-1905/.

46. Duniway addressed the Lewis and Clark Exposition again on October 6, 1905 when the exposition celebrated "Abigail Scott Duniway Day." "Mrs. Duniway's Response," *Oregonian*, October 7, 1905; "Abigail Scott Duniway," *Woman's Tribune*, October 28, 1905, 46. An authenticated text of the speech is available at Abigail Scott Duniway, "Lewis and Clark Exposition—October 6, 1905," "She Flies with Her Own Wings": The Collected Speeches of Abigail Scott Duniway, asduniway.org/lewis-and-clark-exposition-october-6-1905/.

47. Duniway, "'Success in Sight'—February 12, 1900."

48. Duniway, "'How to Win the Ballot'—May 2, 1899."

49. Duniway, "Oregon State Equal Suffrage Association—November 20, 1897."

50. Duniway, "Equal Rights for All—July 17, 1889."

51. Duniway, "Woman in Oregon History—February 14, 1899."

52. Duniway, "'How to Win the Ballot'—May 2, 1899."

53. Kolodny, *The Land Before Her.*

54. Rushing, "Mythic Evolution," 265–266.

55. Dorsey, "The Frontier Myth," 14.

56. Dorsey, "The Frontier Myth," 4.

57. Leroy G. Dorsey and Rachel M. Harlow, "'We Want Americans Pure and Simple': Theodore Roosevelt and the Myth of Americanism," *Rhetoric & Public Affairs* 6 (2003): 55–78; Janice H. Rushing, "The Rhetoric of the American Western Myth," *Communication Monographs* 50 (1983): 19.

58. Dorsey, "The Frontier Myth," 2.

59. Dorsey and Harlow, "We Want Americans Pure and Simple"; Dorsey, "The Frontier Myth."

60. Georgi-Findlay, *The Frontiers of Women's Writing*, 6.

61. Duniway spoke on "Women in Oregon History" at the fortieth anniversary of the statehood of Oregon, Exercises Before the Legislative Assembly at Salem, Oregon, February 14, 1899, https://ir.library. oregonstate.edu.

62. Duniway, "Woman in Oregon History—February 14, 1899."

63. Duniway, "Woman in Oregon History—February 14, 1899."

64. Duniway, "Woman in Oregon History—February 14, 1899."

65. Slotkin, *Gunfighter Nation*, 11.

66. Duniway, "Woman in Oregon History—February 14, 1899." In 1847, Oregon missionaries Marcus and Narcissa Whitman and eleven others were killed by Cuyuse American Indians.

67. Duniway, "Woman in Oregon History—February 14, 1899." Duniway also alludes to Miller's poem in "How to Win the Ballot" (1899) and "Equal Rights for All" (1889). When she spoke to the Idaho Constitutional Convention in 1889, Duniway similarly asserted, "You . . . [are] forgetting, or pretending to forget, that life's hardest battles, everywhere, are fought by the mothers of men in giving existence to the race." Duniway, "Equal Rights for All—July 17, 1889." In her 1899 speech at the NAWSA, she reminded her audience of the frontier heroines who, by "giving existence to the soldiers, and suffer[ing] their full share of the penalties and perils of existence, equaling all the horrors of war."

Duniway, "'How to Win the Ballot'—May 2, 1899."

68. Duniway, "Woman in Oregon History—February 14, 1899."

69. Duniway, "'Success in Sight'—February 12, 1900."

70. Duniway, "'Success in Sight'—February 12, 1900," emphasis added.

71. Duniway, "Equal Rights for All—July 17, 1889."

72. *Pacific Empire*, June 18, 1896, 7.

73. Duniway, "'Ballots and Bullets'—January 23, 1889."

74. Employing what Campbell has termed "explicit enactment," Duniway suggested that she is an example of her argument to enhance her message's urgency to her audience. Campbell, "Enactment as a Rhetorical Strategy," 260.

75. Similarly, Duniway told a NWSA audience in 1884 about the "long, laborious, patient canvass" she had made in both Washington and Oregon by "traveling by stage, rail, steamer, and often afoot." She reported, "the same obstacles have been met and overcome in carrying on the work . . . I have traveled each year many thousands of miles, and spoken in each geographical division an average of seventy times per year, during a period of twelve and a half years duration, making, at a low estimate, 1750 public speeches, or nearly five years of steady speaking." Duniway, "National Woman Suffrage Association Convention—March 4, 1884."

76. Rhetorical scholars call this kind of enactment "implicit enactment." Campbell, "Enactment as a Rhetorical Strategy"; Suzanne M. Daughton, "The Fine Texture of Enactment: Iconicity as Empowerment in Angelina Grimke's Pennsylvania Hall Address," *Women's Studies in Communication* 18 (1995): 19–43.

77. Campbell, "Enactment as a Rhetorical Strategy," 260.

78. Moynihan, "Abigail Scott Duniway," 176.

79. Beverly Beeton, *One Woman, One Vote: Rediscovering the Woman Suffrage Movement*, ed. Marjorie Spruill Wheeler (Syracuse, NY: NewSage Press, 1995).

80. Karlyn Kohrs Campbell and Kathleen Hall Jamieson, *Form and Genre: Shaping Rhetorical Action* (Falls Church: Speech Communication Association, 1978), 9.

81. Campbell and Jamieson, *Form and Genre*.

82. Duniway, *Path Breaking*.

83. Haarsager, *Organized Womanhood*, 265.

84. "Abigail Scott Duniway," *Woman's Tribune*, October 28, 1905, 46.

85. Duniway's introduction and commemoration continued, stating "Her voice and pen have been always eloquent and powerful in any cause in which they were engaged, and many a foe has keenly regretted having called forth her batteries of reasoning, ridicule, and retributive castigation." Oregon Legislative Assembly, *Fortieth Anniversary of the Statehood of Oregon. Exercises before the Legislative Assembly at Salem, Oregon, February 14, 1899* (Salem, OR: W.H. Leeds, State Printer, 1899), ir.library. oregonstate.edu.

86. Livermore and Willard, *American Women*, 264.

87. Joseph Campbell, *The Hero with a Thousand Faces* (Novota, CA: New World Library, 2008).

88. Abigail Scott Duniway, "Journal of a Trip to Oregon," David C. Duniway Collection, Salem, OR, 1852.

89. Duniway, "'Success in Sight'—February 12, 1900."

90. Duniway, "'Success in Sight'—February 12, 1900."

91. Alexander Keyssar, *The Right to Vote: The Contested History of Democracy in the United States* (New York: Perseus, 2008).

92. After the American Revolution, advocates of an expanded franchise contended that men who had served in the army or militia should have the right to vote because their experiences in war had earned them the right to choose their leaders and participate in politics. In the mid-nineteenth century, Keyssar argues, reformers commonly depicted suffrage as "a right that had to be earned: by paying taxes, serving in the militia, or even laboring on the public roads." In 1865, Henry Ward Beecher advocated black men's voting rights by asserting that black men had "earned and deserved" the franchise through their "heroic military service" and "unswerving fidelity to the Union." Similar arguments were made by Republican legislators in the debates about the Fifteenth Amendment to the Constitution. Keyssar, *The Right to Vote*, 14–15, 41, 103; Henry Ward Beecher, *Universal Suffrage, and Complete Equality in Citizenship* (Boston: Geo. C. Rand & Avery, 1865), 9–10.

93. Aileen Kraditor, *The Ideas of the Woman Suffrage Movement*; Karlyn Kohrs Campbell, *Man Cannot Speak for Her*, vol. 1, *A Critical Study of Early Feminist Rhetoric* (Westport, CT: Praeger Publishers, 1989), 9–10.

94. Randall Lake, "'She Flies with Her Own Wings': The Collected Speeches of Abigail Scott Duniway (1834–1915)," asduniway.org/home/.

95. John Locke, *The Two Treatises of Civil Government* (Oxford: Basil Blackwell, 1948); Thomas Hobbes, *Leviathan*, ed. M. Oakeshott (Oxford: Basil Blackwell, 1957).

96. Slotkin, *Gunfighter Nation*, 11, 14.

97. Slotkin, *Gunfighter Nation*, 11, 19.

98. Duniway, "Woman in Oregon History—February 14, 1899." She made a similar claim in her speech delivered at the World's Columbian Exposition in 1893, in which she praised Westerners as "descendants of the hardy stock of Anglo-Saxons who long ago conquered the adverse climatic elements of the Atlantic seaboard." Duniway, "The Pacific Northwest—June 1, 1893."

99. Duniway, "'Success in Sight'—February 12, 1900."

100. Duniway, "The Pioneer Mother—July 6, 1905."

101. Duniway, "Lewis and Clark Exposition—October 6, 1905."

102. Duniway, "The Pioneer Mother—July 6, 1905."

103. Cindy Koenig Richards, "Inventing Sacagawea: Public Women and the Transformative Potential of Epideictic Rhetoric," *Western Journal of Communication* 73 (2009): 5.

104. Moynihan, *Rebel for Rights*, 177.

105. Duniway, "'Success in Sight'—February 12, 1900."

106. Duniway, "'Ballots and Bullets'—January 23, 1889."

107. Duniway, "Equal Rights for All—July 17, 1889.

108. Duniway, "'How to Win the Ballot'—May 2, 1899."

109. Duniway, "'How to Win the Ballot'—May 2, 1899."

110. Duniway told the 1884 NWSA convention that "the hearts of the men of the great Pacific Northwest were right toward women," because, "no sooner had we begun to agitate the question of equal rights than men responded to our plea" by helping her establish her woman suffrage journal. Duniway, "National Woman Suffrage Association

Convention—March 4, 1884."

111. Duniway, "Equal Rights for All—July 17, 1889."

112. Duniway, "'How to Win the Ballot'—May 2, 1899."

113. Duniway, "'Success in Sight'—February 12, 1900."

114. Duniway, "'How to Win the Ballot'—May 2, 1899."

115. Duniway, "Lewis and Clark Exposition—October 6, 1905."

116. Duniway, "Eminent Women I Have Met—June 1, 1900."

117. Duniway, "Oregon State Equal Suffrage Association—November 20, 1897."

118. "Remarks by Mrs. Duniway," *New Northwest*, April 24, 1884.

119. Duniway, "U.S. Senate Select Committee on Woman Suffrage—March 7, 1884."

120. Duniway, "U.S. Senate Select Committee on Woman Suffrage—March 7, 1884."

121. Duniway, "'Success in Sight'—February 12, 1900."

122. Duniway, "'Success in Sight'—February 12, 1900."

123. Rebecca J. Mead, *How the Vote Was Won: Woman Suffrage in the Western United States, 1868-1914* (New York: New York University Press, 2004); Moynihan, "Abigail Scott Duniway"; "Pioneer Oregon Suffragist Is Happy," *Oregon Journal*, October 11, 1912, 14.

124. "Oregon's Pioneer Woman Suffrage Advocate Is Honored," *Oregon Journal*, October 23, 1912, 13.

125. Duniway, *Path Breaking*, 67.

126. Abigail Scott Duniway, letter to Clyde Duniway, Duniway Papers, Box 32, November 18, 1896. University of Oregon Libraries, Special Collections and University Archives, Eugene, OR.

127. Duniway, letter to Clyde Duniway, Duniway Papers, Box 32, November 18, 1896. University of Oregon Libraries, Special Collections and University Archives, Eugene, OR.

128. Duniway, *Path Breaking*, 259.

129. Abigail Scott Duniway, "Editorial Correspondence," *New Northwest*, September 30, 1886, 1; Moynihan, *Rebel for Rights*.

130. Duniway, *Path Breaking*, 203, 227.

131. Abigail Scott Duniway, letter to Anna Howard Shaw, Duniway Papers,

September 18, 1906. University of Oregon Libraries, Special Collections and University Archives, Eugene, OR.

132. Duniway, letter to Anna Howard Shaw.

133. Sarah A. Evans, "Oregon," in *History of Woman Suffrage*, vol. 6, ed. I. H. Harper (New York: National American Woman Suffrage Association, 1922), 538–549.

134. Abigail Scott Duniway, "Editorial Correspondence," *New Northwest*, November 20, 1874, 2.

135. Ethel Smith, *Testimony from Western States on Anti-Party Policy of the Congressional Union*, Records of the National American Woman Suffrage Association 1839–1961, Reel 33 (n.d.). Manuscript Division, Library of Congress, Washington, DC; Mead, *How the Vote Was Won*.

136. Christine A. Lunardini and Thomas J. Knock, "Woodrow Wilson and Woman Suffrage: A New Look," *Political Science Quarterly* 95 (1981): 655–671.

137. "The Spirit of the West," *Votes for Women* (WA), December 1910.

138. Belle Squire, "Suffragists Rejoice Greatly Over the Winning of California," *Chicago Tribune*, October 15, 1911, 8.

139. "The Spirit of the West," *Votes for Women* (WA), December 1910.

140. "National American Convention of 1905," in *History of Woman Suffrage*, vol. 5, ed. I. H. Harper (New York: National American Woman Suffrage Association, 1922), 136.

141. "National American Convention of 1905," 136.

142. Squire, "Suffragists Rejoice Greatly."

143. Leroy Dorsey, "Managing Women's Equality: Theodore Roosevelt, the Frontier Myth, and the Modern Woman," *Rhetoric & Public Affairs* 16 (2013): 423–456.

144. Bertha Rickoff, "Ballad of the 'Vote,'" *San Francisco Call*, October 3, 1911, 7.

Chapter 2. Visualizing the West:
Suffrage Maps' Imagery of Legitimacy, Civilization, and Continental Expansion, 1907–1917

1. The first suffrage map may have been created during the Chicago campaign for municipal woman suffrage that ran from 1905 to 1907. In

1907, Anna Nicholes prepared a map of all the US cities that had enacted municipal suffrage for women, as a means of persuading Chicago voters to do the same. Catharine Waugh McCulloch, *Woman's Journal*, January 18, 1908, 12; "That Suffrage Map," *Woman's Journal*, February 1, 1908, 19; Bertha Damaris Knobe, "That Suffrage Map," *Woman's Journal*, March 14, 1908, 42.

2. These maps often featured Wyoming, Utah, Idaho, and Colorado as states that had fully enfranchised all women. But Idaho's franchise excluded American Indian women, Utah restricted some elections to property owners, and Wyoming required voters to pass literacy tests. Alexander Keyssar, *The Right to Vote: The Contested History of Democracy in the United States* (New York: Basic Books, 2000), 335, 345, 363.

3. Bertha Damaris Knobe, "The Suffragists' Uprising," *Appleton Magazine* (December 1907), 772–779.

4. Knobe, "That Suffrage Map," 42; "Parade to Glow," *Woman's Journal*, February 22, 1913, 62; "Order of March," *Woman's Journal*, March 1, 1913, 72; "Celebrating the 'Ratification' by the Ninth State," parade float in Omaha, Kansas, 1912, from Carrie Chapman Catt Photograph Album (Catt2.13.1b). Carrie Chapman Catt Papers, Special Collections Department, Bryn Mawr College Library. The "Ninth State" was Kansas. "Votes for Women Slogan of Parade," *Sunday Evening Star* (DC), May 4, 1913, 13.

5. "Parade to Glow," 62; "Order of March," 72; "Celebrating the 'Ratification' by the Ninth State"; "Votes for Women Slogan of Parade," *Sunday Evening Star*, May 4, 1913, 13; 1916 Suffrage Billboard, Susan B. Anthony Ephemera Collection, Huntington Library; "Walks and Wins with Two-Ft. Map," *Woman's Journal*, February 1, 1913, 40; "Suffrage Army Trudging on Way to Washington and Miss Lavinia Dock with Her Suffrage Map," *Gulfport Daily Herald*, February 26, 1913, 1.

6. "Map of America Changes: Chance Offered for Clearing Complexions in Many States by November When Question Marks Will Be Removed and Welfare of Whole Country Will Be Affected," *Woman's Journal*, March 23, 1912, 91; "Suffrage Leaders Get Their Innings," *New York Times*, May 19, 1915, 5; "Big Suffrage Party for Mrs. Whitman," *New York Times*, October

10, 1915, 14; Ida Husted Harper, *History of Woman Suffrage*, vol. 6 (New York: National American Woman Suffrage Association, 1922), 398, 405, 463, 471.

7. Christine Dando, "'The Map Proves It': Map Use by the American Woman Suffrage Movement," *Cartographica* 45 (2010): 222.

8. Catherine H. Palczewski, "The 1919 Prison Special: Constituting White Women's Citizenship," *Quarterly Journal of Speech* 102 (2016): 107–132; Michele E. Ramsey, "Inventing Citizens During World War I: Suffrage Cartoons in *The Woman Citizen*," *Western Journal of Communication* 64 (2000): 113–147; Jennifer L. Borda, "The Woman Suffrage Parades of 1910–1913: Possibilities and Limitations of an Early Feminist Rhetorical Strategy," *Western Journal of Communication* 66 (2002): 25–53; Belinda Stillion Southard, "Militancy, Power, and Identity: The Silent Sentinels as Women Fighting for Political Voice," *Rhetoric & Public Affairs* 10 (2007): 399–417; Angela G. Ray, "The Rhetorical Ritual of Citizenship: Women's Voting as Public Performance, 1868–1875," *Quarterly Journal of Speech* 93 (2007): 1–26; Mary Chapman, *Making Noise, Making News: Suffrage Print Culture and U.S. Modernism* (Oxford: Oxford University Press, 2014); Linda J. Lumsden, *Rampant Women: Suffragists and the Right of Assembly* (Knoxville: University of Tennessee Press, 1997); Alice Sheppard, *Cartooning for Suffrage* (Santa Fe: University of New Mexico Press, 1993); Margaret M. Finnegan, *Selling Suffrage: Consumer Culture and Votes for Women* (New York: Columbia University Press, 1999), 58–59.

9. *Woman Suffrage* (Boston, MA: Massachusetts Woman Suffrage Association, 1915).

10. Henrietta Livermore, *Six Arguments from the Suffrage Map* (New York: National Woman Suffrage Publishing Company, Inc, 1917).

11. "First Suffrage Map of US 1869, Last Suffrage Map of US 1917," *Woman's Journal*, September 22, 1917, 317.

12. "Map of America Changes," *Woman's Journal*, March 23, 1912, 91.

13. Timothy Barney, *Mapping the Cold War: Cartography and the Framing of America's International Power* (Chapel Hill: University of North Carolina Press, 2015); Tim Barney, "Power Lines: The Rhetoric of Maps as Social Change in the Post-Cold War Landscape," *Quarterly Journal of Speech* 95 (2009):

412–434; Samantha Senda-Cook, "Materializing Tensions: How Maps and Trails Mediate Nature," *Environmental Communication* 7 (2013): 355–371; Joshua P. Ewalt, "Mapping Injustice: The *World Is Witness*, Place-Framing, and the Politics of Viewing on Google Earth," *Communication, Culture, & Critique* 4 (2011): 333–354.

14. Timothy Barney theorizes that a map possesses a "rhetorical life"—"a lifespan in which it exists as a communicative practice," and has the ability to "reflect and shape" political and historical contexts. Barney, *Mapping the Cold War*, 11–15; Ewalt, "Mapping Injustice."

15. Samantha Senda-Cook's analysis of national park maps demonstrates that park maps shape where visitors go, what they do, and how they think and feel about their experience. Lawrence J. Prelli argues that maps can dispose viewers' attitudes toward supporting legal claims. Senda-Cook, "Materializing Tensions"; Lawrence J. Prelli, "Visualizing a Bounded Sea: A Case Study in Rhetorical Taxis," in *Rhetorics of Display*, ed. Lawrence J. Prelli (University of South Carolina Press, 2006), 90–120; Barney, *Mapping the Cold War*, 14–15; Ewalt, "Mapping Injustice"; J. B. Harley, *The New Nature of Maps: Essays in the History of Cartography,* ed. Paul Laxton (Baltimore, MD: Johns Hopkins University Press, 2001), 112–113.

16. Barney, *Mapping the Cold War*, 2.

17. As Karlyn Kohrs Campbell explains, rhetorical agency is "the capacity to act . . . in a way that will be recognized or heeded by others in one's community," and is "communal . . . and, simultaneously, constituted and constrained by the material and symbolic elements of context and culture." Karlyn Kohrs Campbell, "Agency: Promiscuous and Protean," *Communication and Critical/Cultural Studies* 2, no. 1 (2005): 3.

18. "Our Flag," *Woman's Journal*, September 13, 1890, 289.

19. "Adoption of a New Flag," *Woman's Tribune*, July 11, 1891, 220.

20. "Adoption of a New Flag," *Woman's Tribune*, July 11, 1891, 220.

21. Emma Smith DeVoe, "Wanted a Flag," *Woman's Journal*, August 8, 1891, 254.

22. "Adoption of a New Flag," *Woman's Tribune*, July 11, 1891, 220; "People's Party and Woman Suffrage," *Woman's Journal*, September 3, 1892, 288.

23. "Adoption of a New Flag," *Woman's Tribune*, July 11, 1891, 220.

24. A. S. B., "A Suffrage Exhibit," *Woman's Journal*, September 4, 1909, 142.

25. Denis Wood and John Fels, *The Natures of Maps: Cartographic Constructions of the Natural World* (Chicago: University of Chicago Press, 2008), xvi.

26. Wood and Fels, *The Natures of Maps*, xvi, 7.

27. J. H. Andrews, "Introduction: Meaning, Knowledge, and Power in the Map Philosophy of J.B. Harley," in *The New Nature of Maps: Essays in the History of Cartography*, ed. Paul Laxton (Baltimore: John Hopkins University Press, 2001), 9; Harley, *The New Nature of Maps*, 37; Jeremy Black, *Maps and Politics* (Chicago: University of Chicago Press, 1998), 105.

28. Mark Monmonier, *How to Lie with Maps*, 2nd ed. (Chicago: University of Chicago Press, 1996), 87.

29. Black, *Maps and Politics*, 12, 105; Harley, *The New Nature of Maps*, 37, 163; Judith A. Tyner, "Persuasive Cartography," *Journal of Geography* 81 (1982): 140–144.

30. Wood and Fels, *The Natures of Maps*, 14.

31. Black, *Maps and Politics*, 109.

32. Barney, *Mapping the Cold War*, 6.

33. John Louis Recchiuti, *Civic Engagement: Social Science and Progressive-Era Reform in New York City* (Philadelphia: University of Pennsylvania Press, 2007); Lorraine Daston and Peter Galison, "The Image of Objectivity," *Representations* (1992): 81–128; Cheryl R. Jorgensen-Earp and Darwin D. Jorgensen, "Physiology and Physical Force: The Effect of Edwardian Science on Women's Suffrage," *Southern Journal of Communication* 81 (2016): 136–155.

34. Ellen Fitzpatrick, *Endless Crusade: Women Social Scientists and Progressive Reform* (Oxford: Oxford University Press, 1990); Theda Skocpol, *Protecting Soldiers and Mothers: The Political Origins of Social Policy in the United States* (Cambridge, MA: Harvard University Press, 1992).

35. Carolyn Skinner, "Medical Discovery as Suffrage Justification in Mary Putnam Jacobi's 1894 New York Campaign Rhetoric," *Advances in the History of Rhetoric* 19 (2016): 251–275; Robin E. Jensen, *Dirty Words: The Rhetoric of Public Sex Education, 1870-1924* (Urbana: University of Illinois Press, 2010).

36. Susan Schulten, *Mapping the Nation: History and Cartography in*

Nineteenth-Century America (Chicago: University of Chicago Press, 2012).

37. Knobe, "The Suffragist's Uprising," 772, 774.

38. Wood and Fels, *The Natures of Maps*, xv; Harley, *The New Nature of Maps*, 163.

39. Harley, *The New Nature of Maps*, 54, 165.

40. "A Suffrage Map," *Woman's Journal*, January 11, 1908, 1.

41. Bertha Damaris Knobe, "Votes for Women: An Object-Lesson," *Harper's Weekly*, April 25, 1908; "New Leaflets," *Woman's Journal*, February, 8, 1908, 24.

42. Alice Park, "Suffrage Map Enlarged," *Woman's Journal*, July 18, 1908, 113; Alice Stone Blackwell, "A Suffrage Exhibit: Suffrage Maps," *Woman's Journal*, September 4, 1909, 142; "Walks and Wins with Two-Ft. Map," *Woman's Journal*, February 1, 1913, 40.

43. Park, "Suffrage Map Enlarged," 113.

44. Leone Cass Baer, "News and Gossip of Plays and Players," *Morning Oregonian*, August 8, 1915, 2.

45. "Walks and Wins with Two-Ft. Map," *Woman's Journal*, February 1, 1913, 40.

46. Blackwell, "A Suffrage Exhibit," 142; "Walks and Wins with Two-Ft. Map," *Woman's Journal*, February 1, 1913; "Talk and Suffrage Tea," *Trenton Evening Times*, February 16, 1914, 1; "Observations and Comment," *Macon Daily Telegraph*, June 17, 1915, 4; "Equal Suffrage Meeting," *Trenton Evening Times*, October 18, 1916, 13; Harper, *History of Woman Suffrage*, vol. 6, 405; "Statement of Mrs. Crystal Eastman Benedict, of New York City," *Women Suffrage: Hearings on Woman Suffrage, March 3, 1914*, US Congressional House Committee on the Judiciary (Washington, DC: US Government Printing Office, 1914), 21–24.

47. "New Suffrage Map for 1914," *Trenton Evening Times*, February 20, 1917, 10; "United States Suffrage Map Today!" *Salt Lake Evening Telegram*, November 4, 1914, 13; "Great Advance of Suffrage," *New York Times*, May 4, 1913, SM3; "Three More States of the Union Will Ballot on Suffrage," *San Jose Mercury Herald*, October 28, 1915, 6; "State-Wide Campaign Is Being Waged by Women to Put Missouri on Suffrage Map," *Wilkes-Barre Times Leader* (PA), May 30, 1914, 7; "The World Grows Whiter," *Kalamazoo Gazette*, February 22, 1917, 7; "Very Latest in Suffrage Map," *Duluth*

News Tribune, September 8, 1917, 7; "Suffrage Gets Setback by War and Picketing," *Idaho Daily Statesman*, October 14, 1917, 3; "10,121,931 Women in U.S. Have Vote in Presidential Elections," *Times-Picayune*, December 30, 1917, 42; "Woman Suffrage," *Miami Herald*, April 4, 1917, 8.

48. Schulten, *Mapping the Nation*.

49. Cara A. Finnegan, "The Naturalistic Enthymeme and Visual Argument: Photographic Representation in the 'Skull Controversies,'" *Argumentation and Advocacy* 37 (2001): 133–149.

50. Black, *Maps and Politics*, 104; Schulten, *Mapping the Nation*.

51. Black, *Maps and Politics*, 98.

52. Barney, *Mapping the Cold War*, 33, 107.

53. Alyssa Samek, "Mobility, Citizenship, and 'American Women on the Move' in the 1977 International Women's Year Torch Relay," *Quarterly Journal of Speech* 103 (2017): 207–229; Leslie Harris, "Rhetorical Mobilities and the City: The White Slavery Controversy and Racialized Protection of Women in the U.S.," *Quarterly Journal of Speech* 104 (2018): 22–46; Daniel C. Brouwer, "From San Francisco to Atlanta and Back Again: Ideologies of Mobility in the AIDS Quilt's Search for a Homeland," *Rhetoric & Public Affairs* 10, no. 4 (2007): 701–721.

54. Italics added. "A Suffrage Map," *Woman's Journal*, January 11, 1908, 1.

55. Italics added. "A Suffrage Map," *Woman's Leader and the Common Cause*, August 29, 1913, 353.

56. The four Western suffrage states had a population of 1,070,722 combined, compared to the US population of 76,303,387 (including Alaska, Hawaii, Indian Territory, and Indian reservations). *1900 Census*, vol. 1, *Population, Part 1* (Washington, DC: US Census Bureau, 1901), xviii.

57. "Population Votes, Not Area," *Utica Observer*, July 28, 1915, 5.

58. Mary Radcliffe, "In the Outer Darkness," *New York Times*, April 19, 1915.

59. Schulten, *Mapping the Nation*.

60. Walter Clark, letter to Maud Younger, February 8, 1919, Library of Congress, National Woman's Party Papers, reel 69, frame 165.

61. "Lesson of the Suffrage Map," *Woman's Journal*, November 16, 1912, 1; "The New Suffrage Map," *Suffragist*, November 7, 1914, 1.

62. Ida Husted Harper, *History of Woman Suffrage*, vol. 5 (New York: National

American Woman Suffrage Association, 1922), 531, 532.

63. "First Suffrage Map of U.S. 1869," 317; *Woman's Journal*, March 10, 1917, 1; Flyer titled "Seeing Is Believing!" (New York City: NAWSA Publishing Co., 1919).

64. Harris, "Rhetorical Mobilities," 26.

65. Votes for Women: A Success. Map. (New York: National American Woman Suffrage Association, 1914). The Dobkin Family Collection of Feminist History at the Roosevelt House Public Policy Institute at Hunter College.

66. "Letters to the Telegraph," *Macon Daily Telegraph*, March 19, 1918, 6.

67. Samek, "Mobility, Citizenship," 7–8.

68. Knobe, "The Suffragist's Uprising," 774.

69. During the 1870s and 1880s, the US Census Bureau began mapping their results, and their maps were so popular that they were widely reproduced in government, educational, and commercial contexts. These statistical maps visualized the US population density and other results of the census with shading, which made the information more accessible. The majority of the Census Bureau's maps also reported the location of the ever-advancing "frontier line of settlement" that identified where the settled land ended and the unsettled frontier (land that had fewer than two white residents per square mile) began. These maps of the frontier line and US population were foundational to Frederick Jackson Turner's essay on "The Significance of the Frontier." He studied the maps closely while completing his research on western migration, sent his essay to the director of the Census Bureau, and later credited the maps with shaping his thinking. Even on those that did not include the official "frontier line," the maps depicted the population that moved further westward every year and portrayed the Western half of the continent as unsettled and unpopulated. In 1890, the number of white Americans living in the West was so great that there was no longer a distinct line between settled and unsettled land. As a result, the US Census Bureau announced the "closure of the frontier." The disappearance of the frontier line may have made the 1890 proclamation that much more jarring, as Americans had become accustomed to the visualization of the nation with a line

separating the settled East from the unsettled West. Susan Schulten, *The Geographical Imagination in America, 1880–1950* (Chicago: University of Chicago Press, 2001); Schulten, *Mapping the Nation*; *Report of the Ninth Census*, vol. 1, *The Statistics of the Population of the United States; Compiled from the Original Returns of the Ninth Census, June 1, 1870, under the Direction of the Secretary of the Interior by Francis A. Walker, Superintendent of the Census* (Washington, DC: US Government Printing Office, 1872); *Statistical Atlas of the United States Based on the Results of the Ninth Census 1870; Compiled under Authority of Congress by Francis A. Walker, M.A. Superintendent of the 9th Census*, (Washington, DC: US Government Printing Office, 1874; David M. Wrobel, *The End of American Exceptionalism: Frontier Anxiety from the Old West to the New Deal* (Lawrence, University Press of Kansas, 1993), 30; *Eleventh United States Census, 1890* (Washington: US Government Printing Office, 1892).

70. Belinda A. Stillion Southard, *Militant Citizenship: Rhetorical Strategies of the National Woman's Party, 1913–1920* (College Station: Texas A&M University Press, 2011), 78.

71. John L. O'Sullivan, "The True Title," *Morning News*, December 27, 1845, 1.

72. Amy S. Greenberg, *Manifest Manhood and the Antebellum American Empire* (Cambridge: Cambridge University Press, 2005), 1.

73. Suffragists' verbal arguments often featured woman suffrage as an attribute of civilized cultures. Allison L. Sneider, *Suffragists in an Imperial Age: U.S. Expansion and the Woman Question, 1870–1929* (Oxford: Oxford University Press, 2008).

74. Michael Osborn, "Archetypal Metaphor in Rhetoric: The Light-Dark Family," *Quarterly Journal of Speech* 53 (1967): 117; see also Michael Osborn, *Michael Osborn on Metaphor and Style* (East Lansing: Michigan State University Press, 2018), 59–93; Michael Osborn, "Rhetorical Depiction," in *Form, Genre, and the Study of Political Discourse*, ed. Herbert W. Simons and Aram A. Aghazarian (Columbia: University of South Carolina Press, 1986), 79–107.

75. Harry Osborn, "Two More Bright Spots on the Map," *Maryland Suffrage News*, November 14, 1914.

76. Michael Friendly and Gilles Palsky, "Visualizing Nature and Society," in *Maps: Finding Our Place in the World*, ed. James R. Akerman and Robert

W. Karrow Jr. (Chicago: University of Chicago Press), 240–242; Jeremy
W. Crampton, "GIS and Geographic Governance: Reconstructing
the Choropleth Map," *Cartographica* 39 (2004): 41–43; Susan Schulten,
"Mapping American History," in *Maps: Finding Our Place in the World*, ed.
James R. Akerman and Robert W. Karrow Jr. (Chicago: University of
Chicago Press, 2007), 187.

77. In 1837, abolitionist Julius Rubens Ames created the "Moral Map of the
United States," which shaded the US states that practiced enslavement
in black and other states in white. He paired the map with Lafayette's
quote, "Slavery is a dark spot on the face of the nation." The quote
underlined the visual connotation of using black to represent evil and
white to represent morality. Rubens's map was updated, republished,
and recreated for different purposes. In 1861, Edwin Hergesheimer
made another popular map of enslavement that President Abraham
Lincoln was known to study so regularly that the map was included
in his portrait. Hergesheimer's map used data from the 1860 census to
visualize the spatial distribution of the four million enslaved people
living in the United States by county. Counties with a larger enslaved
population were shaded in black and dark gray. Julius Rubens Ames,
"Moral Map of the United States," in *Liberty: The Image and Superscription on
Every Coin Issued by the United States of America* (New York: American Anti-
Slave Society, 1837), 66; William C. Reynolds, "Reynolds's Political Map
of the United States," 1856, Geography and Map Division, Library of
Congress, Washington, DC; Francis Bicknell Carpenter, *First Reading of
the Emancipation Proclamation of President Lincoln*, 1864, US Senate Collection,
Library of Congress Prints and Photographs Division, Washington,
DC; Susan Schulten, "The Cartography of Slavery and the Authority of
Statistics," *Civil War History* 56 (2010): 5–32.

78. Older Americans encountering the suffrage map may have been familiar
with the black and white imagery of enslavement maps. As Schulten
notes, the enslavement map was copied by a number of other mapmakers
and reproduced widely in newspapers and magazines, "suggest[ing]
that it struck a chord outside the White House as well." But the suffrage
maps were popular fifty years after the enslavement maps, so it's

difficult to know whether Americans would have associated the suffrage maps with the maps of enslavement. Schulten, *Mapping the Nation,* 143; Charles Sumner, "The Barbarism of Slavery," Speech on the Bill for the Admission of Kansas as a Free State, in the United States Senate, June 4, 1860; "The 'Twin Relics of Barbarism,'" *New York Times,* July 18, 1869, 4; "A Relic of Barbarism," *New York Times,* August 8, 1865.

79. Amy Kaplan, "'Manifest Domesticity.' No More Separate Spheres!" *American Literature* 70 (1998): 582; Gail Bederman, *Manliness and Civilization: A Cultural History of Gender and Race in the United States, 1880–1917* (Chicago: University of Chicago Press, 1995). I discuss the discourse of civilization throughout this book, focusing primarily on beliefs about civilization at the turn of the century. For further discussion of civilization discourse throughout US history, see Robert L. Ivie, "Savagery in Democracy's Empire," *Third World Quarterly* 26 (2005): 55–65; Robert L. Ivie, "Democracy, War, and Decivilizing Metaphors of American Insecurity," in *Metaphorical World Politics*, ed. Francis A. Beer and Christ'l De Landtsheer (East Lansing: Michigan State University Press, 2004), 75–90.

80. "Metropolis Fluttering Yellow Sea Thirty-Five Thousand Enthusiasts Tramp through Streets of New York," *Salt Lake Evening Telegram*, May, 3, 1913, 1; "35,000 March in Suffrage Parade," *Fort Worth Star-Telegram*, May 3, 1913, 1; "35,000 Women in Line New York Suffrage Parade the Biggest Demonstration," *Kansas City Times*, May 3, 1913; "35,000 March in Suffrage Parade," *Cleburn Morning Review*, May 4, 1913, 10; "A Square Deal for Women," *Philadelphia North American*, October 30, 1915, n.p., newspaper clipping in Collection of Woman Suffrage Clippings by Mrs. Oliver H. P. Belmont, September 26, 1915, to December 30, 1915, vol. 15, National Woman's Party Collection.

81. "The World Grows Whiter," *Lexington Herald*, March 12, 1917, 8; "Woman Suffrage," *Miami Herald*, April 4, 1917, 8.

82. Angela Y. Davis, *Women, Race, and Class* (New York: Random House, 1981).

83. "Votes for Women a Success," map, Austin Woman Suffrage Association, 1913, Erminia Thompson Folsom Papers, Archives and Information Services Division, Texas State Library and Archives Commission.

84. "Newspaper Sentiment. Woman and the Franchise," *Charlotte Observer*, November 6, 1916, 4.

85. Zornitsa Keremidchieva, "The Congressional Debates on the 19th Amendment: Jurisdictional Rhetoric and the Assemblage of the US Body Politic," *Quarterly Journal of Speech* 99 (2013): 51–73.

86. Samek, "Mobility, Citizenship," 208.

87. "Rains Coin for Cause at Carnegie Hall," *New York Tribune*, February 18, 1913, 3.

88. "Moving Map at Carnegie Hall," *Woman's Journal*, February 8, 1913, 48.

89. "Rains Coin for Cause at Carnegie Hall," *New York Tribune*, February 18, 1913, 3.

90. Nigel Rees, *A Word in Your Shell-Like: 6,000 Curious and Everyday Phrases Explained* (Glasgow: Collins, 2004).

91. Samek, "Mobility, Citizenship," 8.

92. "Eastward the Tide of Woman Suffrage Takes Its Way," *Current Opinion*, November 1915, 297–299.

93. "The Changing Map," *Woman's Journal*, September 23, 1916, 308.

94. "Statement of Mrs. Crystal Eastman Benedict," 21–24.

95. Mrs. William Forse Scott, "Suffrage a Failure: States That Have It Are Declared to be Sorry," *New York Times*, January 24, 1915, 4; "Time to Fight the Folly of Feminism," *Reply: An Anti-Suffrage Magazine* 7 (1915), 19.

96. "Suffrage Moving Steadily East," *Woman's Journal*, November 20, 1915, 369.

97. Alice Stone Blackwell, "The Progress of Woman Suffrage," in *Woman Suffrage* (Boston: Massachusetts Woman Suffrage Association, 1915), 2. History of Women Collection, microfilm reel #950, no. 9140, Arthur and Elizabeth Schlesinger Library on the History of Women in America, Harvard University.

98. Italics added. "Statement of Mrs. Crystal Eastman Benedict, of New York City," *Women Suffrage: Hearings on Woman Suffrage, March 3, 1914*, United States Congressional House Committee on the Judiciary (Washington, DC: US Government Printing Office, 1914), 21–24.

99. "Suffrage Moving Steadily East," *Woman's Journal*, November 20, 1915, 369.

100. Samek, "Mobility, Citizenship."

101. "Our Woman Suffrage Map—July, 1917," *General Federation Bulletin* 16 (1917): 9.

102. George Berkeley, "Verses on the Prospect of Planning Arts and Learning in America," *A Miscellany, Containing Several Tracts on Various Subjects, 1752* (London: J. & R. Tonson and S. Draper), 186–187; John Quincy Adams, "Further Strictures on Mr. Russell's Representations and Estimates," in *The Duplicate Letters, the Fisheries and the Mississippi*, collected by John Quincy Adams (Washington: Davis and Force, 1822), 187; Albert J. Beveridge, "March of the Flag," September 16, 1898, Voices of Democracy: The U.S. Oratory Project, www.voicesofdemocracy.umd.edu.

103. Emanuel Gottlieb Leutze, *Westward the Course of Empire Takes Its Way*, 1861, Smithsonian American Art Museum, Washington, DC; John Gast, *American Progress*, 1872, Museum of the American West, Los Angeles, CA.

104. Greenberg, *Manifest Manhood*, 1.

105. "Our Flag," *Woman's Journal*, September 13, 1890, 289; "Adoption of a New Flag," *Woman's Tribune*, July 11, 1891, 220; "The Lone Star of Suffrage," *Woman's Journal*, July 30, 1892, 246; Woman Suffrage Flag, 1900, at the Smithsonian National Museum of American History, Washington, DC.

106. "Eastward the Tide of Woman Suffrage Takes Its Way," *Current Opinion* 59, no. 5, November 1915, 297–299.

107. Elbert Hubbard, "Ohio Next," *Hearst's Magazine* 22 (1912), 131–132.

108. "Vigorous Fight in Buckeye State," *Woman's Journal and Suffrage News*, October 3, 1914, 1.

109. John T. McCutcheon, "The First One East of the 'Mother of Waters,'" *Chicago Daily Tribune*, June 12, 1913, 1.

110. Henry Mayer, "The Awakening," *Puck Magazine* (February 20, 1915), 14–15.

111. Front cover of the *Suffragist*, January 8, 1916.

112. "Roosevelt Centre of Suffrage Host: Crowded Metropolitan Opera House Cheers the Colonel's Defense of His Faith," *New York Times*, May 3, 1913, 1–2.

113. Jenny Rice argues that "appeals to regional identity may actually be in service to national identity," and sometimes serve as shorthand for

nationalistic claims." "From Architectonic to Tectonics: Introducing Regional Rhetorics," *Rhetoric Society Quarterly* 42, no. 3 (2012): 208.

CHAPTER 3. DISMISSING THE WEST:
ANTISUFFRAGISTS' WILD AND WOOLLY WEST, 1903–1919

1. Walter C. Taylor, "No Eastern States," *New York Times*, May 7, 1913, 10.
2. Antisuffrage periodicals included the *Remonstrance*, the *Anti-Suffragist*, *Woman's Protest*, *Woman Patriot*, and the *Reply*.
3. "The Four Woman-Suffrage States," *Anti-Suffragist* 1, no. 3 (1909): 7.
4. Billie Barnes Jensen, "'In the Weird and Wooly West': Antisuffrage women, gender issues, and woman suffrage in the West," *Journal of the West* 32 (1993): 41–51.
5. Thomas Rosteck, "Form and cultural context in rhetorical criticism: Re-reading Wrage," *Quarterly Journal of Speech* 84 (1998): 471–490.
6. "Suffrage, East and West," *New York Times*, October 16, 1915, 10.
7. "Suffrage, East and West," *New York Times*, October 16, 1915, 10.
8. "Suffrage, East and West," *New York Times*, October 16, 1915, 10.
9. "Suffrage, East and West," *New York Times*, October 16, 1915, 10.
10. "Suffrage, East and West," *New York Times*, October 16, 1915, 10.
11. Kristy Maddux, "When Patriots Protest: The Anti-Suffrage Discourse Transformation of 1917," *Rhetoric & Public Affairs* 7 (2004): 287; Anne M. Benjamin, *A History of the Anti-Suffrage Movement in the United States from 1895 to 1920: Women Against Equality* (Lewiston, NY: Edwin Mellen Press, 1991), 3; Jane J. Camhi, *Women Against Women* (Brooklyn: Carlson Publishing, 1994), 77–79. The Massachusetts Association Opposed to the Further Extension of Suffrage to Women and the New York State Association Opposed to Woman Suffrage were founded in the 1890s. Similar antisuffrage state organizations formed in California, Illinois, New York, Oregon, South Dakota, and Washington by 1900.
12. Thomas Jablonsky, *The Home, Heaven, and Mother Party* (Brooklyn: Carlson Publishing, 1994), 120–121; Jensen, "In the Weird and Wooly West," 41.
13. Manuela Thurner, "'Better Citizens Without the Ballot': American AntiSuffrage Women and Their Rationale During the Progressive Era," *Journal of Women's History* 5 (1993): 33–60.

14. Catherine Palczewski, "The Male Madonna and the Feminine Uncle Sam: Visual Arguments, Icons, and Ideographs in 1909 Anti-Woman Suffrage Postcards," *Quarterly Journal of Speech* 91 (2005): 365–394.
15. Jablonsky, *The Home*, 95–99.
16. Maddux, "When Patriots Protest," 292.
17. Many suffragists believed that antis were motivated or paid by corporations and major industries that were financially threatened by women's potential voting rights, such as liquor, the railroad, textiles, manufacturing, and oil. But the most recent historical scholarship shows that women opposed suffrage according to rationales based on pragmatism, racism, reform, separate spheres ideology, biology, and theology. Maddux, "When Patriots Protest"; Eleanor Flexner and Ellen Fitzpatrick, *Century of Struggle: The Woman's Rights Movement in the United States* (Cambridge: Harvard University Press, 1996); Camhi, *Women Against Women*; Thurner, "'Better Citizens Without the Ballot'"; Jablonsky, *The Home*.
18. Palczewski, "The Male Madonna."
19. Thurner, "'Better Citizens Without the Ballot.'"
20. Palczewski, "The Male Madonna."
21. Aileen Kraditor, *The Ideas of the Woman Suffrage Movement, 1890-1920* (New York: Columbia University Press, 1962).
22. Jablonsky, *The Home*, 48.
23. Maddux, "When Patriots Protest," 288; Kraditor, *The Ideas of the Woman Suffrage Movement*, 15–23.
24. Palczewski, "The Male Madonna," 375–376.
25. Rebecca J. Mead, *How the Vote Was Won: Woman Suffrage in the Western United States, 1868-1914* (New York: New York University Press, 2004), 144.
26. Palczewski, "The Male Madonna"; Maddux, "When Patriots Protest," 292; Kraditor, *The Ideas of the Woman Suffrage Movement*.
27. Palczewski, "The Male Madonna"; Jablonsky, *The Home*; Maddux, "When Patriots Protest."
28. The official name of the Mormon Church is The Church of Jesus Christ of Latter-day Saints, but as other scholars and Mormons do, I will use the more common name of the church.

29. Angela G. Ray, *The Lyceum and Public Culture in the Nineteenth-Century United States* (East Lansing: Michigan State University, 2005); David Brion Davis, "Some Themes of Countersubversion: An Analysis of Anti-Masonic, Anti-Catholic, and Anti-Mormon Literature," in *The Fear of Conspiracy: Images of Un-American Subversion from the Revolution to the Present*, ed. David Brion Davis (Ithaca, NY: Cornell University Press, 1971), 9–22; Rosalyn Collings Eves, "Mapping Rhetorical Frontiers: Women's Spatial Rhetorics in the Nineteenth-Century American West" (diss., Pennsylvania State University, 2008).

30. President Abraham Lincoln signed the Morill Anti-Bigamy Act into law in 1862, and Congress tried to restrict polygamy by passing the Edmunds–Tucker Act in 1887.

31. "The 'Twin Relics of Barbarism,'" *New York Times*, July 18, 1869, 4; "A Relic of Barbarism," *New York Times*, August 8, 1865.

32. Eves, *Mapping Rhetorical Frontiers*; William Mulder and A. Russell Mortensen, eds., *Among the Mormons: Historic Accounts by Contemporary Observers* (New York: Alfred A. Knopf, 1958), 407–408.

33. Leslie J. Harris, *State of the Marital Union: Rhetoric, Identity, and Nineteenth-Century Marriage Controversies* (Waco: Baylor University Press, 2014), 53–67; Justin S. Morrill, *Utah Territory and Its Laws—Polygamy and Its License; Delivered in the House of Representatives, February 23, 1857* (Washington, DC: Office of the Congressional Globe, 1857), 10.

34. This phrase is sometimes also spelled as "wild and wooly." Woolly is sometimes also spelled "woolley," "wolly," or "wooly." *Oxford English Dictionary Online*, s.v. "woolly, adj. and n.," June 2016, https://www.oed.com/view/Entry/230148?redirectedFrom=woolly#eid; Popik, "Wild and Woolly."

35. Gail Bederman, *Manliness and Civilization: A Cultural History of Gender and Race in the United States, 1880–1917* (Chicago: University of Chicago Press, 1995), 27.

36. J. T. "Home Pets," *Ladies' Floral Cabinet* 4 (1875): 121; Arthur Chapman, "The Sheep Herders of the West," *Outlook*, June 24, 1905, 481–488. In an 1881 article in the *Women's Suffrage Journal*, a Virginian woman described an African American "boy" as a "woolly-headed, coffee-coloured animal."

"Negro Versus Woman Suffrage," *Women's Suffrage Journal* 12 (1881): 106.

37. "Woolly" was used when describing "the wild and woolly-haired Negrillo, Alfouron, or Papuan." *Protestant Episcopal Quarterly Review, and Church Register*, July 1855, 378.

38. Shane White and Graham White, "Slave Hair and African American Culture in the Eighteenth and Nineteenth Centuries," *Journal of Southern History* 61, no. 1 (1995): 45–76.

39. Gussie Davis, an African American songwriter, described African Americans' hair as "wool" in his 1894 minstrel song, "When They Straighten All the Colored People's Hair." Neal A. Lester, "Nappy Edges and Goldy Locks: African-American Daughters and the Politics of Hair," *The Lion and the Unicorn* 24, no. 2 (2000): 201–224.

40. Phineas T. Barnum, "Negro Suffrage, May 26, 1865," *Struggles and Triumphs: or, Forty Years' Recollections of P.T. Barnum, Written by Himself* (New York: American News Company, 1871), 621–637; Ida Husted Harper, *History of Woman Suffrage*, vol. 2 (New York: National American Woman Suffrage Association, 1922), 383.

41. Noliwe M. Rooks, *Hair Raising: Beauty, Culture, and African American Women* (New Brunswick, NJ: Rutgers University Press, 1996). In 1913, Sam M. Lewis's song, "Underneath the Cotton Moon," included lines such as:

You's ma little black boy wid a turned up nose,
An' a little bunch o' wool upon yo' head. . . .
You's ma little bit o' wooly headed brown-eyed gal.

42. Ayana Byrd and Lori Tharps, *Hair Story: Untangling the Roots of Black Hair in America* (New York: St. Martin's Press, 2001), 14. In the 1850s, scientist Peter A. Browne maintained that white and black people were different species according to physical differences including the dissimilarity between the "hair" of white men and the "wool" on the heads of black men. Whitney Bellinger, "Why African American Women Try to Obtain 'Good Hair,'" *Sociological Viewpoints* (2007): 63–72; Roy Sieber and Frank Herreman, *Hair in African Art and Culture* (New York: Museum for African Art, 2000).

Influential Darwinian scientist Thomas Henry Huxley classified races according to three physical characteristics: skin color, head size, and hair type. There were two types of hair: *Leiotrichi* was either straight or wavy, and *Ulotrichi* was "crisp, woolly, or tufted hair." Bruce Baum, *The Rise and Fall of the Caucasian Race: A Political History of Racial Identity* (New York: New York University Press, 2006), 133.

43. George Stocking Jr., *Race, Culture, and Evolution* (New York: Free Press, 1968), 122; Rooks, *Hair Raising*, 37–38.

44. Rooks, *Hair Raising*, 38. In 1848, Charles Hamilton Smith, a British typologist of races, used these physical differences to create a hierarchy of races that placed Caucasians at the top and the "wooly haired negro" at the bottom, because of their small brains, dark skin, and woolly hair. Charles Hamilton Smith, *Natural History of the Human Species* (Boston: Gould and Lincoln, 1848); Waldo E. Martin Jr., *The Mind of Frederick Douglass* (Chapel Hill: University of North Carolina Press, 1984), 239.

45. The units of the US Cavalry that were made up entirely of African Americans were formed in 1866 in Fort Leavenworth, Kansas, and were active in the Indian Wars. Between 1866 and 1917, 25,000 black men served in the Ninth and Tenth cavalries and the Twenty-Fourth and Twenty-Fifth Infantry regiments. These men were active in the Indian Wars and were often responsible for defending the white inhabitants of the West. The legend is that the African American soldiers were given their nickname "Buffalo Soldiers" by the American Indians with whom they battled. Frances Roe, the white wife of Lieutenant Fayette Washington Roe of the Third Infantry, in a letter home to relatives in the East in 1872, wrote, "The officers say that the negroes make good soldiers and fight like fiends. They certainly manage to stick on their horses like monkeys. The Indians call them 'buffalo soldiers,' because their woolly heads are so much like the matted cushion that is between the horns of the buffalo." Frances Marie Antoinette Mack Roe, *Army Letters from an Officer's Wife, 1871-1888* (New York: D. Appleton, 1909), 76.

Some historians argue that the Buffalo Soldiers embraced the name with pride because they knew how much respect American Indians had for buffalo. Bruce A. Glasrud and Michael N. Searles, eds., *Buffalo Soldiers in the West: A Black Soldier's Anthology* (College Station: Texas A&M

University Press, 2007); Charles L. Kenner, *Buffalo Soldiers and Officers of the Ninth Cavalry, 1867-1898: Black and White Together* (Norman: University of Oklahoma Press, 1990); Gerald Horne, *Black and Brown: African Americans and the Mexican Revolution, 1910-1920* (New York: New York University Press, 2005); Quintard Taylor, *In Search of the Racial Frontier: African Americans in the American West, 1528-1990* (New York: W. W. Norton & Company, 1999).

46. Kenner, *Buffalo Soldiers*; Taylor, *In Search of the Racial Frontier*.

47. Bederman, *Manliness and Civilization*, 20–23.

48. Adair Welcker, *Tales of the "Wild & Woolly West"* (London: Leadenhall Press, 1891).

49. Welcker, *Tales of the "Wild & Woolly West"*; Andrew Jackson Sowell, *Rangers and Pioneers of Texas* (San Antonio: Shepard Bros. & Co., Printers and Publishers, 1884); "Woolly West," *Judge's Library: A Monthly Magazine of Fun* 48, March 1893, 1.

50. In 1916, Bray Productions released a film titled *The Wild and Woolly West*. In February 1917, L-KO Company released *Fearless Freddie in the Woolly West*. In June 1917, a silent Western comedy film was released titled *Wild and Woolly*.

51. "Wild West Show for Stony Wold," *New York Times*, April 13, 1909.

52. "Inkowa Powwow at a Council Fire," *New York Times*, November 14, 1915, 5.

53. Liza Nicholas, *Becoming Western: Stories of Culture and Identity in the Cowboy State* (Lincoln: University of Nebraska Press, 2006).

54. William F. Cody, "In the West, Theodore Roosevelt Won His Health and Strenuousness," *Success* (January 1902): 9.

55. George P. White, "Failure of Suffrage in Great Chicago Test," *Woman's Protest* 6, no. 5 (1915).

56. "'Buffalo Bill'—a Scout Who Knew No Fear," *The Boy Scouts' Year Book* (New York: D. Appleton and Company, 1917), 179–180.

57. William R. Lighton, "Where Is the West?" *Outlook*, July 18, 1903, 702–704.

58. Leslie Harris, "Rhetorical Mobilities and the City: The White Slavery Controversy and Racialized Protection of Women in the U.S.," *Quarterly Journal of Speech* 104 (2018): 22–46. Tim Cresswell explains that movement involves both time and space, for movement "is the spatialization of time

and the temporalization of space." Tim Cresswell, *On the Move: Mobility in the Modern Western World* (New York: Routledge, 2006).

59. Defining a community as "developing" or "backward" constituted them "as moving at a different rate from another space." Harris, "Rhetorical Mobilities."

60. Nicholas, *Becoming Western*, 4–5.

61. "What Has Become of the Wild and Woolly West," *Chicago Tribune*, January 25, 1903, A3.

62. "Population Votes, Not Area; Suffrage Map a Fraud," *Utica Observer*, July 28, 1915, 5.

63. "Facts That Speak for Themselves," *Anti-Suffragist* 3, no. 3 (1911): 4.

64. "The Four Woman-Suffrage States," *Anti-Suffragist* 1, no. 3 (1909): 6–7.

65. "Population Diagram," Women's Anti-Suffrage Association of Massachusetts, 1916, Persuasive Maps: The PJ Mode Collection, Division of Rare & Manuscript Collections, Cornell University Library.

66. Michael Bunce, *The Countryside Ideal: Anglo-American Images of Landscape* (Routledge, 2005); Paul Cloke, Terry Marsden and Patrick H. Mooney, eds., *The Handbook of Rural Studies* (Thousand Oaks, CA: Sage, 2006).

67. Harris, "Rhetorical Mobilities"; Stephen M. Underhill, "Urban Jungle, Ferguson: Rhetorical Homology and Institutional Critique," *Quarterly Journal of Speech* 102 (2016): 396–417.

68. Mrs. Simon Baruch, "Reasons for Anti-Suffrage," *General Federation Bulletin* 14, no. 10 (1915): 14.

69. "The Ladies' Battle," *Atlantic Monthly*, September 1910, 290.

70. "The Ladies' Battle," *Atlantic Monthly*, September 1910, 299.

71. "The Four Woman-Suffrage States," *Anti-Suffragist* 1, no. 3 (1909): 6.

72. Baruch, "Reasons for Anti-Suffrage," 14.

73. *Population Votes—Not Area* (New York: National Association Opposed to Woman Suffrage, 1915). Cornell University Library, Division of Rare and Manuscript Collections, PJ Mode Collection of Persuasive Cartography, ID # 1171.

74. Harris, "Rhetorical Mobilities," 25.

75. "The Four Woman-Suffrage States," *Anti-Suffragist* 1, no. 3 (1909): 7.

76. "Facts That Speak for Themselves," *Anti-Suffragist* 3, no. 3 (1911): 4.

77. "A Woman Voter's Views," *Woman's Protest Against Women's Suffrage* 8, no. 4 (February 1916): 9.

78. "A Woman Voter's Views," *Woman's Protest Against Women's Suffrage* 8, no. 4 (February 1916): 9.

79. "Some Facts about Suffrage and Anti-Suffrage," *National League for the Civic Education of Women*, May 1910, 503.

80. "Anti-Suffragist and Convention Plan Dual Fight Against Federal Suffrage Amendment and Red Flag," *Woman Patriot*, January 11, 1919, 3.

81. "Anti-Suffragist and Convention," 4.

82. Jensen, "In the Weird and Wooly West," 44.

83. Michael P. Malone and Richard W. Etulain, *The American West: A Twentieth-Century History* (Lincoln: University of Nebraska Press, 1989), 56.

84. As cited in David Edwin Harrell Jr., Edwin S. Gaustad, John B. Boles, and Sally Foreman Griffith, *Unto a Good Land: A History of the American People* (Grand Rapids, MI: Wm. B. Eerdmans Publishing, 2005), 774.

85. "Mrs. Guide's Answer," *Anti-Suffragist* 1, no. 2 (1908): 15.

86. "Statement of Miss Phoebe W. Couzins, in Opposition to Woman Suffrage," *Anti-Suffragist* 2, no. 4 (1910): 2–3.

87. "Some Facts about Suffrage," *National League for the Civic Education of Women*, May 1910, 503.

88. "Some Facts about Suffrage," *National League for the Civic Education of Women*, May 1910, 501.

89. Kate C. Towle, "Woman Suffrage in California," *Reply* 1 (Nov. 1913): 156.

90. "Extracts from Papers Read at Albany N.Y., February 24, 1909," *Anti-Suffragist* 1, no. 4 (1909): 7.

91. "A Woman Voter's Views," *The Woman's Protest Against Women's Suffrage* 8, no. 4 (February 1916): 9; "Mrs. Guide's Answer," *Anti-Suffragist* 1, no. 2 (1908): 15.

92. Jensen, "In the Weird and Wooly West," 47; US Congress, Senate. *Woman Suffrage, Hearings before the Committee on Woman Suffrage*, 64th Cong., 1st Session (1915), 69–70.

93. "Some Facts about Suffrage," *National League for the Civic Education of Women*, May 1910, 501.

94. "Some Facts about Suffrage," *National League for the Civic Education of Women*,

May 1910, 501.

95. "A Woman Voter's Views," *Woman's Protest Against Women's Suffrage* 8, no. 4 (February 1916): 9.

96. "Anti-Suffragist and Convention Plan Dual Fight Against Federal Suffrage Amendment and Red Flag," *Woman Patriot*, January 11, 1919, 3.

97. "The Ladies' Battle," *Atlantic Monthly*, September 1910, 290.

98. Verna Witherell, "The Woman's Protest: Letter from Excelsior Spring's (Mo.) Daily Call," *Woman's Protest* 1 (September 1912): 12.

99. Elizabeth McCracken, "The Women of America: Fourth Paper—Woman's Suffrage in Colorado," *Outlook*, November 28, 1903, 740.

100. As Leslie Harris explains, at the turn of the century, women's ability to enact idealized expectations of femininity through their status as wives and enactment of morality and values, functioned as "an enforcement of the line between civilization and barbarism." Harris, *State of the Marital Union*, 2. Also see Bederman, *Manliness and Civilization*, 25.

101. McCracken, "The Women of America," 740.

102. "Suffrage Hearing Before the Joint Judiciary Committee," *Anti-Suffragist* 1, no. 3 (1909): 1; "Mrs. Howe's Article in the Outlook," *Anti-Suffragist* 2, no. 1 (1909): 8.

103. Bederman, *Manliness and Civilization*, 25; Jensen, "In the Weird and Wooly West," 41.

104. Anna Steese Richardson, "What the Ballot That I Had Did Not Do for Me," *New York Times Magazine*, October 31, 1915, 7.

105. "Mrs. Howe's Article in the Outlook," *Anti-Suffragist* 2, no. 1 (1909): 8.

106. McCracken, "The Women of America," 742–744.

107. "Suffrage Leader Says Vote Kills Woman's Charms," *Reply* 1 (December 1913): 180.

108. "American Anti-Slavery Meeting," *Liberator*, May 16, 1850, 88. Also see "Society Library, Tuesday Evening, May," *Liberator,* May 16, 1850, 88; "American Anti-Slavery Society," *Liberator,* May 16, 1850, 88.

109. Catherine H. Palczewski, "The 1919 Prison Special: Constituting White Women's Citizenship," *Quarterly Journal of Speech* 102 (2016): 107–132.

110. "Suffrage in Washington," *Anti-Suffragist* 3, no. 2 (1910): 4–5.

111. "Mrs. Howe's Article in the Outlook," *Anti-Suffragist* 2, no. 1 (1909): 8.

112. Palczewski, "The Male Madonna."

113. "Editorial," *Reply* 2 (June 1914): 26.

114. *The Case Against Woman Suffrage* (Boston: National Antisuffrage Association, n. d.), 18.

115. A. S. B., "Biennial Notes from Colorado," *Woman's Journal*, July 9, 1898, 220.

116. "Visiting Suffragists Find Women of Illinois are Not Masculine," *Chicago Herald*, April 11, 1916.

117. "A 'Message from Western Women Voters,'" *Woman's Protest* 9, no. 2 (1916): 11–12.

Chapter 4. Defending the West:
Helen Ring Robinson's and Jeannette Rankin's
Western Domestication and Boosterism, 1913–1918

1. "Talk on Suffrage Stirs Eager Crowd," *New York Times*, January 20, 1914, 18. The audience for the debate included about nine hundred men and four hundred women. After the debate was over, antisuffragists thought that "the papers spoke very well of Mrs. George's speech [the antisuffragist who Robinson debated] and all reports were most encouraging." Meeting Minutes for the Education and Organization Committee of the Massachusetts Association Opposed to the Further Extension of Suffrage to Women, December 17, 1913, Boston, MA. Massachusetts Association Opposed to the Further Extension of Suffrage to Women Records, 1894–1920, carton 2, folder 22, 1913.

2. "Jeannette Rankin Cheered by 3,000 for Speech Here," *New York Tribune*, March 3, 1917, 11; Cindy Koenig Richards and Paul McKean, "'Government is an Instrument in Their Hands': Jeanette Rankin on Progressive Technologies of Democracy," *Advances in the History of Rhetoric* 20 (2017): 75–85; Paul Stob, "Jeannette Rankin's Democratic Errand to Washington," *Advances in the History of Rhetoric* 20 (2017): 86–98.

3. Maria Hughes Cannon was the fourth of Angus M. Cannon's plural wives. Pat Pascoe, *Helen Ring Robinson: Colorado Senator and Suffragist* (Boulder: University Press of Colorado, 2011), 44.

4. Robinson was an activist senator who helped pass a minimum-wage

law and endorsed many progressive causes, including the protection of
children in state homes, the right of women to sit on juries, a minimum
wage for men, and improvements in education and care for those with
mental disabilities. Pascoe, *Helen Ring Robinson*, xi.

5. Robinson attended Wellesley College for one year and taught for
twenty years in Colorado. She also wrote regular columns and feature
articles in Colorado newspapers. Robinson's successful election was
enabled by the growing national support for the progressive and woman
suffrage movements that were especially strong in Colorado, the active
women's club movement in Colorado that prepared women to vote and
promoted women candidates for political office, and the modeling of
a few other Colorado women who had become elected officials before
her. In addition to serving as president of the Denver Woman's Press
Club, Robinson was also a member of the Woman's Club of Denver, the
Wellesley Club, the Artists' Club, the Monday Literary Club, and the
Writers' Club. Pascoe, *Helen Ring Robinson*.

6. "Woman Dons Her Toga," *Washington Post*, January 3, 1913, 1.

7. "Woman Senator Visits New York," *Daily News* (NY), May 9, 1913.

8. "Senator Helen Robinson Finishes Stumping Tour," *Daily News* (NY),
July 10, 1913.

9. "Woman Senator Visits New York," *Daily News* (NY), May 9, 1913;
"Woman Legislator Defends Suffrage," *New York Times*, May 10, 1913, 9.

10. "Senator Helen Robinson Finishes Stumping Tour," *Daily News* (NY),
July 10, 1913.

11. Robinson returned to the East Coast at the end of 1913 and spoke in
Massachusetts, Pennsylvania, Washington, DC, and New Hampshire.
Her 1914 tour included performances in Boston's Symphony Hall and
New York City's Hotel Astor, in addition to lectures in Connecticut,
West Virginia, and Canada. In 1915, she did another lecture tour through
New York, New Jersey, and Indiana, and in 1916 took this message to
Atlanta. "Senator Helen Ring Robinson Talks on 'Woman Suffrage in
Practice,'" *Portsmouth Herald* (NH), December 10, 1913, 4; "News Notes,"
Wellesley College News, January 22, 1914, 8; Lillian Green, "East Changes
Suffrage View" *Rocky Mountain News*, March 10, 1914; "Talk on Suffrage

Stirs Eager Crowd," *New York Times*, January 20, 1914, 18; Pascoe, *Helen Ring Robinson*, 79; "Senator Helen Robinson Finishes Stumping Tour," *Daily News* (NY), July 10, 1913; "Talk on Suffrage Stirs Eager Crowd," *New York Times*, January 20, 1914, 18.

12. James J. Lopach, and Jean A. Luckowski, *Jeannette Rankin: A Political Woman* (Boulder: University Press of Colorado, 2005), 5, 102–106.

13. The *Evening Star* reported: "Every mail brings a fresh crop of proposals. They come from all over the United States. One man, a lawyer from Oklahoma. . . . a toothpaste company wanted to photograph Miss Rankin's teeth" and was "willing to pay $5,000 for the picture. An automobile company asked the privilege of presenting a new model car to Miss Rankin if she would merely consent to having her ownership used for advertising purposes. The latest excitement is a motion picture sharpshooter from California who has dug himself near the Rankin homestead." "Her Victory at Polls Proves Peril at Gate," *Evening Star* (Washington, DC), November 21, 1916. See also Rene Bache, "When Miss Rankin Goes to Congress," *New York Sunday American*, November 26, 1916, 2; Louis Levine, "First Woman Member of Congress Well Versed in Politics," *New York Times*, November, 1916, 4; "Nervous? Not I, Says Woman Elected to U.S. Congress," *Seattle Sunday Times*, November 26, 1916, 31; Lisetta Noukom, "Our First Congresswoman Is Dainty Bit of Femininity," *Los Angeles Sunday Times*, November 26, 1916, 18; "Good Bread Maker as Well as Vote Getter," *Portsmouth Times*, November 21, 1916; "The Lady from Montana Is Entitled to the Floor," *Chicago Daily Tribune*, November 11, 1916, 2; "Is Able and Womanly," *Washington Post*, November 12, 1916, 5; Bert Lennon, "The Lady from Montana: An Intimate Pen Picture of Miss Jeannette Rankin Presented by a Reporter for This Newspaper Who Was Sent Especially to Interview Her After Her Election to Congress," *San Francisco Sunday Chronicle*, December 10, 1916, 3.

14. "Jeannette Rankin Is Cheered by Tremendous Home Crowd," *Daily Missoulian*, November 7, 1916, 12; "Her Victory at Polls Proves Peril at Gate," *Evening Star* (Washington, DC), November 21, 1916; "Jeannette Rankin Gives First Public Statement," *Daily Missoulian*, November 18, 1916, 10; "First Public Talk for Miss Rankin," *Missoulian-Sentinel*, January

17, 1917, 3; "Jeannette Rankin Declares War on 'Movie' Men," *Hartford Courant*, November 17, 1916, 1.

15. "First Public Talk for Miss Rankin," *Missoulian-Sentinel*, January 17, 1917, 3.
16. "Women Demand Ballot at Once," *Colorado Springs Gazette*, December 1, 1913, 1.
17. "Miss Rankin Elected," *New York Times*, November 11, 1916, 2.
18. Lopach and Luckowski, *Jeannette Rankin*, 6.
19. "Miss Jeannette Rankin, of Montana, the First Woman Elected to Serve in Congress," *Outlook*, November 22, 1916, 650; "Jeannette Rankin Is Congresswoman: Newly Elected Member Ardent Suffragists and 'Very Feminine,'" *Hartford Courant*, November 13, 1916; "Miss Rankin Elected," *New York Times*, November 11, 1916, 2; "First 'Congresswoman' Gets Shower of Congratulations," *Detroit Free Press*, November 11, 1916.
20. "First Public Talk for Miss Rankin," *Missoulian-Sentinel*, January 17, 1917, 3.
21. Eleanor Flexner and Ellen Fitzpatrick, *Century of Struggle: The Woman's Rights Movement in the United States* (Cambridge: Harvard University Press, 1968), 276.
22. Paul Achter, "Unruly Bodies: The Rhetorical Domestication of Twenty-First-Century Veterans of War," *Quarterly Journal of Speech* 96 (2010): 48. See also Amy Kaplan, "'Manifest Domesticity': No More Separate Spheres!" *American Literature* 70 (1998): 582.
23. Rosalyn Collings Eves, "Mapping Rhetorical Frontiers: Women's Spatial Rhetorics in the Nineteenth-Century American West" (PhD diss., Pennsylvania State University, 2008), 5.
24. Kaplan, "'Manifest Domesticity,'" 582, 591. See also Amy Kaplan, *The Anarchy of Empire in the Making of U.S. Culture* (Cambridge, MA: Harvard University Press, 2005).
25. Annette Kolodny's analysis of nineteenth-century women's literature shows the way women helped make the land that was strange to them more familiar and habitable by figuring it in domestic terms, often viewing and speaking of it as a garden. Gardening itself was viewed by many Americans as a civilizing and Americanizing force, as they tamed the natural land and made it productive. Annette Kolodny, *The Land Before Her: Fantasy and Experience of the American Frontiers, 1630–1860*

(Chapel Hill: University of North Carolina Press, 1984). See also Eves, "Mapping Rhetorical Frontiers," 72–73, 213, 244; Brigitte Georgi-Findlay, *The Frontiers of Women's Writing: Women's Narratives and the Rhetoric of Western Expansion* (Tucson: University of Arizona Press, 1996); Karen M. Morin, *Frontiers of Femininity: A New Historical Geography of the Nineteenth-Century American West* (Syracuse, NY: Syracuse University Press, 2008); Martha M. Allen, *Traveling West: 19th Century Women on the Overland Routes* (El Paso: Texas Western Press, 1987); Susan J. Rosowski, *Birthing a Nation: Gender, Creativity, and the West in American Literature* (Lincoln: University of Nebraska Press, 1999); Douglas Cazaux, *Orange Empire: California and the Fruits of Eden* (Berkeley: University of California Press, 2005).

26. Kaplan, "Manifest Domesticity," 582.

27. Marguerite S. Shaffer, *See America First: Tourism and National Identity, 1880–1940* (Washington, DC: Smithsonian Institution Press, 2001).

28. Thomas Goebel, *A Government by the People: Direct Democracy in America, 1890-1940* (Chapel Hill: University of North Carolina Press, 2002), 2–4; Robert V. Hine and John Mack Faragher, *The American West: A New Interpretive History* (New Haven: Yale University Press, 2000), 348–349.

29. Liza Nicholas, *Becoming Western: Stories of Culture and Identity in the Cowboy State* (Lincoln: University of Nebraska Press, 2006), 22; David M. Wrobel, *Promised Lands: Promotion, Memory, and the Creation of the American West* (Lawrence: University Press of Kansas, 2002).

30. George H. Beasley, "The Great Inland Empire," *Sketch Book* 1 (March 1907), n. p.; Richard B. Roeder, "Montana Progressivism Sound and Fury—and One Small Tax Reform," *Montana: The Magazine of Western History* 20 (1970), 24.

31. Shaffer, *See America First*.

32. Brenda D. Frink, "San Francisco's Pioneer Mother Monument: Maternalism, Racial Order, and the Politics of Memorialization, 1907–1915," *American Quarterly* 64 (2012): 96; John Gonzalez, "The Warp of Whiteness: Domesticity and Empire in Helen Hunt Jackson's Ramona," *American Literary History* 16, no. 3 (2004): 437–465; Jason E. Pierce, *Making the White Man's West: Whiteness and the Creation of the American West* (Boulder: University Press of Colorado, 2016).

33. Promoters also boosted Western black towns and promoted land to African Americans who sought freedom from enslavement, persecution, or Jim Crow laws, in addition to the opportunities for agriculture and business. Founders of these black towns and black Western authors often featured the West as an opportunity for a better quality of life and political representation for African American men. Dan Moos, *Outside America: Race, Ethnicity, and the Role of the American West in National Belonging* (Hanover, NH: Dartmouth College Press, 2005); Emily Lutenski, *West of Harlem: African American Writers and the Borderlands* (Lawrence: University Press of Kansas, 2016); Kenneth Marvin Hamilton, *Black Towns and Profit: Promotion and Development in the Trans-Appalachian West, 1877–1915* (Champaign: University of Illinois Press, 1991); William Loren Katz, *The Black West*, rev. ed. (Golden, CO: Fulcrum Publishing, 2019).

34. Wrobel, *Promised Lands*, 2–7, 71, 176; Pierce, *Making the White Man's West*.

35. Between the turn of the century and America's entry into World War I in 1917, more homesteads were filed than in the thirty-eight-year time between the Homestead Act of 1862 and the end of the nineteenth century. But in the first decades of the 1900s, after the economic depression of the 1890s, new farming methods, machines, and dryland farming propaganda brought "floods" of homesteaders to Eastern Montana to settle and farm the land in the second decade of the twentieth century. These twentieth-century settlers "created great excitement" as a new wave of homesteaders promised Montana "a once-given opportunity to build a good rural community for the well-being not just of the state but perhaps of the nation as well." Wrobel, *Promised Lands*, 56; Roeder, "Montana Progressivism," 25–26.

36. "Woman Senator Visits New York," *Daily News* (NY), May 9, 1913.

37. In 1913, the *New York Times* headline read "Woman Legislator Defends Suffrage." Before 1,100 men and women in the grand ballroom of the Hotel Astor in New York City in 1914, "Mrs. Robinson Ridicule[d] Anti-Suffrage Arguments." "Woman Legislator Defends Suffrage," *New York Times*, May 10, 1913, 9; "Talk on Suffrage Stirs Eager Crowd," *New York Times*, January 20, 1914, 18.

38. "Woman Legislator Defends Suffrage," *New York Times*, May 10, 1913, 9.

39. Lillian Green, "East Changes Suffrage View," *Rocky Mountain News*, March 10, 1914.

40. "Senator Helen R. Robinson Goes East," *Weekly Ignacio Chieftain*, August 20, 1915, 4.

41. "Woman Senator on Stump," *New York Times*, September 22, 1915, 1.

42. "Senator Robinson asks $5000 for Gambling Story," *Denver Express*, September 8, 1915, 1.

43. "Woman Legislator Defends Suffrage," *New York Times*, May 10, 1913, 9.

44. "Senator Robinson Talks Suffrage to Councilmen," *Daily News* (NY), May 28, 1913.

45. "Woman Legislator Defends Suffrage," *New York Times*, May 10, 1913, 9.

46. "Woman Legislator Defends Suffrage," *New York Times*, May 10, 1913, 9.

47. "Helen Ring Robinson Defends Women and Threatens Hecker with Expulsion from Senate," *Rocky Mountain View*, February 6, 1913, 2; "Says Women Drink More," *New York Times*, February 6, 1913, 7.

48. "Woman Senator Defends Denver Women against Charge of Highball Drinking," *Denver Express*, February 5, 1913, 1.

49. "Helen Ring Robinson Defends Women and Threatens Hecker with Expulsion from Senate," *Rocky Mountain View*, February 6, 1913, 2; "Woman Senator Defends Denver Women against Charge of Highball Drinking," *Denver Express*, February 5, 1913, 1.

50. "Woman Senator on Stump," *New York Times*, September 22, 1915, 1.

51. Rankin delivered "Democracy and Government" in Carnegie Hall and throughout the Northeast on her 1917 lecture tour. Jeannette Rankin, "'Democracy and Government,' Carnegie Hall, New York, 2 March 1917," ed. Tiffany Lewis, *Advances in the History of Rhetoric* 20 (2017): 57–74. Rankin's Carnegie Hall performance was also covered in eight newspaper reports. "Miss Rankin Addresses 3000," *Woman's Journal*, March 10, 1917, 55–56; "Jeannette Rankin Cheered by 3,000 for Speech Here," *New York Tribune*, March 3, 1917, 11; "'Lady From Montana' Talks," *New York Times*, March 3, 1917, 4; "First Woman M.C. Makes Her Bow to New York," *Irish World*, March 3, 1917; "Lady from Montana Makes Her Bow Here," *New York World*, March 3, 1917, 16; "Lady Congressman Knows Everything," *New York City Mail*, March 3, 1917, 11; "Miss Rankin Urges Direct Vote to

Elect President," *New York American*, March 3, 1917, 6; "Woman Member of Congress Has Rousing Welcome," *New York City Herald,* March 3, 1917, 3.

52. "Jeannette Rankin Cheered by 3,000 for Speech Here," *New York Tribune*, March 3, 1917, 11; Lopach and Luckowski, *Jeannette Rankin*, 135.

53. "Jeannette Rankin Cheered by 3,000 for Speech Here," *New York Tribune*, March 3, 1917, 11.

54. Rankin, "Democracy and Government," 57.

55. "Jeannette Rankin Cheered by 3,000 for Speech Here," *New York Tribune*, March 3, 1917, 11.

56. Rankin, "Democracy and Government," 57.

57. Rankin, "Democracy and Government" 58–59.

58. Wrobel, *Promised Lands*, 2, 68.

59. Eves, "Mapping Rhetorical Frontiers," 244. Also see Douglas Cazaux, *Orange Empire: California and the Fruits of Eden* (Berkeley: University of California Press, 2005).

60. Rankin, "Democracy and Government," 58–59. Rankin made a similar argument in an interview just the week before her speech. Montana produces "as much as either Iowa or Illinois, and we are doing wonderfully well as raisers of wheat. Why, last year we raised 33,500,000 bushels of Wheat, or sufficient to supply each man, woman and child in the city of New York with 306 loaves of bread. Now if a single State of the Far West can supply that much of a single foodstuff, why should there be food disturbances and unusually high prices either in New York or any other city? There should be no food problem in this country, considering all of the things to eat raised here . . . if the supplies of the Far West were brought East and distributed as they should be." "There Would Be No Food Gambling if Women Were in Congress, Says 'Lady from Montana,'" *Evening Telegram* (NY), February 27, 1917.

61. Rankin, "Democracy and Government," 58.

62. Alan Trachtenberg, *The Incorporation of America* (New York: Hill and Wang, 1982), 41, 57.

63. Trachtenberg, *The Incorporation of America*, 57.

64. Rankin, "Democracy and Government," 58.

65. In this case, I quote the report of Rankin's speech in the *New York Times*.

"'Lady from Montana' Talks," *New York Times*, March 3, 1917, 4. The quote in the composition-text read instead as: "Some of the reports of my election in the eastern papers said that I campaigned on horseback. To us campaigning on horseback is very commonplace. We are amazed and delighted that we can reach almost every point by train or automobile. I traveled 6000 miles by train and over 1500 miles by automobile but I wonder if any candidate in any other state could ride 500 miles through the mountains on an electrified train. The last Saturday night in the Primary I spoke at Roundup, then went to bed in a comfortable sleeper and arrived at my home 380 miles distant in time for Sunday dinner." Rankin, "Democracy and Government," 58.

66. Roeder, "Montana Progressivism," 20. The Australian ballot ensured citizens the right to cast their votes secretly. To limit the power of state legislators, who could be bribed by corporations to select senators, reformers advocated for the direct election of United States senators so "the people [could] choose their senators by popular ballot." Michael P. Malone, and Richard B. Roeder, *Montana: A History of Two Centuries* (Seattle: University of Washington Press, 1976), 196–197.

67. Goebel, *A Government by the People*; Steven L. Piott, *Giving Voters a Voice: The Origins of the Initiative and Referendum in America* (Columbia: University of Missouri Press, 2003), 51–52.

68. Nathaniel Persily, "The Peculiar Geography of Direct Democracy: Why the Initiative, Referendum and Recall Developed in the American West," *Michigan Law & Policy Review* 2 (1997); Michael P. Malone and Dianne G. Dougherty, "Montana's Political Culture: A Century of Evolution," *Montana: The Magazine of Western History* 31 (1981), 44–58.

69. Rankin, "Democracy and Government," 65–66, 71.

70. Rankin, "Democracy and Government," 59–60.

71. In contrast to the traditional ideals of femininity as pious and pure, women's participation in the "crooked," "corrupt," and masculine political world was "considered unnatural and degrading to the 'fairer sex.'" Deborah G. Felder, *A Century of Women: The Most Influential Events in Twentieth-Century Women's History* (New York: Kensington Publishing Corp., 1999), 82; Linda Witt, Karen M. Paget, and Glenna Matthews, *Running*

as a Woman: Gender and Power in American Politics (New York: The Free Press, 1994), 30; Dorothy M. Brown, *Setting a Course: American Women in the 1920s* (Boston: Twayne Publishers, 1987), 68.

72. Felder, *A Century of Women*, 82; Witt, Paget, and Matthews, *Running as a Woman*, 31; Judith Butler, *Gender Trouble: Feminism and the Subversion of Identity* (New York: Routledge, 1990); Karen Foerstel and Herbert N. Foerstel, *Climbing the Hill: Gender Conflict in Congress*. (Westport, CT: Praeger, 1996), 4.

73. "There Would Be No Food Gambling if Women Were in Congress, Says 'Lady from Montana,'" *Evening Telegram* (NY), February 27, 1917.

74. Lennon, "The Lady from Montana," 3.

75. "There Would Be No Food Gambling if Women Were in Congress, Says 'Lady from Montana,'" *Evening Telegram* (NY), February 27, 1917.

76. "Colorado's 'Lady Senator' Jars East Because She's No Freak," *Denver Republican*, July 19, 1913, 1.

77. "Suffrage Is Live Issue," *Grand Traverse Herald and Traverse Bay Eagle*, July 31, 1913, 1.

78. "How the First 'Petticoated' Member May Upset Congressional Traditions and Change the Personal Habits of the Trouser-Wearing Majority—What I Expect to Do When I Get to Congress," *New York Sunday American*, November 26, 1916.

79. Donald Wilhelm, "The Lady from Missoula," *Independent*, April 2, 1917, 25.

80. "Jeannette Rankin Is Congresswoman: Newly Elected Member Ardent Suffragists and 'Very Feminine,'" *Hartford Courant*, November 13, 1916; Lisetta Noukom, "Our First Congresswoman Is Dainty Bit of Femininity," *Los Angeles Sunday Times*, November 26, 1916, 18.

81. "Miss Rankin Elected," *New York Times*, November 11, 1916; "Good Bread Maker as Well as Vote Getter," *Portsmouth Times*, November 21, 1916; "Jeannette Rankin Is Congresswoman: Newly Elected Member Ardent Suffragists and 'Very Feminine,'" *Hartford Courant*, November 13, 1916; "The Lady from Montana Is Entitled to the Floor," *Chicago Daily Tribune*, November 11, 1916, 2. Also see "Nervous? Not I, Says Woman Elected to U.S. Congress," *Seattle Sunday Times*, November 26, 1916, 31; Lisetta Noukom, "Our First Congresswoman Is Dainty Bit of Femininity," *Los Angeles Sunday Times*, November 26, 1916, 18.

82. "Nervous? Not I, Says Woman Elected to U.S. Congress," *Seattle Sunday Times*, November 26, 1916, 31. Also see reports of her ability to make her own clothes and hats in Lisetta Noukom, "Our First Congresswoman Is Dainty Bit of Femininity," *Los Angeles Sunday Times*, November 26, 1916, 18; "Miss Rankin Elected," *New York Times*, November 11, 1916; "The Lady from Montana Is Entitled," *Chicago Daily Tribune*, November 11, 1916.

83. "Nervous? Not I, Says Woman Elected to U.S. Congress," *Seattle Sunday Times*, November 26, 1916, 31. Also see her statements in Lisetta Noukom, "Our First Congresswoman Is Dainty Bit of Femininity," *Los Angeles Sunday Times*, November 26, 1916, 18; "The Lady from Montana Is Entitled," *Chicago Daily Tribune*, November 11, 1916, 2.

84. Gail Bederman, *Manliness and Civilization: A Cultural History of Gender and Race in the United States, 1880–1917* (Chicago: University of Chicago Press, 1995), 25.

85. Three days after her election, she told the *Denver Republican*, "I am going to be the housewife of the senate . . . There will be so many men there that I shall let them look after themselves and I shall take it upon myself to look after the women and children. I wish to be a spokeswoman of the women and children in Colorado in the legislature, and I shall feel honored to introduced any laws drawn up for their welfare and protection . . . I believe a woman who has qualified as a capable mother and housewife can qualify as a capable legislator. I hold my new responsibilities to the people of the state as sacred as I hold my responsibilities to my husband and my daughter." "She Calls Herself 'Housewife of Colorado Senate' and Will Work for Women and Children," *Denver Republican*, November 8, 1912, 10.

86. "Suffrage Is Live Issue," *Grand Traverse Herald and Traverse Bay Eagle*, July 31, 1913, 1.

87. "News Notes," *Wellesley College News*, January 22, 1914, 8.

88. Mary P. Ryan, *Womanhood in America: From Colonial Times to the Present*, 3rd ed. (New York: Franklin Watts, 1983), 198–210; Kraditor, *The Ideas of Woman Suffrage*, 52–55.

89. Jane Addams, "Women and Public Housekeeping" (New York: National Woman Suffrage Publishing Co., Inc., 1910); "Woman Senator

Becomes Arizona State Leader," *Tacoma Times,* December 31, 1914, 5; "Woman Elected to Legislature," *Graham Guardian*, November 13, 1914, 1; Heidi J. Osselaer, *Winning Their Place: Arizona Women in Politics, 1883-1950* (Tuscon: University of Arizona Press, 2009); Tiffany Lewis, "Municipal Housekeeping in the American West: Bertha Knight Landes's Entrance into Politics," *Rhetoric & Public Affairs* 14 (2011): 465-492.

90. n.t., *Woman Citizen*, October 7, 1922.

91. Kristi Andersen, *After Suffrage: Women in Partisan and Electoral Politics before the New Deal* (Chicago: University of Chicago Press, 1996), 133; Nancy Woloch, *Women and the American Experience* (New York: Alfred A. Knopf, Inc., 1984), 299; Karen M. Mason, "Mary McDowell and Municipal Housekeeping: Women's Political Activism in Chicago, 1890-1920," in *Midwestern Women: Work, Community, and Leadership at the Crossroads*, ed. Lucy Eldersveld Murphy and Wendy Hamand Venet (Bloomington: Indiana University Press, 1997), 61.

92. Karen Blair, *The Clubwoman as Feminist: True Womanhood Redefined, 1868-1914* (New York: Holmes & Meier Publishers, 1980), 74.

93. "Women Demand Ballot at Once," *Colorado Springs Gazette*, December 1, 1913, 1.

94. "News Notes," *Wellesley College News*, January 22, 1914, 8.

95. "Women Legislature Should Be Womanly," *New York Times*, November 23, 1913, 12.

96. "News Notes," *Wellesley College News*, January 22, 1914, 8.

97. "Women Demand Ballot at Once," *Colorado Springs Gazette*, December 1, 1913, 1.

98. Bonnie J. Dow, "The Womanhood Rationale in the Woman Suffrage Rhetoric of Frances E. Willard," *Southern Communication Journal* 56 (1991): 298-307; Amy R. Slagell," The Rhetorical Structure of Frances E. Willard's Campaign for Woman Suffrage, 1876-1896," *Rhetoric & Public Affairs* 4 (2001): 1-23; Amy R. Slagell, "'Making the World More Homelike': The Reform Rhetoric of Frances E. Willard," in *The Rhetoric of Nineteenth-Century Reform*, vol. 5, *A Rhetorical History of the United States*, ed. Martha S. Watson and Thomas R. Burkholder (East Lansing: Michigan State University Press, 2008).

99. "News Notes," *Wellesley College News*, January 22, 1914, 8.

100. "Woman Legislator Defends Suffrage," *New York Times*, May 10, 1913, 9.

101. "News Notes," *Wellesley College News*, January 22, 1914, 8.

102. "Women Legislature Should Be Womanly," *New York Times*, November 23, 1913, 12.

103. Aileen Kraditor, *The Ideas of the Woman Suffrage Movement, 1890–1920* (New York: Columbia University Press, 1962); Karlyn Kohrs Campbell, *Man Cannot Speak For Her*, vol. 1, *A Critical Study of Early Feminist Rhetoric* (Westport, CT: Praeger Publishers, 1989); Dow, "The Womanhood Rationale."

104. Sara Hayden, "Negotiating Femininity and Power in the Early Twentieth-Century West: Domestic Ideology and Feminine Style in Jeannette Rankin's Suffrage Rhetoric," *Communication Studies* 50 (1999): 83–102; "Whole Nation Observes Suffrage Day," *Missoulian*, May 2, 1914, 6; "Talk Made by Jeannette Rankin, Chairman of the Montana Equal Suffrage State Central Committee, at the State Federation of Women's Clubs, at Lewistown," June 4, 1914, speech notes in Jeannette Rankin Papers, Montana Historical Society, Small Collection 567.

105. Jeannette Rankin, "Why Women Should Share in the Making of Our Laws," *Boston Traveller*, December 30, 1916.

106. Rankin, "Democracy and Government," 63.

107. Jeannette Rankin, "Why Women Should Share in the Making of Our Laws," *Boston Traveller*, December 30, 1916.

108. "How the First 'Petticoated' Member May Upset Congressional Traditions and Change the Personal Habits of the Trouser-Wearing Majority—What I Expect to Do When I Get to Congress," *New York Sunday American*, November 26, 1916. Rankin makes a similar argument in Jeannette Rankin, "Children's Bureau Proves Value of Women in Politics," *San Francisco Chronicle*, February 25, 1917, 7.

109. "How the First 'Petticoated' Member May Upset Congressional Traditions and Change the Personal Habits of the Trouser-Wearing Majority—What I Expect to Do When I Get to Congress," *New York Sunday American*, November 26, 1916.

110. Witt, Paget, and Matthews, *Running as a Woman*, 30.

111. "How the First 'Petticoated' Member May Upset Congressional

Traditions and Change the Personal Habits of the Trouser-Wearing Majority—What I Expect to Do When I Get to Congress," *New York Sunday American*, November 26, 1916.

112. Rankin, "Democracy and Government," 63.

113. "There Would Be No Food Gambling if Women Were in Congress, Says 'Lady from Montana,'" *Evening Telegram* (NY), February 27, 1917.

114. Kraditor, *The Ideas of the Woman Suffrage Movement*; Campbell, *Man Cannot Speak For Her*, vol. 1.

115. "There Would Be No Food Gambling if Women Were in Congress, Says 'Lady from Montana,'" *Evening Telegram* (NY), February 27, 1917.

116. Dow, "The Womanhood Rationale"; Carmen Heider, "Suffrage, Self Determination, and the Woman's Christian Temperance Union in Nebraska, 1879–1882," *Rhetoric & Public Affairs* 8 (2005): 85–107.

117. John M. Sloop, *Disciplining Gender: Rhetorics of Sex Identity in Contemporary U.S. Culture* (Amherst, MA: University of Massachusetts Press, 2004), 11–12.

118. "How the First 'Petticoated' Member May Upset Congressional Traditions and Change the Personal Habits of the Trouser-Wearing Majority—What I Expect to Do When I Get to Congress," *New York Sunday American*, November 26, 1916.

119. Rankin, "Democracy and Government, 63."

120. "Nervous? Not I, Says Woman Elected to U.S. Congress," *Seattle Sunday Times*, November 26, 1916, 31.

121. "The Lady from Montana Is Entitled," *Chicago Daily Tribune*, November 11, 1916, 2.

122. Carol Mattingly, *Appropriate[ing] Dress: Women's Rhetorical Style in Nineteenth-Century America* (Carbondale: Southern Illinois University Press, 2002), 5–7.

123. Mattingly, *Appropriate[ing] Dress*, 111, 122–123.

124. "Woman Legislator Defends Suffrage," *New York Times*, May 10, 1913, 9.

125. "Suffrage Is Live Issue," *Grand Traverse Herald and Traverse Bay Eagle*, July 31, 1913, 1.

126. "Colorado's Woman Senator Is Here," *Providence Journal*, June 16, 1913, 2.

127. Lopach and Luckowski, *Jeannette Rankin*, 134.

128. Jeannette Rankin, interview with Hannah Josephson, transcript,

Montana Historical Society; Lopach and Luckowski, *Jeannette Rankin*, 134.

129. "Woman Member of Congress Has Rousing Welcome," *New York City Herald,* March 3, 1917, 3.

130. "Jeannette Rankin Cheered by 3,000 for Speech Here," *New York Tribune*, March 3, 1917, 11.

131. "Woman Member of Congress Has Rousing Welcome," *New York City Herald,* March 3, 1917, 3.

132. "Jeannette Rankin Cheered by 3,000 for Speech Here," *New York Tribune*, March 3, 1917, 11.

133. "There Would Be No Food Gambling if Women Were in Congress, Says 'Lady from Montana,'" *Evening Telegram* (NY), February 27, 1917.

134. "Woman Member of Congress Has Rousing Welcome," *New York City Herald,* March 3, 1917, 3.

135. "There Would Be No Food Gambling if Women Were in Congress, Says 'Lady from Montana,'" *Evening Telegram* (NY), February 27, 1917.

136. Lisetta Noukom, "Our First Congresswoman Is Dainty Bit of Femininity," *Los Angeles Sunday Times*, November 26, 1916, 18.

137. Also see Barbara Handy-Marchello's discussion of Linda Slaughter, a woman booster of the Great Plains. Slaughter was hired by the Northern Pacific Railroad to write letters for Eastern newspapers about life in the Dakotas. She also used her position as a "well-bred woman with a taste for silk dresses and champagne" to prove that genteel society existed in the West. Barbara Handy-Marchello, "Gendered Boosterism: The 'Doctor's Wife' Writes from the New Northwest," in *Regionalism and the Humanities*, ed. Timothy R. Mahoney and Wendy J. Katz (Lincoln: University of Nebraska Press, 2008), 112.

138. Wrobel, *Promised Lands*, 3; Handy-Marchello, "Gendered Boosterism," 111.

139. "Flowers Sent to Woman Senator," *Denver Express*, February 7, 1913, 3.

140. "Flowers Sent to Woman Senator," *Denver Express*, February 7, 1913, 3.

141. "Work of Colorado Women in 1913 Stands out Like Beacon Light," *Denver Post*, December 28, 1913, 7.

142. Pascoe, *Helen Ring Robinson*, 75; "Helen Ring Robinson Is Paid High Tribute," *St. Louis Star*, March 1913.

143. Pascoe, *Helen Ring Robinson*, 75, 145–156.

144. "Jeannette Rankin Cheered by 3,000 for Speech Here," *New York Tribune*, March 3, 1917, 11.

145. "Jeannette Rankin Takes Place in House," *Woman's Journal*, April 7, 1917.

146. "Jeannette Blushes When Roll," no publication title, April 2, 1917, Scrapbook, JR Papers, Library of Congress.

147. "Miss Rankin Stands by the Republicans," *New York Times*, April 2, 1917, 11.

148. After Rankin opened the debate on woman suffrage, the federal amendment passed in the House by a single extra vote, but was not passed by the Senate. Jeannette Rankin, "Woman Suffrage. Speech of Hon. Jeannette Rankin, of Montana, in the House of Representatives," January 10, 1918. *Congressional Record*, House, 65th Congress, 2nd session (Washington: Government Printing Office, 1918).

149. Goebel, *A Government by the People*, 132.

150. For more on Rankin's public memory, see Shane Borrowman and Marcia Kmetz, "Divided We Stand: Beyond Burkean Identification," *Rhetoric Review* 30 (2011): 275–292; Jennifer A. Jackson and Leland G. Spencer, "Remembering Rural Rankin: Feminism, Pacifism, and Rurality in Jeannette Rankin's Identity," in *City Places, Country Spaces: Rhetorical Explorations of the Urban/Rural Divide*, ed. Wendy Atkins-Sayre and Ashli Quesinberry Stokes (New York: Peter Lang Publishing, 2020), 53–69.

Chapter 5. Embodying the West:
The Women Voters' Envoys' Transcontinental Car Travel, 1915

1. "Suffrage Car Racing from Pacific Coast to White House with Long Petition," *Day Book*, November 20, 1915.

2. "From Boston to New York," *Suffragist*, December 4, (1915), 5.

3. For a thorough analysis of the history and rhetorical strategies of the cuws, see Belinda A. Stillion Southard, *Militant Citizenship: Rhetorical Strategies of the National Woman's Party, 1913–1920* (College Station: Texas A&M University Press, 2011).

4. Robert W. Rydell, *All the World's a Fair: Visions of Empire at American International Expositions* (Chicago: University of Chicago Press, 1984); Georgine Clarsen, *Eat My Dust: Early Women Motorists* (Baltimore: Johns

Hopkins University Press, 2008), 90.

5. "Suffrage Car Racing from Pacific Coast to White House with Long Petition," *Day Book*, November 20, 1915.

6. Stillion Southard, *Militant Citizenship*, 109.

7. "The Farewell to the Woman Voters' Envoys," *Suffragist*, October 2, 1915, 5; "Mass Meeting to Welcome Women Voters' Envoys," *Suffragist*, December 18, 1915, 3; "Hearing before National Democratic Committee," *Suffragist*, December 11, 1915, 10; "Suffrage Envoy Will Lead Parade," *Des Moines Register and Leader*, October 30, 1915; "Women Voters Bring Their Message to Congress," *Suffragist*, October 9, 1915, 5.

8. "1,000 Suffs on 3,000-Mile Trek," *New York Evening Mail*, September 4, 1915; "Hard Auto Trip Taken to Aid Suffrage Cause," *San Francisco Call*, December 4, 1915.

9. "Suffrage Envoy Will Lead Parade," *Des Moines Register and Leader*, October 30, 1915; "Called on the Governor," *Nebraska State Journal*, October 28, 1915; "Woman Voters' Envoys Reach Unfree States," *Suffragist*, October 30, 1915, 3.

10. Newspaper reports often explained Frances Jolliffe's absence according to poor health or an ill family member. "50 Cars to Meet Suffrage Envoys," *New York Press*, November 26, 1915; "Women Voters Bring Their Message to Congress," *Suffragist*, October 9, 1915, 5.

11. "Suffrage Envoys on Transcontinental Trip to Capital by Auto Lose Way on Arizona Deserts," *Washington Herald*, December 5, 1915, 10; "Suffrage Envoy Will Lead Parade," *Des Moines Register and Leader*, October 30, 1915; "Women Voters Bring Their Message to Congress," *Suffragist*, October 9, 1915, 5; "Women's Suffragist Writes to the Standard," *Ogden Standard* (UT), October 6, 1915.

12. Clarsen, *Eat My Dust*, 93–94.

13. "Messengers Bearing Tidings of Suffrage across Country Only Needed Mere Man Once and He Proved Much of a Failure," *Cheyenne State Leader*, October 8, 1915.

14. Clarsen, *Eat My Dust*, 92–93, 96–97.

15. "Eastern Journey of the Women Voters' Envoy," *Suffragist*, October 23, 1915, 5.

16. "Women Voters' Envoy in Utah," *Suffragist*, October 16, 1915, 5; "Champ Clark Sidesteps Efforts to Bind Him to Suffrage Cause," *Denver Post*, October 14, 1914; "Women Voters Bring Their Message to Congress," *Suffragist*, October 9, 1915, 5; "Rousing Welcome Given Envoys of the Women Voters," *Suffragist*, November 6, 1915, 3; "Suffragists Given Rousing Welcome," *Des Moines Register and Leader*, October 31, 1915; "Energy Women Are Using To Gain Vote Would Secure Many Reforms," *Colorado Springs Gazette*, October 15, 1915; "Eastern Journey of the Women Voters' Envoy," *Suffragist*, October 23, 1915, 5; "Illinois Greets Women Voters' Envoy," *Suffragist*, November 13, 1915, 3; "Women Voters' Envoys Reach the East," *Suffragist*, November 20, 1915, 3; "Signs Suffrage Petition," *Washington Herald*, November 20, 1915.

17. "Champ Clark Sidesteps Efforts to Bind Him to Suffrage Cause," *Denver Post*, October 14, 1914.

18. "Suffragists Given Rousing Welcome," *Des Moines Register and Leader*, October 31, 1915; "Called on the Governor," *Nebraska State Journal*, October 28, 1915.

19. "Rousing Welcome Given Envoys of the Women Voters," *Suffragist*, November 6, 1915, 3; "Called on the Governor," *Nebraska State Journal*, October 28, 1915.

20. Many of the newspaper articles examined in this chapter were located in the Collection of Congressional Union for Woman's Suffrage Clippings by Mrs. Oliver H. P. Belmont, May 18, 1915 to Dec. 31, 1916, Florence Bayard Hilles Feminist Library.

21. Angela G. Ray, "The Rhetorical Ritual of Citizenship: Women's Voting as Public Performance, 1868–1875," *Quarterly Journal of Speech* 93 (2007): 1–26; Catherine H. Palczewski, "The 1919 Prison Special: Constituting White Women's Citizenship"; Jennifer L. Borda, "The Woman Suffrage Parades of 1910–1913: Possibilities and Limitations of an Early Feminist Rhetorical Strategy," *Western Journal of Communication* 66 (2002): 25–53; Belinda A. Stillion Southard, "Militancy, Power, and Identity: The Silent Sentinels as Women Fighting for Political Voice," *Rhetoric & Public Affairs* 10 (2007): 399–418.

22. Linda J. Lumsden, *Rampant Women: Suffragists and the Right of Assembly*

(Knoxville: University of Tennessee Press, 1997); Borda, "The Woman Suffrage Parades"; Sarah J. Moore, "Making a Spectacle of Suffrage: The National Woman Suffrage Pageant, 1913," *Journal of American Culture* 20 (1997): 89–103; Stillion Southard, *Militant Citizenship.*

23. Suffragists began parading as early as 1908 in New York City. From 1910 to 1917, women paraded down Fifth Avenue for voting rights annually and organized smaller parades in many cities around the country. In 1913 in Washington, DC, the Congressional Committee of the NAWSA timed one of the most famous suffrage parades to coincide with and mimic President Wilson's inaugural parade. Mary P. Ryan, "The American Parade: Representations of the Nineteenth-Century Social Order," in *The New Cultural History*, ed. Lynn Hunt (Berkeley: University of California Press, 1989), 132–133; Lumsden, *Rampant Women*, 71; Stillion Southard, *Militant Citizenship*, 75–90.

24. Lumsden, *Rampant Women*, 96–97; Moore, "Making a Spectacle of Suffrage"; Katherine H. Adams, Michael L. Keene, and Jennifer C. Koella, *Seeing the American Woman, 1880-1920: The Social Impact of the Visual Media Explosion* (London: McFarland & Company Inc.), 14–15.

25. Adams, Keene, and Koella, *Seeing the American Woman*, 14–15; Moore, "Making a Spectacle of Suffrage."

26. Suffragists' participation in parades challenged ideals of respectability and femininity for middle- and upper-class women, and at times were met with violence. The 1913 parade in Washington, DC, faced mobs of men who "spat upon women, slapped them in the face, tripped them, pelted them with cigar stubs, pulled them off floats, tore off their skirts, and cursed them" while "the police stood by and did nothing." Women were warned they could lose their jobs for participating in the parades. In 1909, even Carrie Chapman Catt was averse to women parading, contending that "we do not have to win sympathy by parading ourselves like the street cleaning department." Lumsden, *Rampant Women*, 75, 79; Borda, "The Woman Suffrage Parades," 26, 32; Eleanor Flexner and Ellen Fitzpatrick, *Century of Struggle: The Woman's Rights Movement in the United States* (Cambridge: Harvard University Press, 1996); Lumsden, *Rampant Women*; Hazel Mackaye, "Pageants as a Means of Suffrage Propaganda,"

Suffragist, November 28, 1914, 6.

27. The suffrage parades, pageants, and tableaus regularly featured their triumph by celebrating the Western suffrage states with floats or women's bodies. In June 1912, Maryland's first suffrage parade in Baltimore had six floats representing each of the existing free states in 1912, each driven by a suffragist "dressed in flowing robes of ancient Greece . . . [that] made a most beautiful and impressive picture." Each float represented the existence of women's voting rights and reiterated the successes and growing numbers of the suffrage movement. "One Thousand Women March," *Woman's Journal*, July 6, 1912, 209. Also see "New States to Lead in Suffrage Parade," *New York Times*, November 9, 1912, 22.

28. In a 1916 parade in Philadelphia, a suffrage float included eleven young marching women dressed in white, each of whom represented one of the eleven equal suffrage states that surrounded a Victory figure holding high the light of the suffrage torch. "Advertising Suffrage among the Advertisers," *Woman's Journal*, July 8, 1916, 1. In a 1915 Philadelphia parade, those "representing the suffrage states were robed white, non-suffrage in black and partial suffrage in black-and-white frocks." Rose D. Weston, "Women in Brilliant Street Pageant Make Striking Plea for Passage of Suffrage Amendment," *Philadelphia North American*, May 2, 1915.

29. "Parade to Glow like Rainbow," *Woman's Journal and Suffrage News*, February 22, 1913, 1, 62.

30. Robert P. J. Cooney, *Winning the Vote: The Triumph of the American Woman Suffrage Movement* (Half Moon Bay, CA: American Graphic Press, 2005), 309.

31. Untitled newspaper clipping from *Philadelphia North-American*, April 25, 1915, in the Collection of Woman Suffrage Clippings by Mrs. Oliver H. P. Belmont, Florence Bayard Hilles Feminist Library. Also see Rose D. Weston, "Women in Brilliant Street Pageant Make Striking Plea for Passage of Suffrage Amendment," *Philadelphia North American*, May 2, 1915.

32. "Torches in Hair to Guide Parade," *New York Times*, November 8, 1912, 7.

33. "New States to Lead in Suffrage Parade," *New York Times*, November 9, 1912, 22.

34. Similarly, women in a St. Louis suffrage tableau in 1916 personified the

non-suffrage states by dressing in black and wearing chains on their wrists. Cooney, *Winning the Vote*, 273, 309.

35. "Suffragists' 'Slavery' Parade," no publication name, newspaper clipping, National Woman's Party, May 18, 1916.

36. "Suffs to Present Tableaux in Park," *New York Sun*, September 20, 1916.

37. Joyce E. McConnell argues that "no matter how rhetorically useful this metaphor may have seemed, . . . it was and remains grossly inaccurate and inherently racist." "Beyond Metaphor: Battered Women, Involuntary Servitude and the Thirteenth Amendment," *Yale Journal of Law & Feminism* 4 (1991): 207–253; Susan Sniader Lanser, *Fictions of Authority: Women Writers and Narrative Voice* (Ithaca, NY: Cornell University Press, 1992).

38. "New States to Lead in Suffrage Parade," *New York Times*, November 9, 1912, 22.

39. "Wanted: 47 Adonises," *New York Tribune*, April 11, 1913, 6.

40. "Suffrage Tableau to Be Shown in Park," *New York Tribune*, September 20, 1916, 7.

41. "Suffs to Present Tableaux in Park," *New York Sun*, September 20, 1916.

42. E. Michele Ramsey, "Driven from the Public Sphere: The Conflation of Women's Liberation and Driving in Advertising from 1910 to 1920," *Women's Studies in Communication* 29 (2006): 88–112; Michele Ramsey, "Selling Social Status: Woman and Automobile Advertisements from 1910–1920," *Women and Language* 28 (2005): 26–38; Clarsen, *Eat My Dust*; Virginia Scharff, *Taking the Wheel: Women and the Coming of the Motor Age* (Albuquerque: New Mexico Press, 1992); Margaret M. Finnegan, *Selling Suffrage: Consumer Culture and Votes for Women* (New York: Columbia University Press, 1999).

43. College Equal Suffrage League of Northern California, *Winning Equal Suffrage in California; Reports of the Committees of the College Equal Suffrage League of Northern California in the Campaign of 1911* (San Francisco: National College Equal Suffrage League, 1913).

44. Scharff, *Taking the Wheel*, 80.

45. "More Suffrage Parades," *Woman's Journal*, May 25, 1912, 164.

46. Clarsen, *Eat My Dust*, 78.

47. Scharff, *Taking the Wheel*, 75–77. Clarsen argues that Americans found

women's interest in cars—as owners, drivers, and mechanics—so surprising and entertaining that early automobile discourse frequently made claims about "the first woman to . . ." These sponsored car trips often imitated the silent film stars of the early twentieth century that glamorized brave and athletic heroines who completed stunts and took risks, often around automobiles, trains, or planes. Clarsen argues that automobile manufactures used the serial queen genre to depict women driving across the country in their automobiles as courageous, adventurous, and attractive. Clarsen, *Eat My Dust*, 67.

48. "Written on the Screen," *New York Times*, September 19, 1915, x6. After driving from Los Angeles to the Panama Pacific Exposition in San Francisco and displaying her KisselKar on stage at the Imperial Theatre, she drove the Lincoln Highway to New York City in forty-nine days, stopping at one hundred Paramount Theatres along the way to speak on filmmaking. She received media attention across the country for her "solo" trip, despite the many members of the press with whom she traveled. Her trip was such a success with audiences that the following year she starred in *The Race*, a Paramount movie about her cross-country trip. These publicity trips also hired press agents to travel ahead of the driving women to arrange promotional events and press coverage, like the suffragists did. Clarsen, *Eat My Dust*, 73–76.

49. Marguerite S. Shaffer, *See America First: Tourism and National Identity, 1880–1940* (Washington, DC: Smithsonian Institution Press, 2001), 137.

50. Shaffer, *See America First*, 137.

51. Clarsen, *Eat My Dust*, 91.

52. Emily Post, "By Motor to the Fair," *Colliers*, September 4, 11, and 18, 1915; Clarsen, *Eat My Dust*, 91.

53. Shaffer, *See America First*, 141.

54. Good Roads Committee of the Missouri DAR, *The Old Trails Road: The National Highway as a Monument to the Pioneer Men and Women* (Kansas City: Missouri Chapter of Daughters of the American Revolution, 1911).

55. Shaffer, *See America First*, 141–142.

56. "National Old Trails Road," *Better Roads*, August 1912, 56–58.

57. Arthur R. Pardington, "Following the Path of Progress," *American Motorist*,

January 1915, 28–29; Shaffer, *See America First*, 148.

58. Pardington, "Following the Path of Progress," 28–29.

59. Shaffer, *See America First*, 153; *The Complete Official Road Guide of the Lincoln Highway* (Detroit: Lincoln Highway Association, 1915).

60. Shaffer, *See America First*; Pardington, "Following the Path of Progress," *American Motorist*, January 1915, 28–29.

61. Shaffer, *See America First*, 141–142.

62. W. D. Rishel, "What Transcontinental Touring Really Means," *American Motorist*, May 1913, 395–398.

63. Caroline Poole, *A Modern Prairie Schooner on the Transcontinental Trail: The Story of a Motor Trip* (San Francisco: privately published, 1919).

64. Poole, *A Modern Prairie Schooner*, 1.

65. David M. Wrobel, *Promised Lands: Promotion, Memory, and the Creation of the American West* (Lawrence: University Press of Kansas, 2002), 104–106.

66. Clarsen, *Eat My Dust*, 90.

67. "Suffrage Envoys on Transcontinental Trip to Capital by Auto Lose Way on Arizona Deserts," *Washington Herald*, December 5, 1915, 10.

68. Leroy G. Dorsey, *We Are All Americans, Pure and Simple: Theodore Roosevelt and the Myth of Americanism* (Tuscaloosa: University of Alabama Press, 2007); Slotkin, *Gunfighter Nation*.

69. "From Boston to New York," *Suffragist*, December 4, 1915, 5.

70. "Suffrage Envoys on Transcontinental Trip to Capital by Auto Lose Way on Arizona Deserts," *Washington Herald*, December 5, 1915, 10.

71. "Suffrage Advance Guard Here Paves Way for Campaign," *Kansas City Post*, October 18, 1915.

72. "Envoys for Suffrage Arrive Friday After Exciting Adventures," *Kansas City Post*, October 20, 1915.

73. "Suffragists Here Today," *Lincoln Nebraska Journal*, October 27, 1915, Congressional Union Suffrage Clippings.

74. "Suffragettes in Overland: Long Distance Tour in Aid for the Cause," *Boston Sunday Post*, December 5, 1915.

75. "Three Lone, Lorn Weemin': A Suffrage Delegation from the Pacific, Pass through Town Today in a Motorcar," *Emporia Gazette*, October 20, 1915.

76. "Suffrage Envoy Will Lead Parade," *Des Moines Register and Leader*, October

30, 1915.

77. "New York Greets Suffrage Envoys," *New York Tribune*, November 27, 1915, 3.

78. "Suffrage Envoys on Transcontinental Trip to Capital by Auto Lose Way on Arizona Deserts," *Washington Herald*, December 5, 1915, 10; "Messengers Bearing Tidings of Suffrage across Country Only Needed Mere Man Once and He Proved Much of a Failure," *Cheyenne State Leader*, October 8, 1915. This story was also repeated in the following articles: "Women's Suffragist Writes to the Standard," *Ogden Standard* (UT), October 6, 1915; "Envoys for Suffrage Arrive Friday After Exciting Adventures," *Kansas City Post*, October 20, 1915; "Envoys from Women Voters' Convention to President Will Visit in Dayton," *Dayton Ohio News*, November 4, 1915; "New York Greets Suffrage Envoys," *New York Tribune*, November 27, 1915, 3.

79. "Envoys from Women Voters' Convention to President Will Visit in Dayton," *Dayton Ohio News*, November 4, 1915.

80. "Messengers Bearing Tidings of Suffrage across Country Only Needed Mere Man Once and He Proved Much of a Failure," *Cheyenne State Leader*, October 8, 1915.

81. "Suffrage Envoys on Transcontinental Trip to Capital by Auto Lose Way on Arizona Deserts," *Washington Herald*, December 5, 1915, 10.

82. "Women's Suffragist Writes to the Standard," *Ogden Standard* (UT), October 6, 1915.

83. "New York Greets Suffrage Envoys," *New York Tribune*, November 27, 1915, 3.

84. Clarsen, *Eat My Dust*, 95.

85. "Called on the Governor," *Nebraska State Journal*, October 28, 1915.

86. "Suffrage Envoys on Transcontinental Trip to Capital by Auto Lose Way on Arizona Deserts," *Washington Herald*, December 5, 1915, 10; "New York Greets Suffrage Envoys," *New York Tribune*, November 27, 1915, 3.

87. "Three Suffrage Pilgrims Here from the West," *Boston Herald*, November 23, 1915.

88. "Suffrage Envoys on Transcontinental Trip to Capital by Auto Lose Way on Arizona Deserts," *Washington Herald*, December 5, 1915, 10.

89. "To Demand Suffrage from Uncle Sam," *Rochester N.Y. Democrat and Chronicle*, November 18, 1915.

90. "Called on the Governor," *Nebraska State Journal*, October 28, 1915.

91. "To Demand Suffrage from Uncle Sam," *Rochester N.Y. Democrat and Chronicle*, November 18, 1915.

92. "Auto Envoys Here," *Baltimore M.D. News*, December 4, 1915.

93. "New York Greets Suffrage Envoys," *New York Tribune*, November 27, 1915, 3.

94. "Suffrage Envoy Warmly Greeted in Wilmington," *Wilmington D.E. Every Evening*, December 4, 1915.

95. "Mayor Signs Long Suffrage Petition for Auto Visitors," *Philadelphia Ledger*, December 3, 1915.

96. "The Women Voters' Envoy in the Eastern States," *Suffragist*, November 27, 1915, 3.

97. "New York Greets Suffrage Envoys," *New York Tribune*, November 27, 1915, 3.

98. "Cheer Envoys on Suffrage Mission," *San Francisco Bulletin*, September 17, 1915.

99. Perry Miller, *Errand into the Wilderness* (Cambridge, MA: Belknap Press, 1956); Stephen H. Browne, "Samuel Danforth's Errand into the Wilderness and the Discourse of Arrival in Early American Culture," *Communication Quarterly* 40 (1992): 91–101; Paul Stob, "Jeannette Rankin's Democratic Errand to Washington," *Advances in the History of Rhetoric* 20 (2017): 86–98.

100. "Mass Meeting to Welcome Women Voters' Envoys," *Suffragist*, December 18, 1915, 3; "Suffrage Envoys on Transcontinental Trip to Capital by Auto Lose Way on Arizona Deserts," *Washington Herald*, December 5, 1915, 10; "Cheer Envoys on Suffrage Mission," *San Francisco Bulletin*, September 17, 1915.

101. "State Suffs See Wilson," *New Haven Register*, December 12, 1915; "Receptions to Envoys and Delegates," *Suffragist*, December 18, 1915, 5.

102. "The Farewell to the Woman Voters' Envoys," *Suffragist*, October 2, 1915, 5.

103. "Mayor Signs Long Suffrage Petition for Auto Visitors," *Philadelphia*

Ledger, December 3, 1915.

104. "The Farewell to the Woman Voters' Envoys," *Suffragist*, October 2, 1915, 5.

105. "Messengers Speed on to Washington," *San Francisco Bulletin*, September 18, 1915, Congressional Union Suffrage Clippings; "The Dawn of a Great Tomorrow," *San Francisco Bulletin*, September 18, 1915.

106. "The Farewell to the Woman Voters' Envoys," *Suffragist*, October 2, 1915, 5.

107. "From Boston to New York," *Suffragist*, December 4, 1915, 5.

108. "Suffrage Advance Guard Here Paves Way for Campaign," *Kansas City Post*, October 18, 1915.

109. "Suffrage Envoys Get Warm Reception Here," *Philadelphia Record*, December 4, 1915.

110. "Suffrage Envoys on Transcontinental Trip to Capital by Auto Lose Way on Arizona Deserts," *Washington Herald*, December 5, 1915, 10.

111. "The Dawn of a Great Tomorrow," *San Francisco Bulletin*, September 18, 1915.

112. "Three Lone, Lorn Weemin': A Suffrage Delegation from the Pacific, Pass through Town Today in a Motorcar," *Emporia Gazette*, October 20, 1915.

113. European Americans advocated their "civilization" programs as a means of "helping" American Indians. These programs were often hurtful and were rooted in the belief that European Americans were more civilized than American Indians, and therefore their way of life was better. Andrew Jackson argued that the violent and deadly removal of American Indians in 1830 was actually a "benevolent policy of the Government . . . toward the red man" that was "not only liberal, but generous." Andrew Jackson, "State of the Union address, 1830," PresidentialRhetoric.com, presidentialrhetoric.com/historicspeeches.

114. "The Dawn of a Great Tomorrow," *San Francisco Bulletin*, September 18, 1915.

115. "Three Suffrage Pilgrims Here from the West," *Boston Herald*, November 23, 1915. Congressional Union Suffrage Clippings.

116. "Suffrage Envoys to Arrive To-day," *New York Tribune*, November 26, 1915, 5.

117. "New York Greets Suffrage Envoys," *New York Tribune*, November 27, 1915, 3.

118. "The Dawn of a Great Tomorrow," *San Francisco Bulletin*, September 18, 1915, Congressional Union Suffrage Clippings.

119. "The Farewell to the Woman Voters' Envoys," *Suffragist*, October 2, 1915, 5.

120. "Mrs. Noel Attends Suffrage Convention," *Los Angeles Citizen*, September 17, 1915, Congressional Union Suffrage Clippings.

121. "Battle for Suffrage Is the Biggest Job," *San Francisco Bulletin*, September 13, 1915.

122. "Eastern Journey of the Women Voters' Envoy," *Suffragist*, October 23, 1915, 5.

123. "As Seen by a Washington Woman," *Washington Herald*, December 7, 1915.

124. "Wilson Extends Hope to Woman Suffrage Chiefs," *Omaha Daily Bee*, December 7, 1915, 1.

125. "State Suffs See Wilson," *New Haven Register*, December 12, 1915.

126. "President Greets Suffrage Envoys," *New York Press*, December 7, 1915.

127. "The Women Voters' Envoys Present Their Message to the President and to Congress," *Suffragist,* December 15, 1915, 4–5.

128. "Suffs Petition, Parade and Plead for Votes; Wilson Promises to Think It Over Once Again," *New York Sun*, December 7, 1915.

129. "President Greets Suffrage Envoys," *New York Press*, December 7, 1915.

130. "As Seen by a Washington Woman," *Washington Herald*, December 7, 1915.

131. "Suffs Petition, Parade and Plead for Votes; Wilson Promises to Think It Over Once Again," *New York Sun*, December 7, 1915.

132. "Vote Plea Scene Gay," *Washington Post*, December 7, 1915, 1.

133. "As Seen by a Washington Woman," *Washington Herald*, December 7, 1915.

134. "Suffragists Urge Committeemen to Support the Cause," *New York Telegraph*, December 8, 1915; "House Bars Women in Appeals on Suffrage," *Philadelphia North American*, December 15, 1915, Congressional Union Suffrage Clippings; "Hearing before the House Judiciary Committee," *Suffragist*, December 25, 1915, 5.

135. "House Bars Women in Appeals on Suffrage," *Philadelphia North American*, December 15, 1915.

136. "Suffrage Party May Be Next: Sarah B. Field Says Women May Organize If Further Denied Ballot," *San Francisco Bulletin*, March 16, 1916.

137. "From Boston to New York," *Suffragist*, December 4, 1915, 5.

138. "Suffrage Envoy Will Lead Parade," *Des Moines Register and Leader*, October 30, 1915.

139. "Called on the Governor," *Nebraska State Journal*, October 28, 1915.

140. "Suffs Petition, Parade and Plead for Votes; Wilson Promises to Think It Over Once Again," *New York Sun*, December 7, 1915.

141. "All Suffragists in City Meet Tonight," *Washington Times*, December 8, 1915.

142. "As Seen by a Washington Woman," *Washington Herald*, December 7, 1915.

143. "Suffragists Open National Convention," *Washington Times*, December 8, 1915.

AFTERWORD

1. "The West—A New Factor," *Woman's Journal and Suffrage News*, November 11, 1916, 1.

2. Alice Stone Blackwell's editorial in the *Woman's Journal* in the days after the election also focused on "The Power of the West." Alice Stone Blackwell, "The Power of the West," *Woman's Journal*, November 11, 1916, 364.

3. Rollin Kirby, "Pauline Revere," *New York World*, November 9, 1916. Suffragists liked this visualization of Western women's power so much that they reprinted it in the *Woman's Journal*, and the NAWSA made it into a flyer paired with a quote from the *New York Herald*: "We do know that it is little short of national scandal that women should be allowed to vote in some States and not in others." When suffragists adapted the cartoon, they made one change to Kirby's original design: they replaced the word "Wilson" with "The Election."

4. In 1916, the twelve suffrage states included eleven equal suffrage states, plus Illinois, which granted women the right to vote in presidential elections.

5. Belinda A. Stillion Southard, *Militant Citizenship: Rhetorical Strategies of the National Woman's Party, 1913-1920* (College Station: Texas A&M University

Press, 2011), 112.

6. Charles A. Beard, "The Woman's Party," *New Republic*, July 29, 1916.

7. Congressional Union for Woman Suffrage, "Farewell to the Women Envoys to the West," flyer, 1916. Collection of Congressional Union for Woman's Suffrage Clippings, Florence Bayard Hilles Feminist Library.

8. "The Washington Press on the Demonstration," *Suffragist*, April 15, 1916, 7.

9. "The Envoys to the West," *Suffragist*, April 15, 1916, 5.

10. "The Envoys to the West," *Suffragist*, April 15, 1916, 5.

11. "Only One Man in Suffrage Train," unidentified article in Collection of Congressional Union for Woman's Suffrage Clippings, May 18, 1915, to December 31, 1916, Florence Bayard Hilles Feminist Library.

12. The conference sent three voting women from their conference to Washington to present their resolution demanding action to Congress. The *Suffragist* reported that the suffragists' return journey to the East was met by a "dramatic welcome home from the crowds that gathered on the Capitol steps" and "great crowds greeted the travelers at [Union] station." This time, the envoys who had traveled from the West by train with their message from Western voters were heard within the Capitol by many members of Congress.

13. "Voting Women Launch a Woman's Party, *Suffragist,* June 10, 1916, 6–7.

14. "Voting Women Launch a Woman's Party, *Suffragist,* June 10, 1916, 6–7.

15. "Review of the Year," *Suffragist*, January 10, 1917; Stillion Southard, *Militant Citizenship*.

16. S. D. Lovell, *The Presidential Election of 1916* (Carbondale: Southern Illinois University Press, 1980).

17. "California Decides," *Daily Telegraph*, November 11, 1916, 9.

18. "Reform Issues Rise in Political Shift," *New York Times*, November 13, 1916, 6.

19. "Reform Issues Rise in Political Shift," *New York Times*, November 13, 1916, 6.

20. "Review of the Year," *Suffragist*, January 10, 1917, 4, 57.

21. Stillion Southard, *Militant Citizenship*; Christine A. Lunardini, *From Equal Suffrage to Equal Rights: Alice Paul and the National Woman's Party, 1910–1928*

(New York: New York University, 1986).

22. Catherine H. Palczewski, "The 1919 Prison Special: Constituting White Women's Citizenship," *Quarterly Journal of Speech* 102 (2016): 107–132.

23. "The Melancholy Map," *Remonstrance Against Woman Suffrage*, October 1919, 1.

Index

Figures are indicated by page numbers in *italics*.

19, 24–25, 112; embodying
through appearance, 118–122;
public housekeeping arguments,
111–114; suffrage parades and, 261
(n. 26); traditional ideals of, xvii,
242 (n. 100), 251 (n. 71); Western
suffragists and, 96, 99, 110–111,
117–118, 124
Field, Sara Bard: on accomplishing
errand, 152; on civilizing mission
to the East, 154–155, 180; on
frontier challenges, 148–149;
rallies and speeches, 131–132,
134, 156, 159; on self-reliance,
147–148; on suffrage petition,
156; transcontinental car travel,
128, 131–132, *133*, 147–149, *150*; on
voting strength of Western women,
160–161; on Wilson, 158–159
Finnegan, Cara, 43
"First One East of 'The Mother of
Waters', The" (McCutcheon), *60*
Fitzpatrick, Ellen, 39, 98
flags, 36–38
Flexner, Eleanor, 98
Fowler, Bertha W., *133*
Franklin, Benjamin, xxiii
Fremont, John, 142
frontier myth: Americanization and,
4–5, 143, 208 (n. 21); conflict
with American Indians, 4–5, 9,
17, 142; conflict with civilization,
17–18; continental expansion
and, 5–6, 129, 151; cosmogonic

cycle and, 15; cultural power of,
4–6; exceptionalism and, xxiii,
xxiv, 4, 8–9, 11, 143; hegemonic
masculinity and, 210 (n. 27), 211
(n. 32); heroism and, xxiv, 4–9,
17; as regional rhetoric, 2–5,
8; Roosevelt and, 211 (n. 32);
use for women's suffrage, 6–13,
15–17, 27–30, 144–145, 161–162, 179;
violence in, 11, 49; West and, 2–7;
white masculinity and, 6–7, 20–24,
28–29, 207 (n. 20), 208 (n. 21), 210
(n. 29); white women and, 7–13,
24, 29; whiteness and, 17

G

Gast, John, 49, *50*, 58, 61
General Federation of Women's
Clubs, 92
Gilman, Charlotte Perkins, xx
Gordon, Laura DeForce, xx
Greeley, Horace, 166
Grimke, Angelina, xvii
Grimke, Sarah, xvii

H

Handy-Marchello, Barbara, 257 (n.
137)
Harper, Ida Husted, 28–29, 161
Harris, Leslie, 46, 78
Haskell, Ella Knowles, xx
Hecker, John, 103
Hergesheimer, Edwin, 230 (n. 77)
House Judiciary Committee, 159

(n. 72); in protest, xxvi, xxviii, xxix, 30, 179, 181–183; rhetorical mobility and, 78; social change and, xvi; social movements and, xxviii, xxix, 181–183; symbolic role and, 182

regional rhetoric: antisuffragists and, xxix, 63; domestic ideology and, 124; frontier myth as, 2–5, 8; historic context and, 183; mobility-based, 66, 78, 180; persuasive resource, xvii, xxviii, xxx; opposition to woman suffrage in, 67; place relationships and, xxviii, 202 (n. 65); suffrage maps and, 35–36; suffragists and, xxix, xxx, 123–124; transcontinental car travel, 128–129; West and, xxvi-xxviii, xxix, xxx, 65, 78, 178–179, 183–184; Western liberty and, 27; woolly West and, 65–66, 78

Reichert Powell, Douglas, xxvii, xxix, 202 (n. 67)

Remington, Frederic, 5, 77

Remonstrance, 71, 176

Reply, 57, 90, 91

Republican National Convention, 137, 176

Republican Party, 74, 159

Rice, Jenny, xxviii, xxix

Richards, Cindy, 18, 186 (n. 5)

Robinson, Helen Ring: appearances in the East, 96–97, 101–105, 119, 180, 244 (n. 11); on Colorado's progressive politics, 104–105; defense of Colorado, 101–105, 122; early years of, 96; femininity and, 110–111, 114, 118–119, 124; political leadership and, 96–99, 111, 114, 122–123, 244 (n. 5); public housekeeping arguments, 111–114, 124, 253 (n. 85); regional rhetoric and, 123–125; social activism and, 243 (n. 4); on suffrage and protection of the home, 113–114, 117; suffrage speeches and, 95, 97, 118; Western boosterism and, 125; Western domesticating rhetoric, 99–101, 124

Roosevelt, Theodore, 5, 6, 29, 61, 77, 82, 105, 211 (n. 32)

Rosteck, Thomas, 66

rurality: frontier myth and, 6; populism and, 86–87; separate spheres ideology and, 73; the West's, 67, 80–84, 93–94; western boosterism and, 248 (n. 35); women's rights journals and, xxi

Rushing, Janice Hocker, 8

S

Sacagawea, 18–19

Sacajawea statue unveiling (1905), 7, 18

Salt Lake Trail, 142

Samek, Alyssa, 47, 55, 56

Santa Fe Trail, 141

Scharff, Virginia, 140

Schulten, Susan, 45, 230 (n. 78)